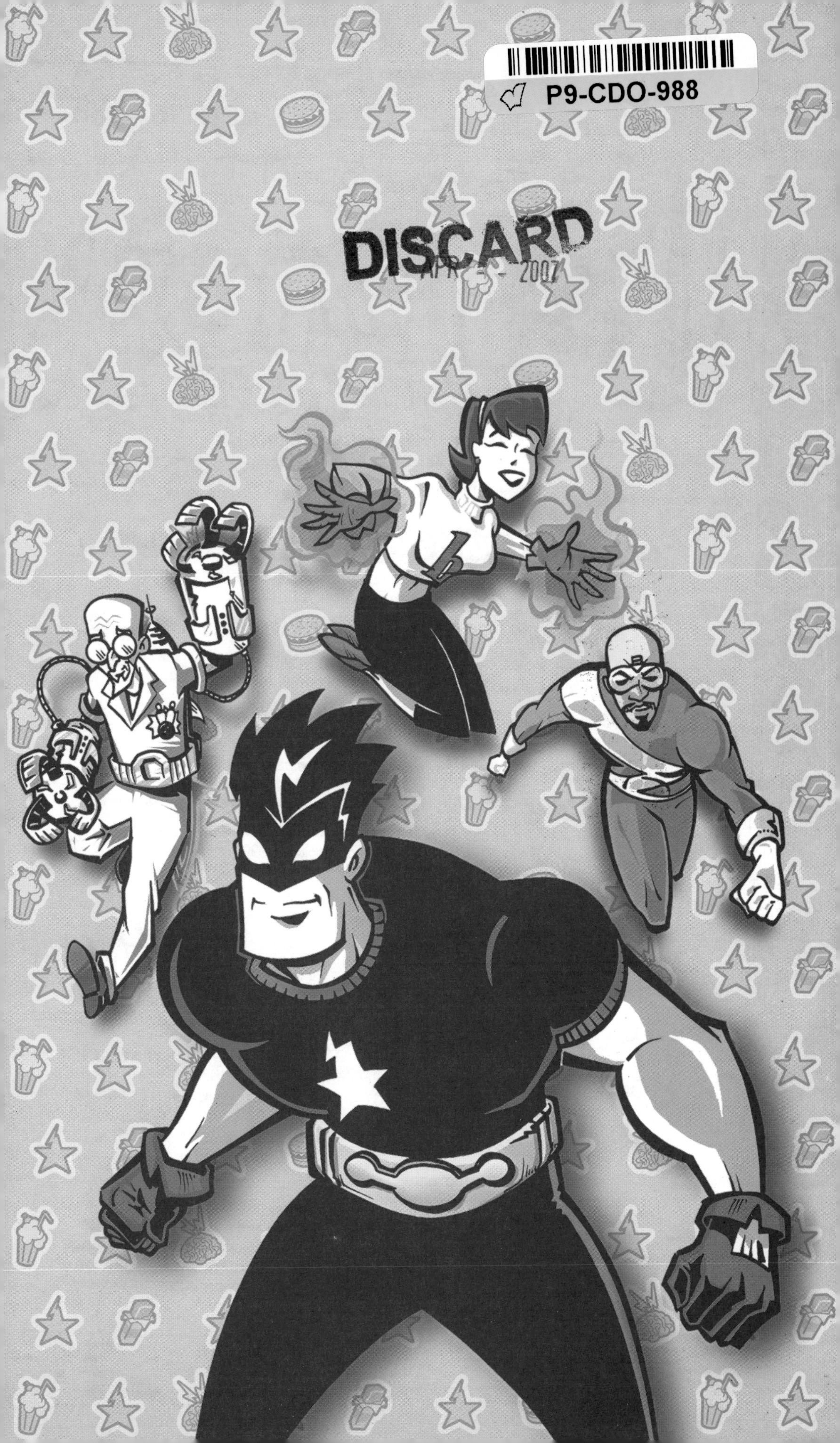

Today's Special

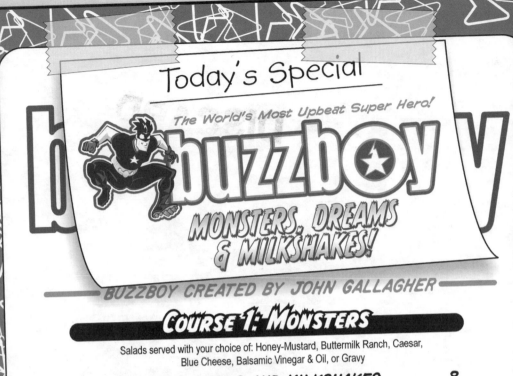

The World's Most Upbeat Super Hero!

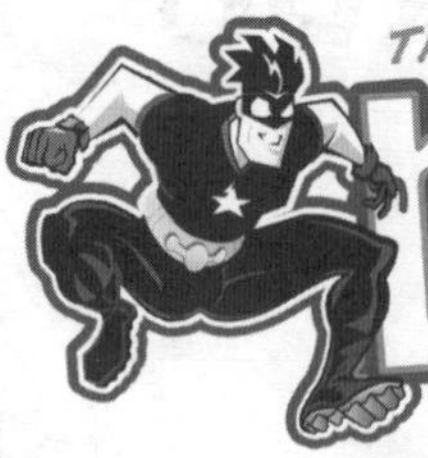

buzzboy

MONSTERS, DREAMS & MILKSHAKES!

BUZZBOY CREATED BY JOHN GALLAGHER

COURSE 1: MONSTERS

Salads served with your choice of: Honey-Mustard, Buttermilk Ranch, Caesar, Blue Cheese, Balsamic Vinegar & Oil, or Gravy

Just Added:

FRONT COVER BY NEIL VOKES,
COLORS BY HI-FI,
DESIGN ASSIST BY VINCE SNEED

BACK COVER ART BY GENE HA

BOOK DESIGN BY JOHN GALLAGHER

No Substitutions, Please!

sky★dog

Published by Sky Dog Press
7948 Freehollow Drive
Falls Church VA 22042
www.buzzboy.com
www.skydogcomics.com

First Edition: August 2003
ISBN: 0-9721831-1-6

Printed in the USA

Buzzboy Volume II: Monsters, Dreams & Milkshakes

COURSE 2: DREAMS

We grill our USDA Choice Beef Burgers medium to medium-well* and serve with shoe-string fries, w/ gravy.

COURSE 3: MILKSHAKES

All deserts are home-made, and come with gravy, if requested.

SIDE DISHES

Don't forget to add the gravy!

— **EAT, AND GET OUT!** —

FIRST COURSE

"...IF I ONLY HAD A BRAIN..."
- THE SCARECROW
WIZARD OF OZ

MONSTERS

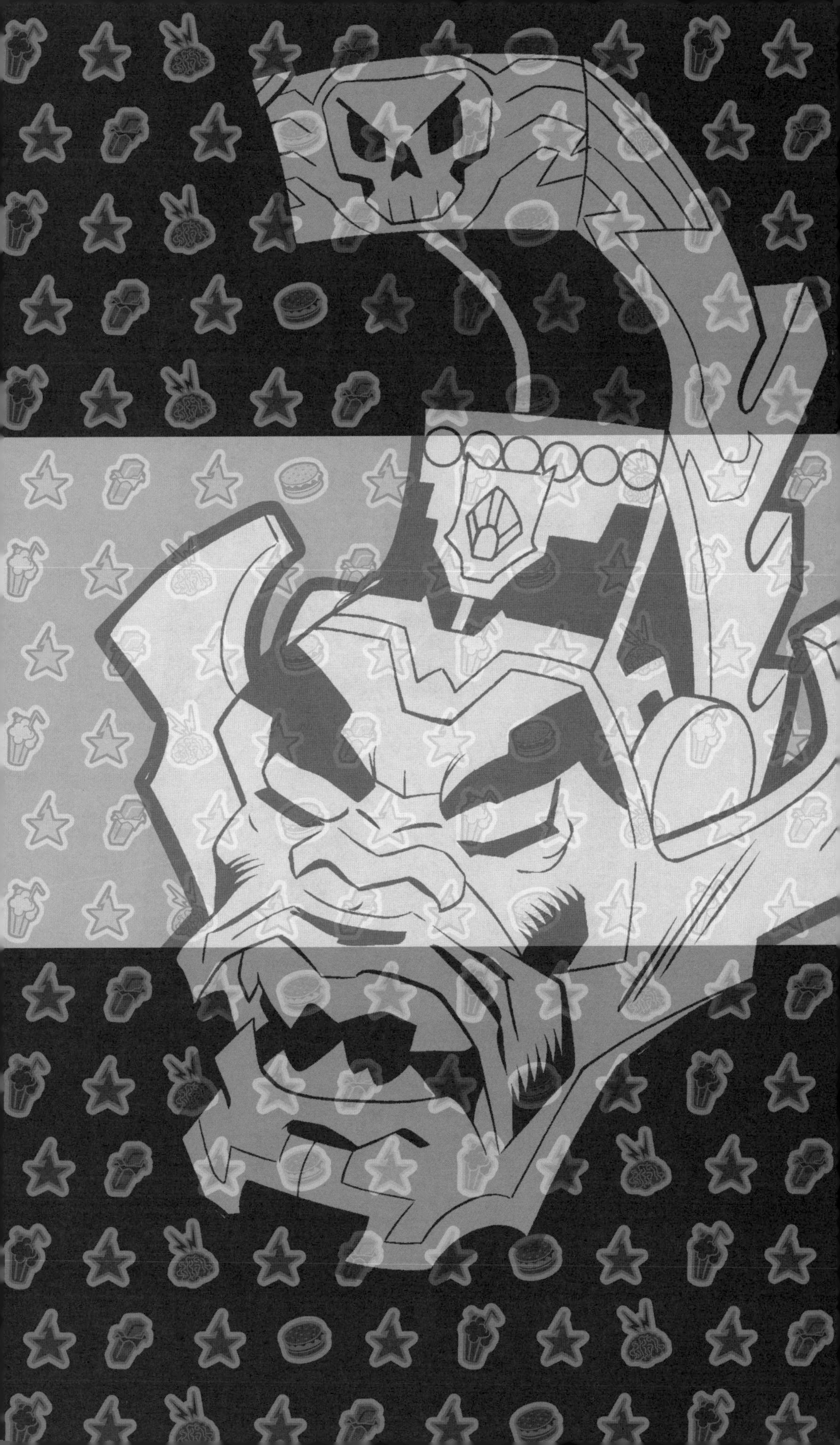

Dedicated To my parents, Joe & Jane Gallagher,
for letting me stay up late and watch TV...

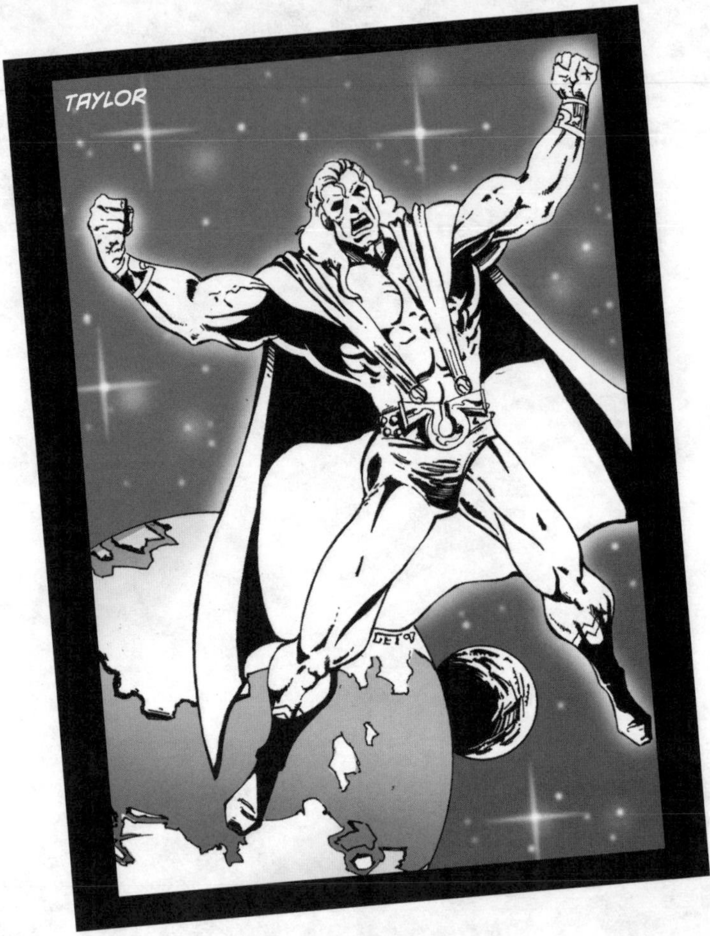
TAYLOR

And In Memory of

George Taylor, 1962-2003

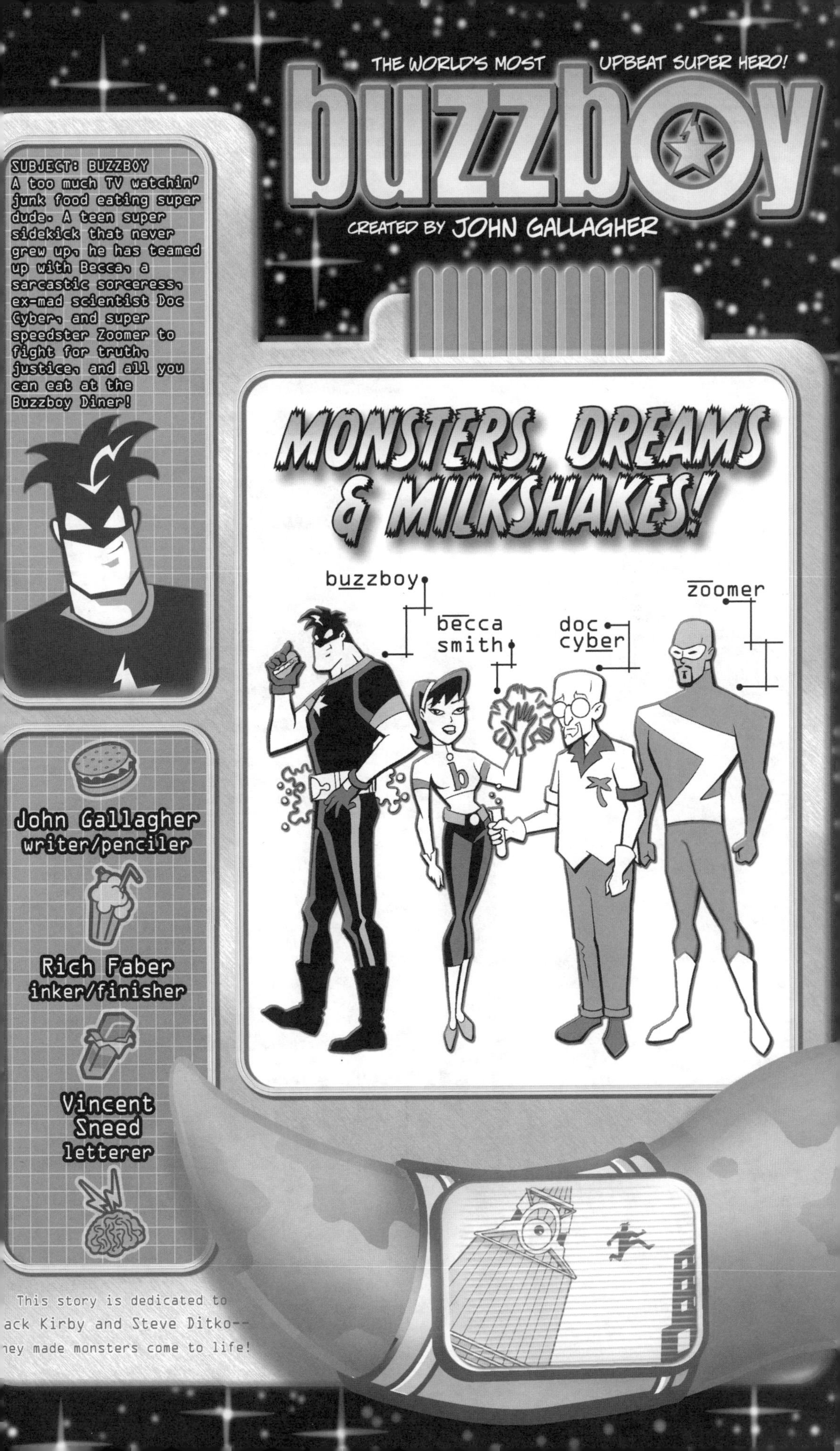
THE WORLD'S MOST UPBEAT SUPER HERO!
buzzboy
CREATED BY JOHN GALLAGHER
SUBJECT: BUZZBOY
A too much TV watchin' junk food eating super dude. A teen super sidekick that never grew up, he has teamed up with Becca, a sarcastic sorceress, ex-mad scientist Doc Cyber, and super speedster Zoomer to fight for truth, justice, and all you can eat at the Buzzboy Diner!
MONSTERS, DREAMS & MILKSHAKES!
buzzboy
becca smith
doc cyber
zoomer
John Gallagher
writer/penciler
Rich Faber
inker/finisher
Vincent Sneed
letterer
This story is dedicated to
ack Kirby and Steve Ditko--
ey made monsters come to life!

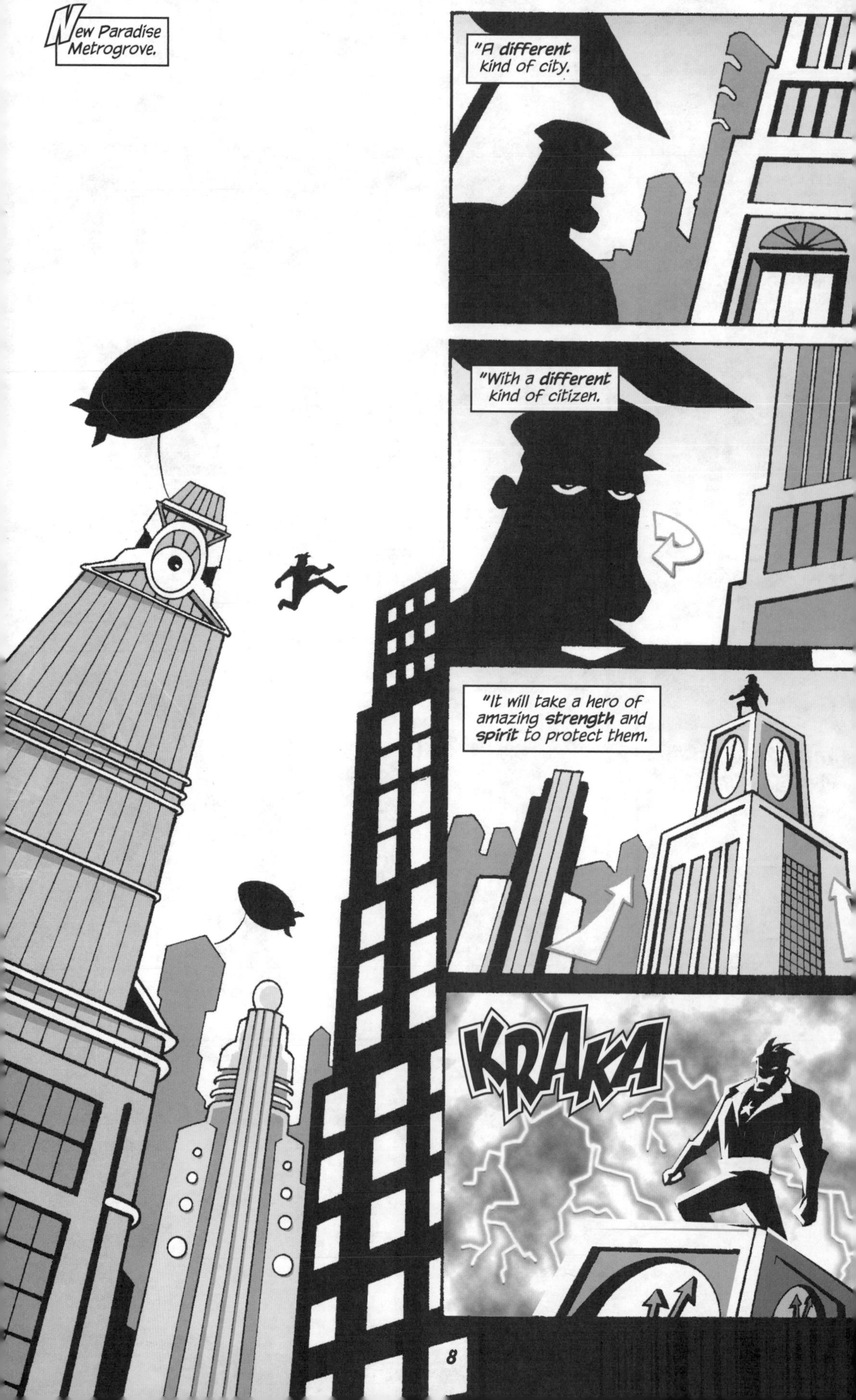
New Paradise Metrogrove.
"A different kind of city.
"With a different kind of citizen.
"It will take a hero of amazing strength and spirit to protect them.
KRAKA

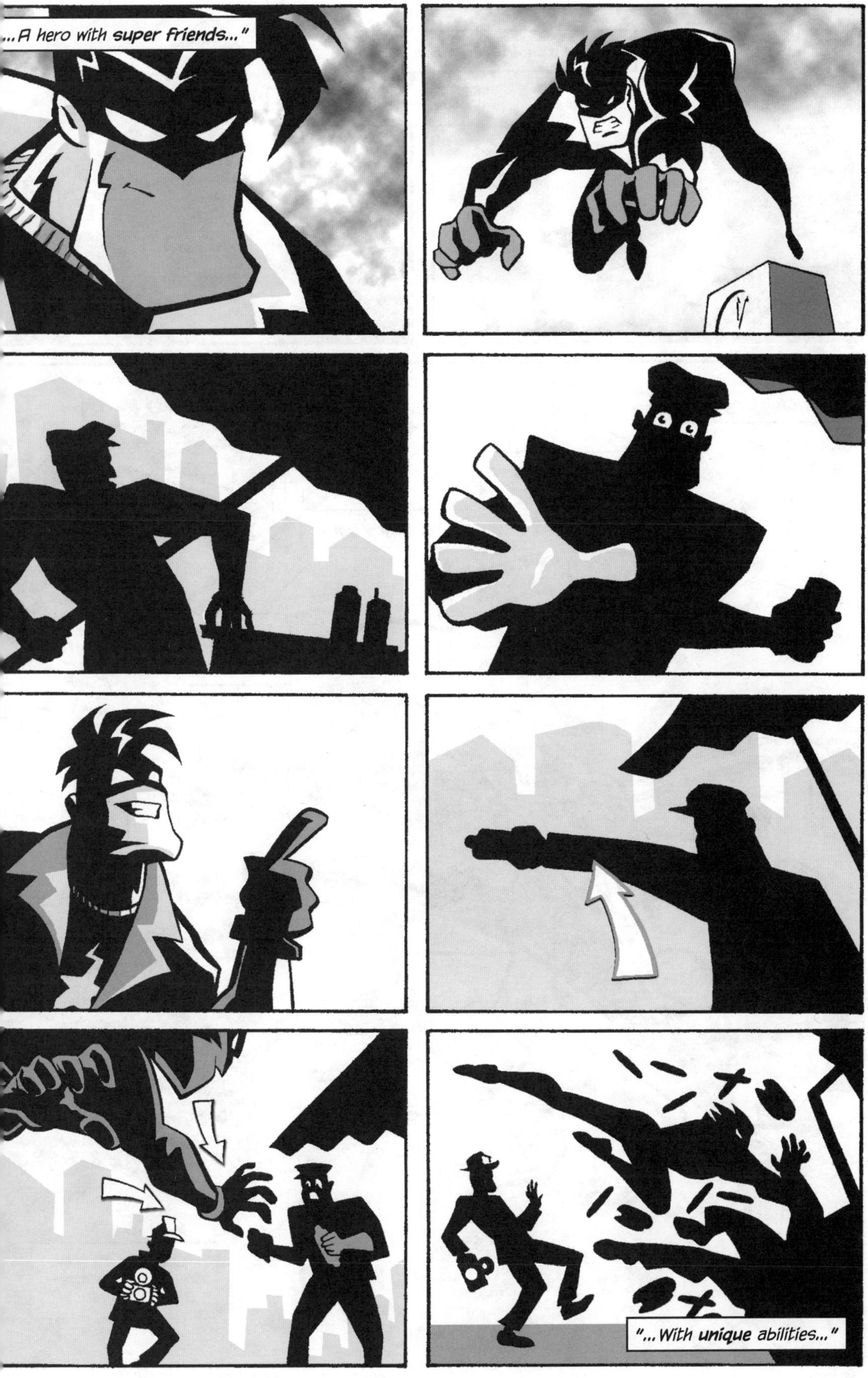
...A hero with super friends..."
"...With unique abilities..."

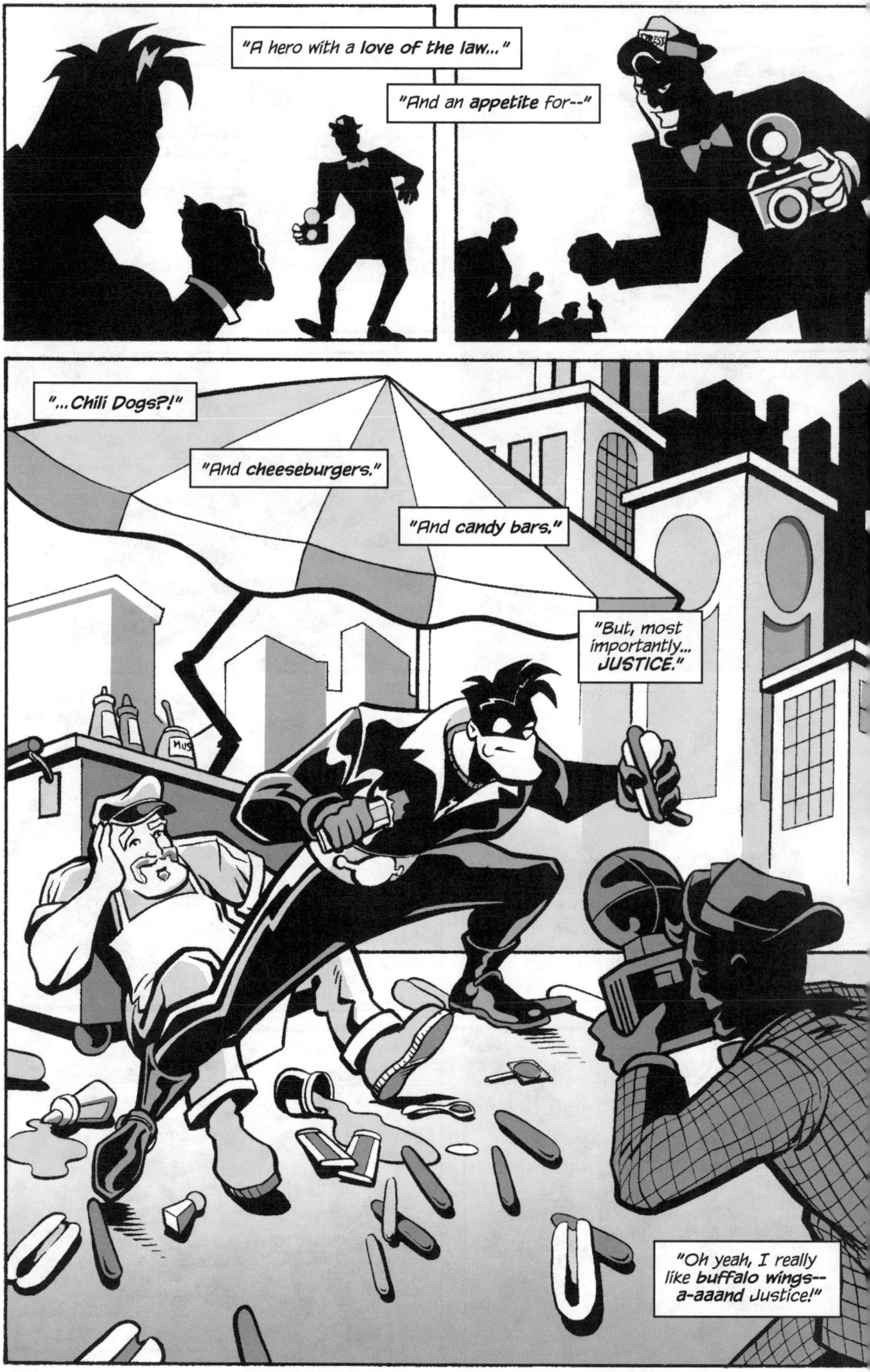
"A hero with a love of the law..."
"And an appetite for--"
PRESS
"...Chili Dogs?!"
"And cheeseburgers."
"And candy bars."
"But, most importantly... JUSTICE."
"Oh yeah, I really like buffalo wings--a-aaand Justice!"

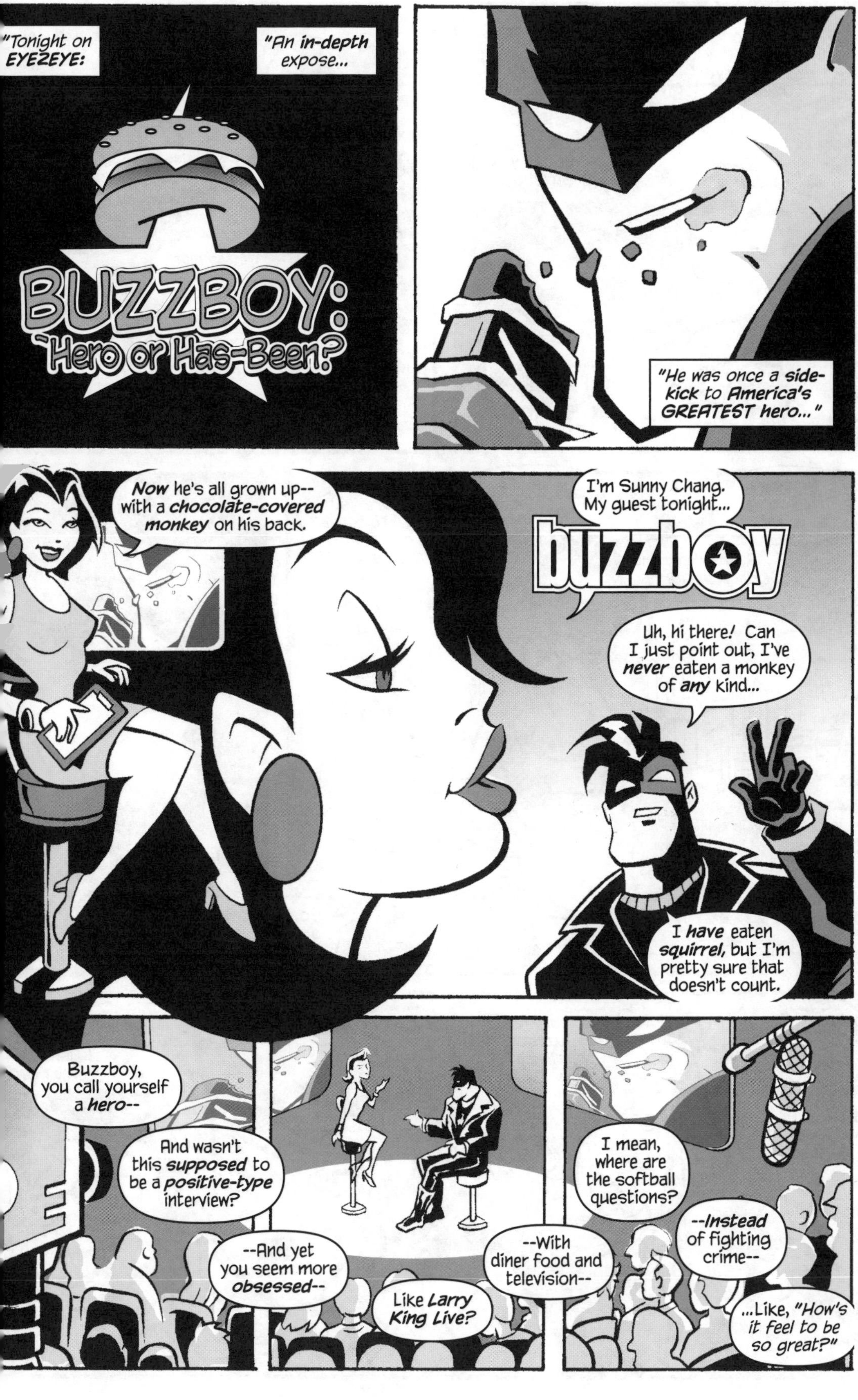
"Tonight on EYEZEYE:
"An in-depth expose...
BUZZBOY: Hero or Has-Been?
"He was once a side-kick to America's GREATEST hero..."
Now he's all grown up--with a chocolate-covered monkey on his back.
I'm Sunny Chang. My guest tonight...
buzzboy
Uh, hi there! Can I just point out, I've never eaten a monkey of any kind...
I have eaten squirrel, but I'm pretty sure that doesn't count.
Buzzboy, you call yourself a hero--
And wasn't this supposed to be a positive-type interview?
--And yet you seem more obsessed--
Like Larry King Live?
--With diner food and television--
I mean, where are the softball questions?
--Instead of fighting crime--
...Like, "How's it feel to be so great?"

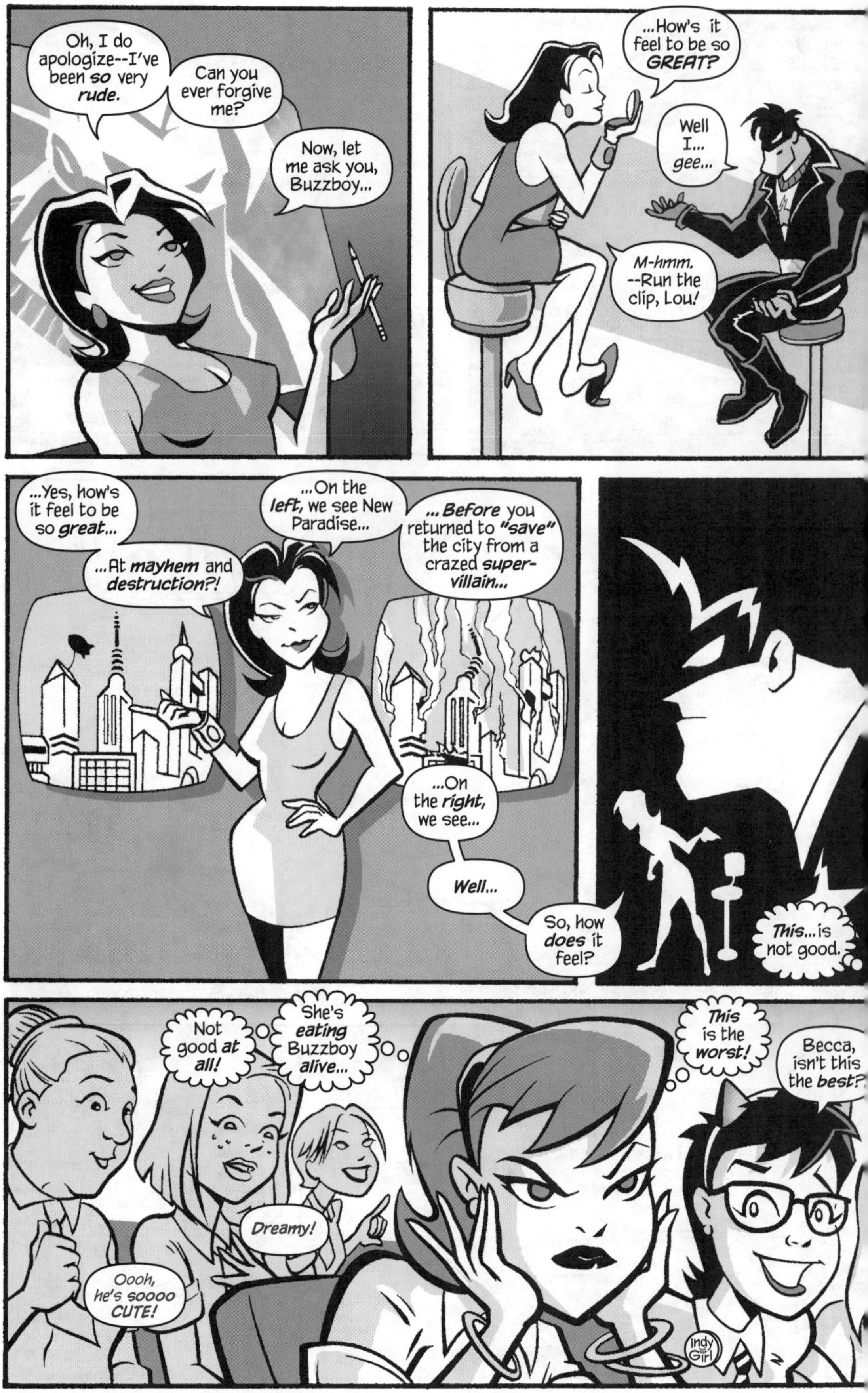
Oh, I do apologize--I've been *so* very ***rude.***
Can you ever forgive me?
Now, let me ask you, Buzzboy...
...How's it feel to be so ***GREAT?***
Well I... *gee...*
M-hmm. --Run the clip, Lou!
...Yes, how's it feel to be so ***great...***
...At ***mayhem*** and ***destruction?!***
...On the ***left,*** we see New Paradise...
...Before you returned to ***"save"*** the city from a crazed ***super-villain...***
...On the ***right,*** we see...
Well...
So, how ***does*** it feel?
This... is not good.
Not good ***at all!***
She's ***eating*** Buzzboy ***alive...***
Dreamy!
Oooh, he's ***soooo CUTE!***
This is the ***worst!***
Becca, isn't this the ***best?***
Indy Girl

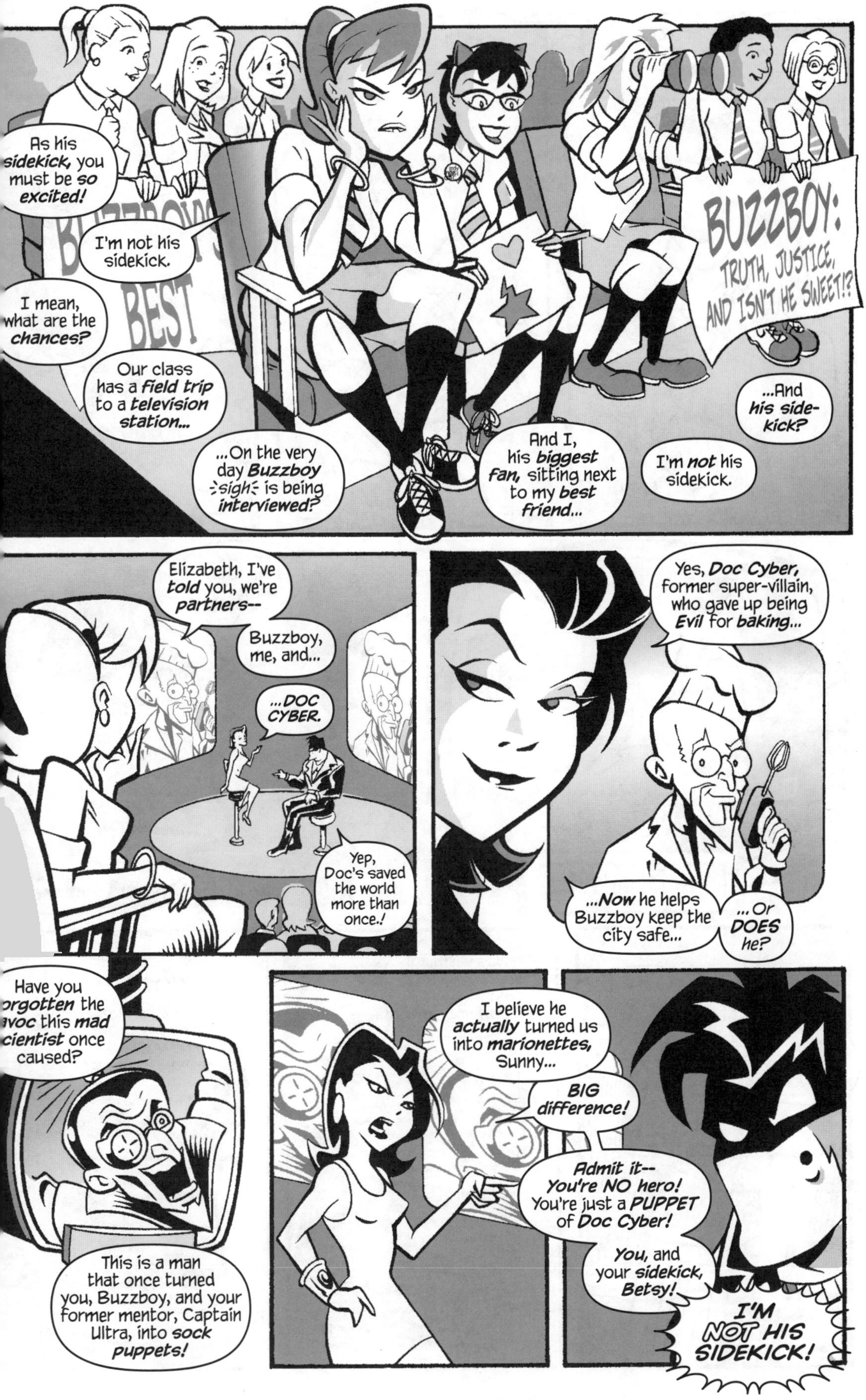
As his *sidekick,* you must be *so excited!*
I'm not his sidekick.
BEST
I mean, what are the *chances?*
Our class has a *field trip* to a *television station...*
...On the very day *Buzzboy* -sigh- is being *interviewed?*
And I, his *biggest fan,* sitting next to my *best friend...*
I'm *not* his sidekick.
...And *his side-kick?*
BUZZBOY: TRUTH, JUSTICE, AND ISN'T HE SWEET!?
Elizabeth, I've *told* you, we're *partners--*
Buzzboy, me, and...
...DOC CYBER.
Yep, Doc's saved the world more than once.!
Yes, *Doc Cyber,* former super-villain, who gave up being *Evil* for *baking...*
...Now he helps Buzzboy keep the city safe...
...Or *DOES* he?
Have you orgotten the avoc this *mad* cientist once caused?
This is a man that once turned you, Buzzboy, and your former mentor, Captain Ultra, into *sock puppets!*
I believe he *actually* turned us into *marionettes,* Sunny...
BIG difference!
Admit it-- You're NO hero! You're just a *PUPPET* of *Doc Cyber!*
You, and your *sidekick, Betsy!*
I'M NOT HIS SIDEKICK!

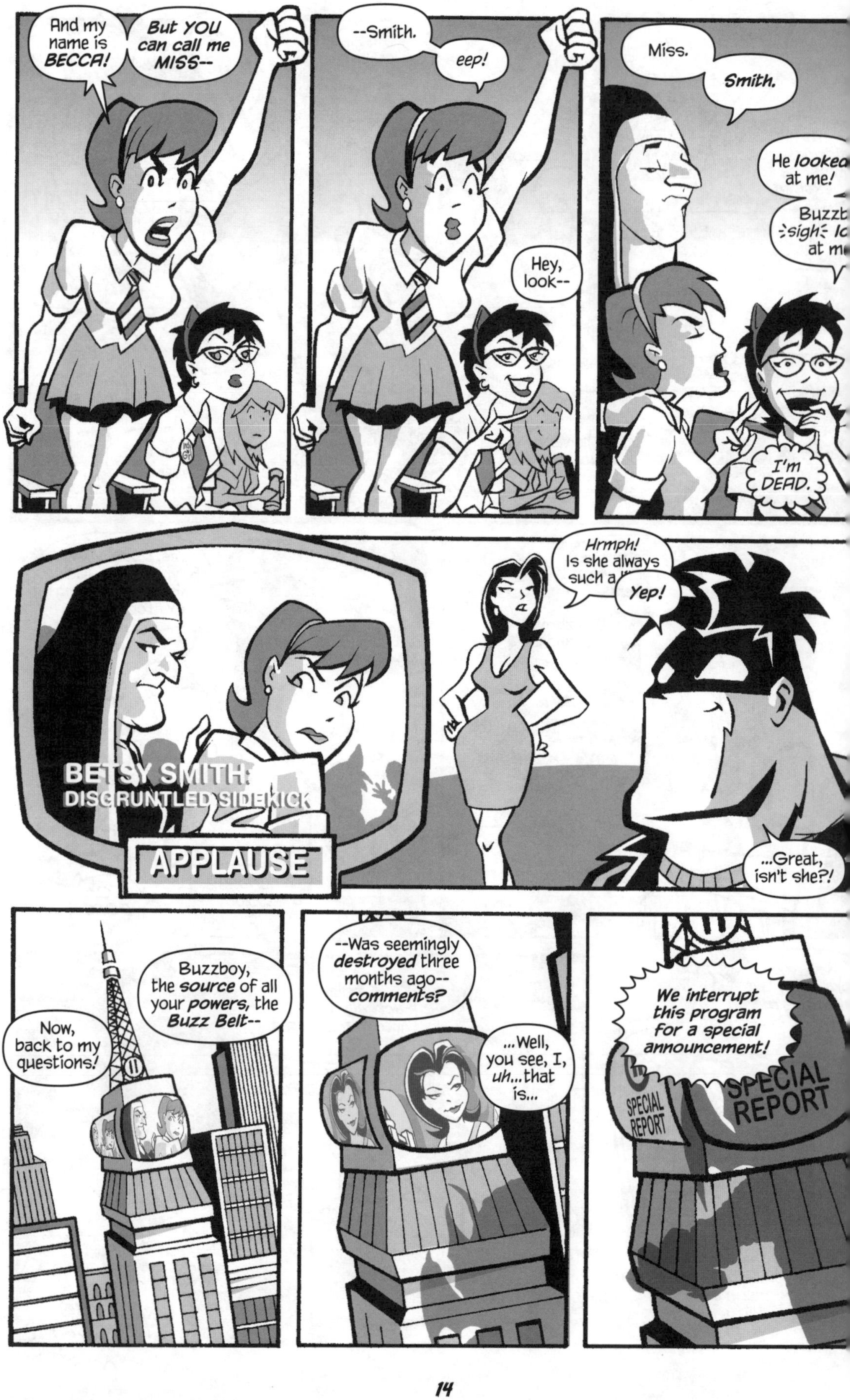

And my name is BECCA!
But YOU can call me MISS--
--Smith.
eep!
Hey, look--
Miss.
Smith.
He looked at me!
Buzzb :sigh: lo at m
I'm DEAD.
BETSY SMITH: DISGRUNTLED SIDEKICK
APPLAUSE
Hrmph! Is she always such a
Yep!
...Great, isn't she?!
Now, back to my questions!
Buzzboy, the source of all your powers, the Buzz Belt--
--Was seemingly destroyed three months ago-- comments?
...Well, you see, I, uh...that is...
We interrupt this program for a special announcement!
SPECIAL REPORT
SPECIAL REPORT

I'm Brink Knightly, with a Knightly News Special Report!

SPECIAL REPORT

A giant monster is storming the city!

Reports are sketchy at this time...

...But it is reported a dragon-like behemoth--

Perfect.

--Appeared in the Channel 11 parking lot just moments ago--

Hey! My new *Jag* is parked out there!

SP REPORT

--Has anyone seen my car?

...Anyone?

Look, can someone just go check...

Brink, we're still on...

What?

Look, I don't care if the *Pope* is watching...

Start up the chopper, boys...

I want everyone to make a *concerted* effort...

...and look *outside* the window...

SPECIAL REPORT

Do you know how *much* that car *cost me?*

Can't somebody check this out for me?

...Can't somebody help?

Yes, somebody can...

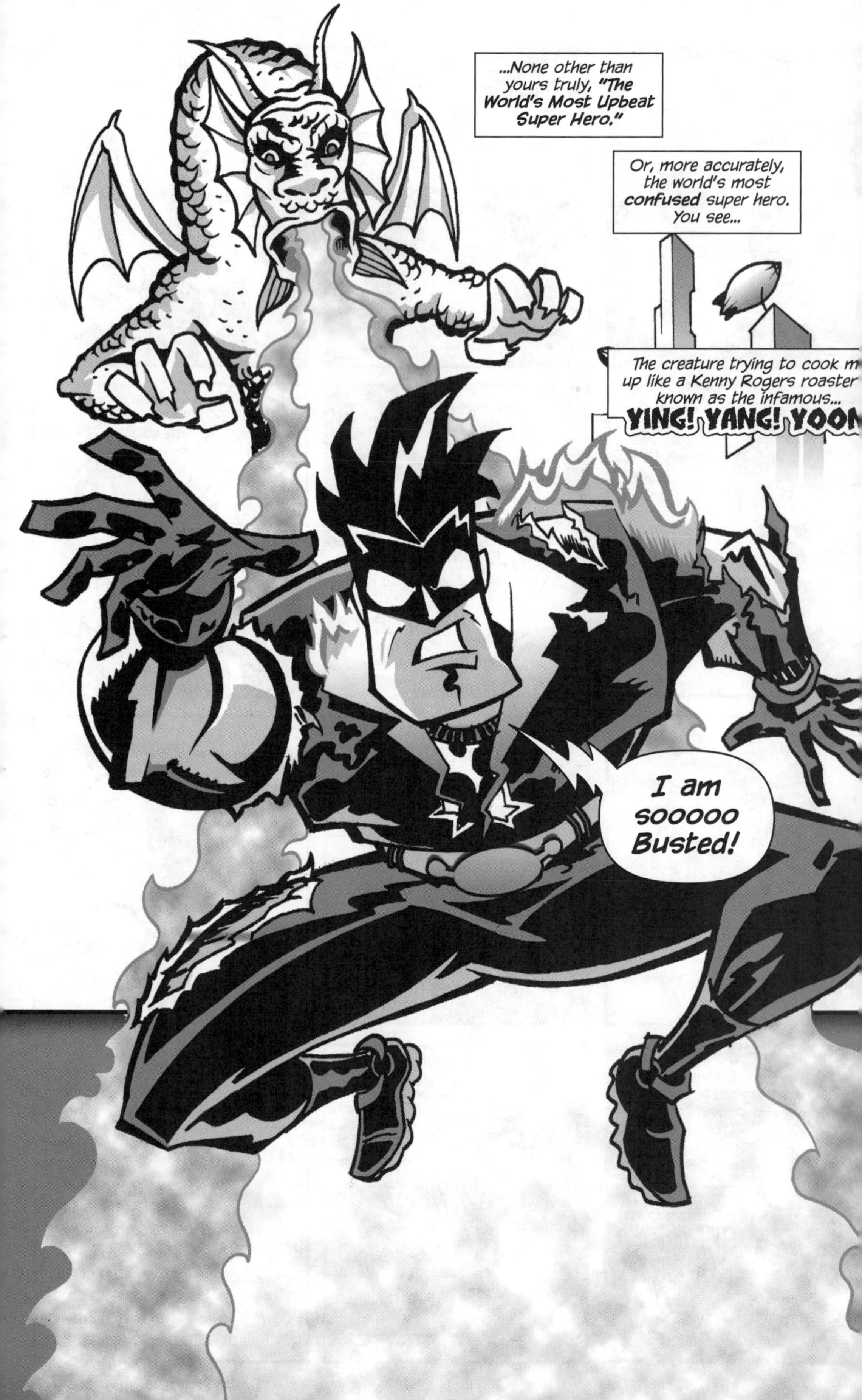
...None other than yours truly, "The World's Most Upbeat Super Hero."
Or, more accurately, the world's most confused super hero. You see...
The creature trying to cook m up like a Kenny Rogers roaster known as the infamous...
YING! YANG! YOON
I am sooooo Busted!

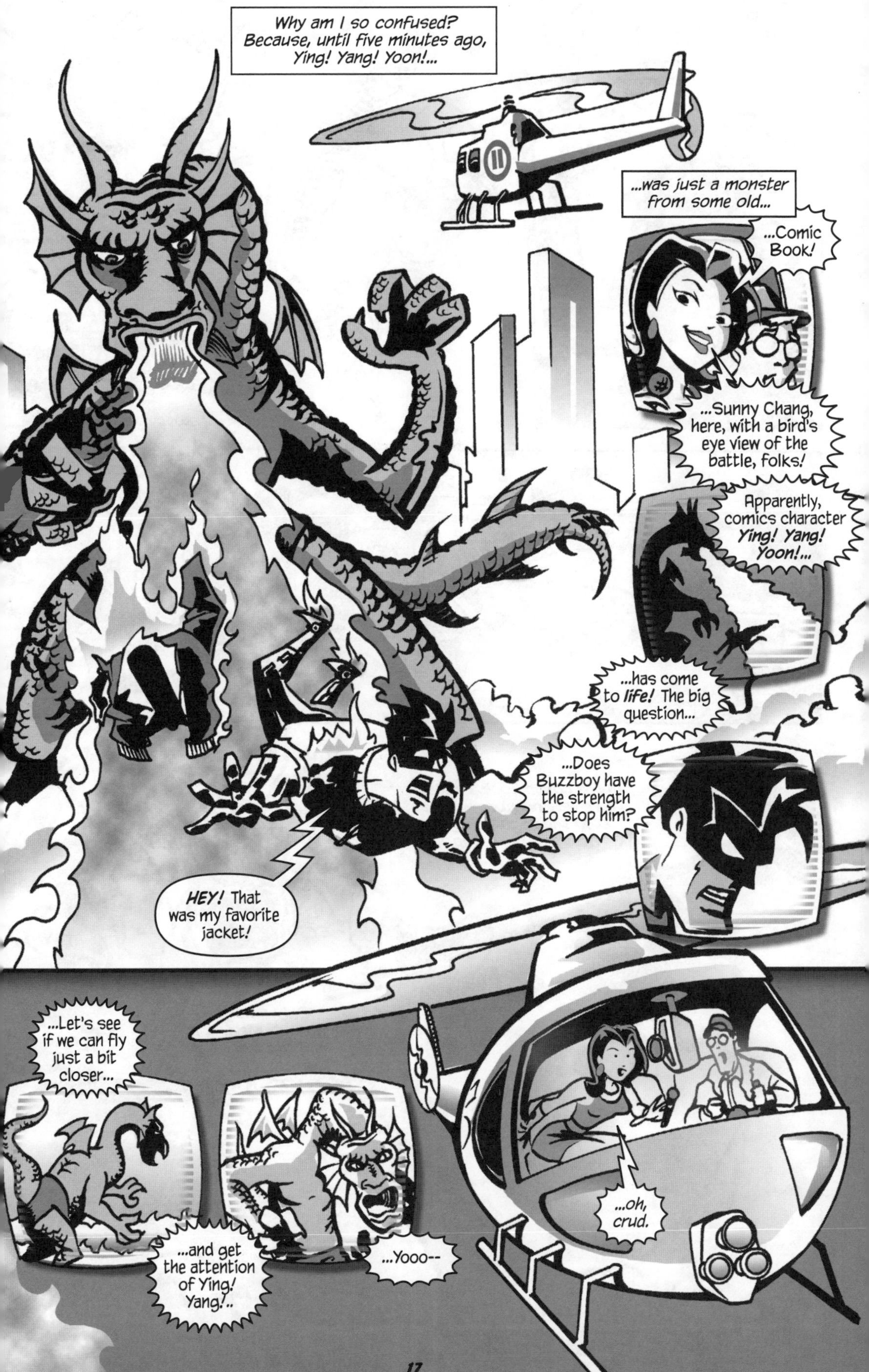

Why am I so confused? Because, until five minutes ago, Ying! Yang! Yoon!...
...was just a monster from some old...
...Comic Book!
...Sunny Chang, here, with a bird's eye view of the battle, folks!
Apparently, comics character *Ying! Yang! Yoon!*...
...has come to *life!* The big question...
...Does Buzzboy have the strength to stop him?
HEY! That was my favorite jacket!
...Let's see if we can fly just a bit closer...
...and get the attention of Ying! Yang!..
...Yooo--
...oh, crud.

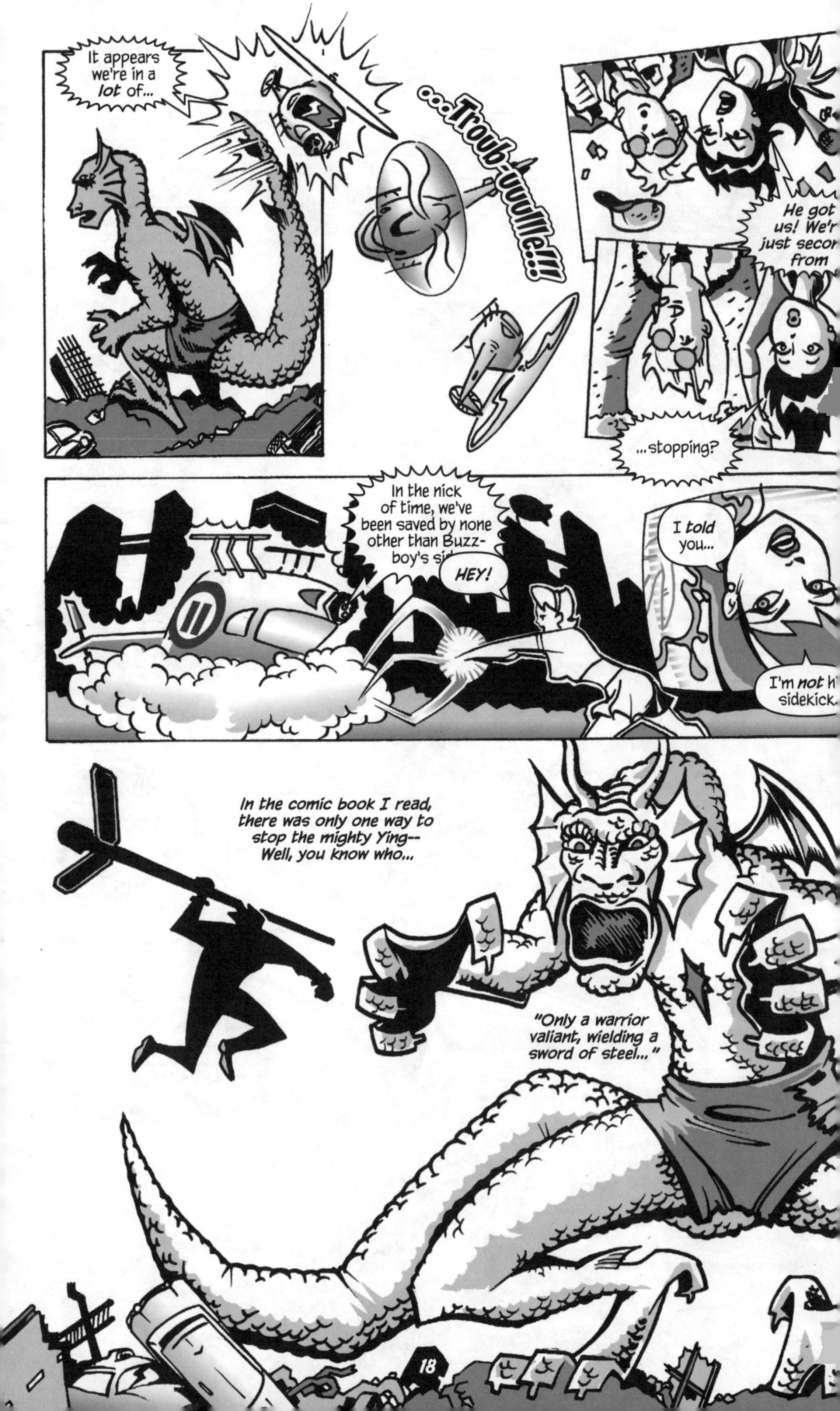
It appears we're in a *lot* of...
...Troub-uuulle!!!
He got us! We'r just secor from
...stopping?
In the nick of time, we've been saved by none other than Buzz-boy's si
HEY!
I *told* you...
I'm *not* h sidekick.
In the comic book I read, there was only one way to stop the mighty Ying-- Well, you know who...
"Only a warrior valiant, wielding a sword of steel..."

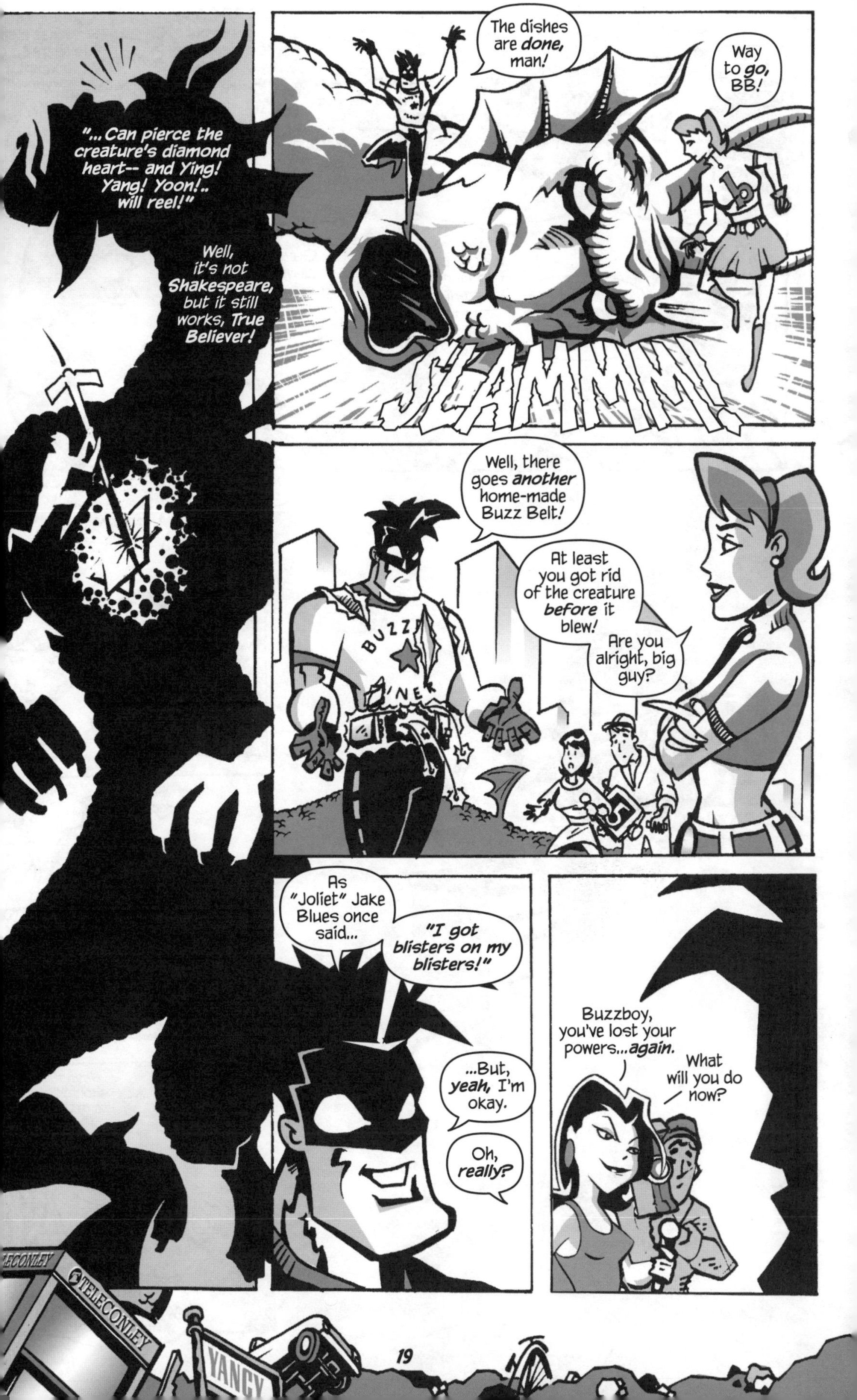
"...Can pierce the creature's diamond heart-- and Ying! Yang! Yoon!.. will reel!"
Well, it's not Shakespeare, but it still works, True Believer!
The dishes are done, man!
Way to go, BB!
SLAMMM!
Well, there goes another home-made Buzz Belt!
At least you got rid of the creature before it blew!
Are you alright, big guy?
As "Joliet" Jake Blues once said...
"I got blisters on my blisters!"
...But, yeah, I'm okay.
Oh, really?
Buzzboy, you've lost your powers...again.
What will you do now?
TELECONLEY
TELECONLEY
YANCY

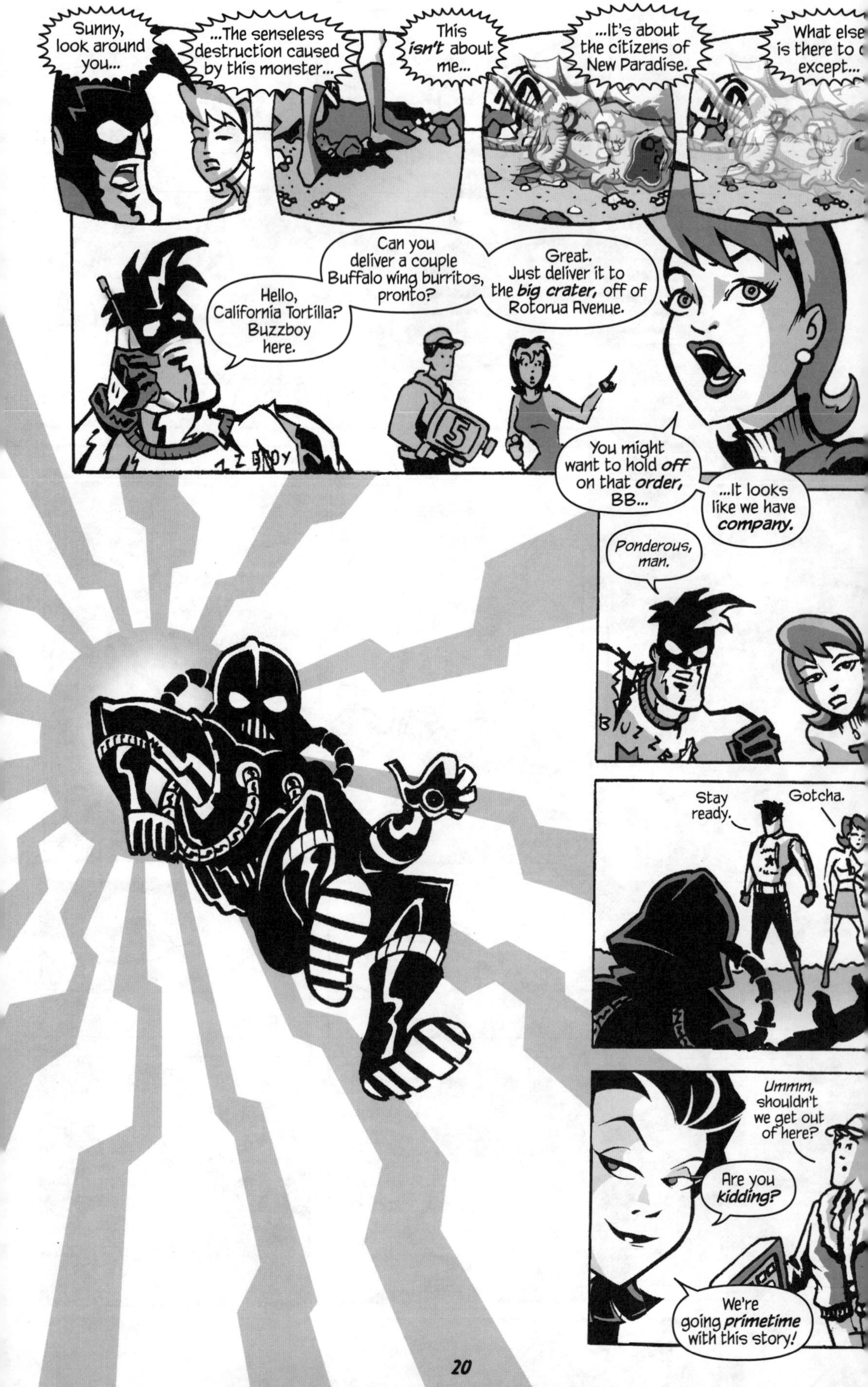
Sunny, look around you...
...The senseless destruction caused by this monster...
This *isn't* about me...
...It's about the citizens of New Paradise.
What else is there to c except...
Hello, California Tortilla? Buzzboy here.
Can you deliver a couple Buffalo wing burritos, pronto?
Great. Just deliver it to the *big crater,* off of Rotorua Avenue.
You might want to hold *off* on that *order,* BB...
...It looks like we have *company.*
Ponderous, man.
Stay ready.
Gotcha.
Ummm, shouldn't we get out of here?
Are you *kidding?*
We're going *primetime* with this story!

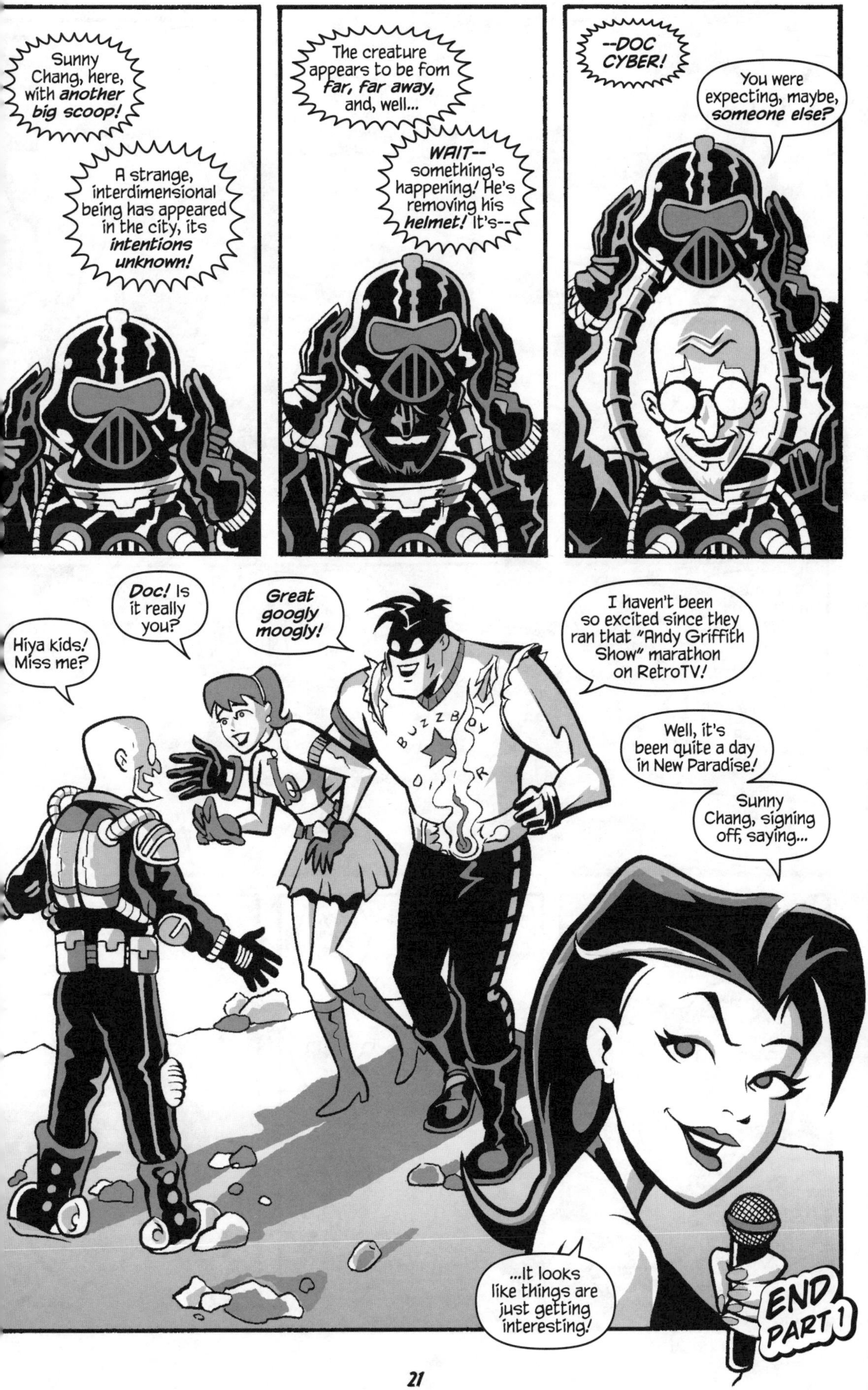

Sunny Chang, here, with **another big scoop!**
A strange, interdimensional being has appeared in the city, its **intentions unknown!**
The creature appears to be fom **far, far away,** and, well...
WAIT-- something's happening! He's removing his **helmet!** It's--
--DOC CYBER!
You were expecting, maybe, **someone else?**
Hiya kids! Miss me?
Doc! Is it really you?
Great googly moogly!
I haven't been so excited since they ran that "Andy Griffith Show" marathon on RetroTV!
Well, it's been quite a day in New Paradise!
Sunny Chang, signing off, saying...
...It looks like things are just getting interesting!
END PART 1

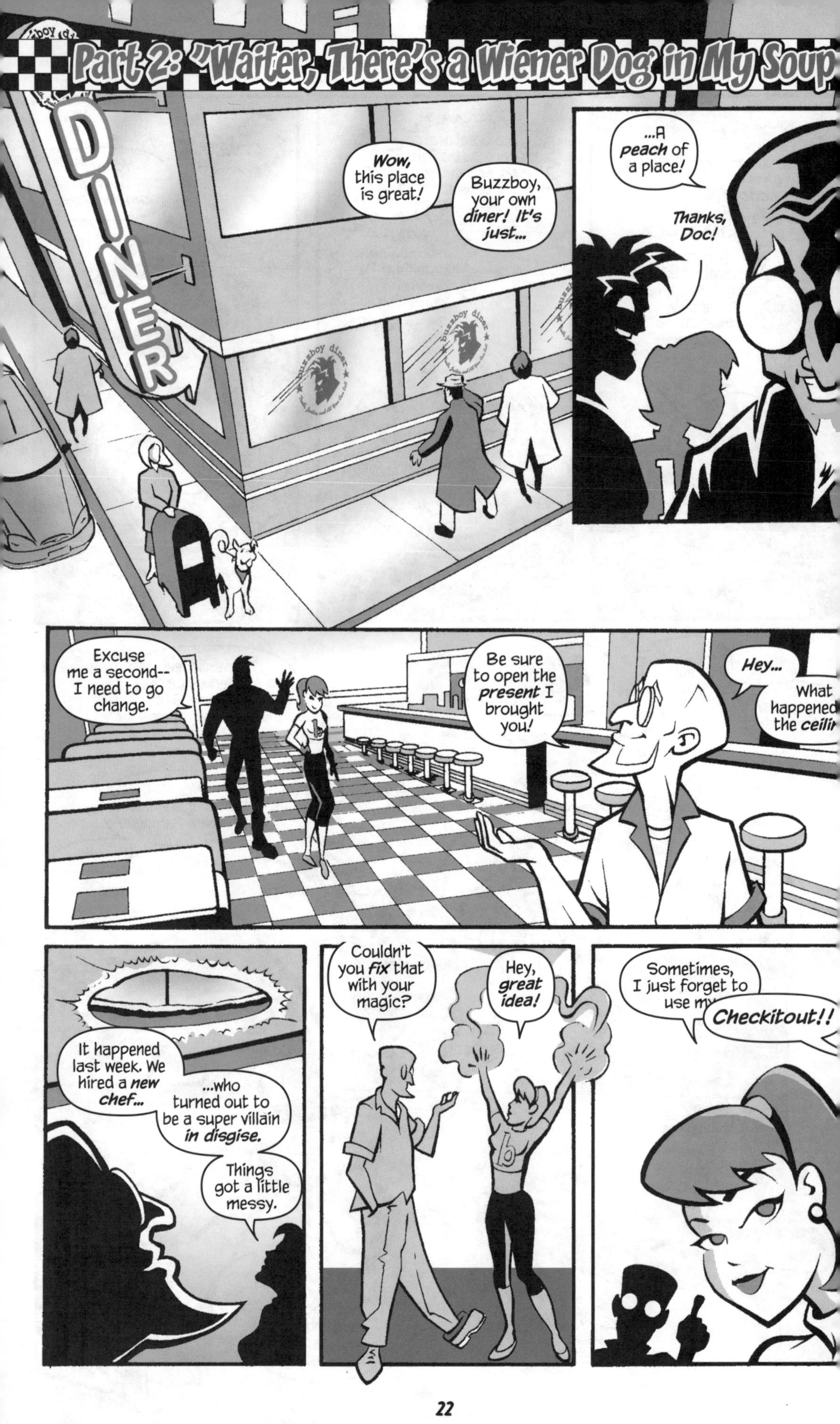
Part 2: "Waiter, There's a Wiener Dog in My Soup
DINER
Wow, this place is great!
Buzzboy, your own diner! It's just...
...A peach of a place!
Thanks, Doc!
Excuse me a second-- I need to go change.
Be sure to open the present I brought you!
Hey...
What happened the ceil
It happened last week. We hired a new chef...
...who turned out to be a super villain in disgise.
Things got a little messy.
Couldn't you fix that with your magic?
Hey, great idea!
Sometimes, I just forget to use my
Checkitout!!

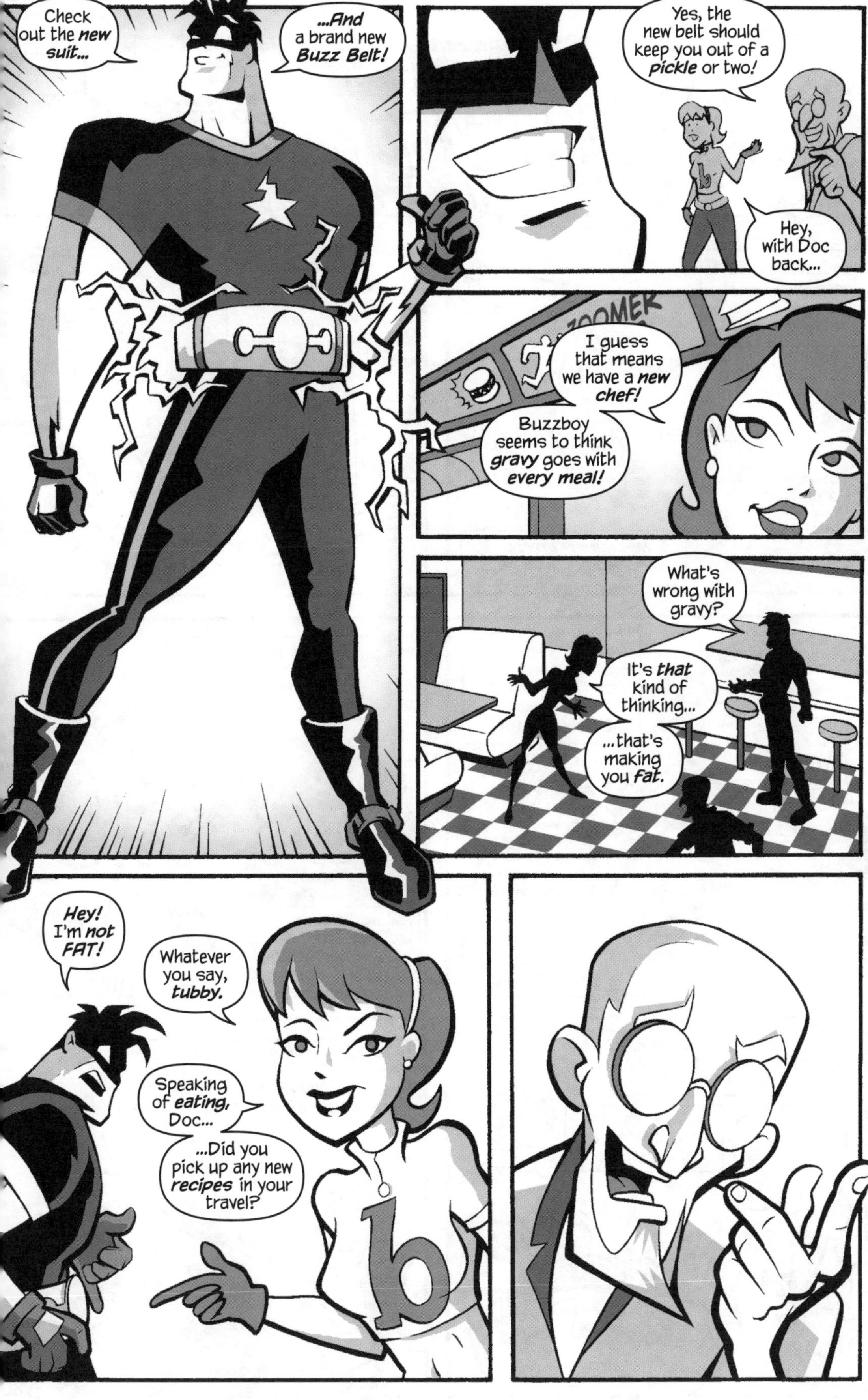
Check out the ***new suit...***
...And a brand new ***Buzz Belt!***
Yes, the new belt should keep you out of a ***pickle*** or two!
Hey, with Doc back...
ZOOMER
I guess that means we have a ***new chef!***
Buzzboy seems to think ***gravy*** goes with ***every meal!***
What's wrong with gravy?
It's ***that*** kind of thinking...
...that's making you ***fat.***
Hey! I'm ***not FAT!***
Whatever you say, ***tubby.***
Speaking of ***eating,*** Doc...
...Did you pick up any new ***recipes*** in your travel?

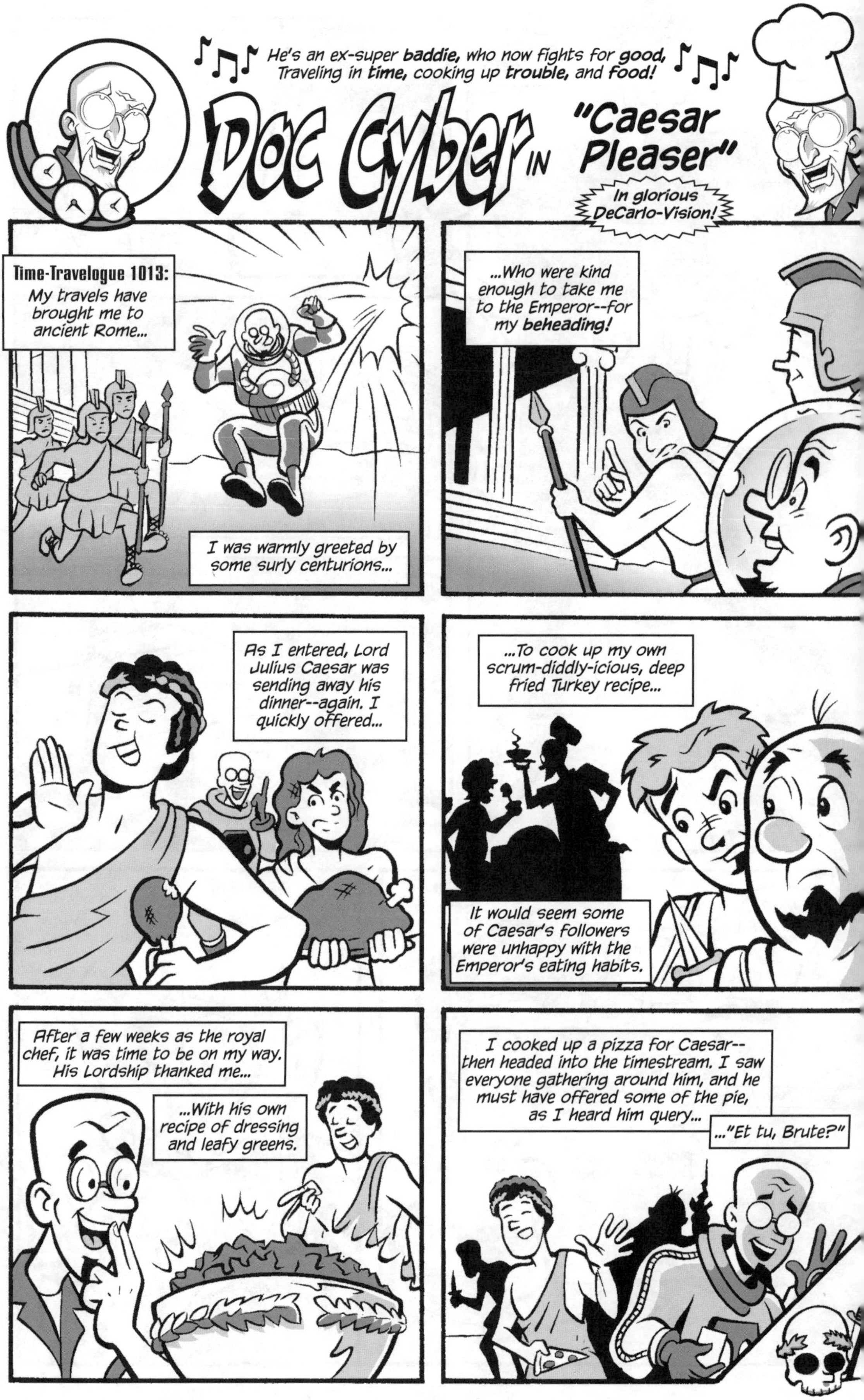

He's an ex-super baddie, who now fights for good,
Traveling in time, cooking up trouble, and food!
Doc Cyber IN "Caesar Pleaser"
In glorious DeCarlo-Vision!
Time-Travelogue 1013: My travels have brought me to ancient Rome...
I was warmly greeted by some surly centurions...
...Who were kind enough to take me to the Emperor--for my beheading!
As I entered, Lord Julius Caesar was sending away his dinner--again. I quickly offered...
...To cook up my own scrum-diddly-icious, deep fried Turkey recipe...
It would seem some of Caesar's followers were unhappy with the Emperor's eating habits.
After a few weeks as the royal chef, it was time to be on my way. His Lordship thanked me...
...With his own recipe of dressing and leafy greens.
I cooked up a pizza for Caesar--then headed into the timestream. I saw everyone gathering around him, and he must have offered some of the pie, as I heard him query...
..."Et tu, Brute?"

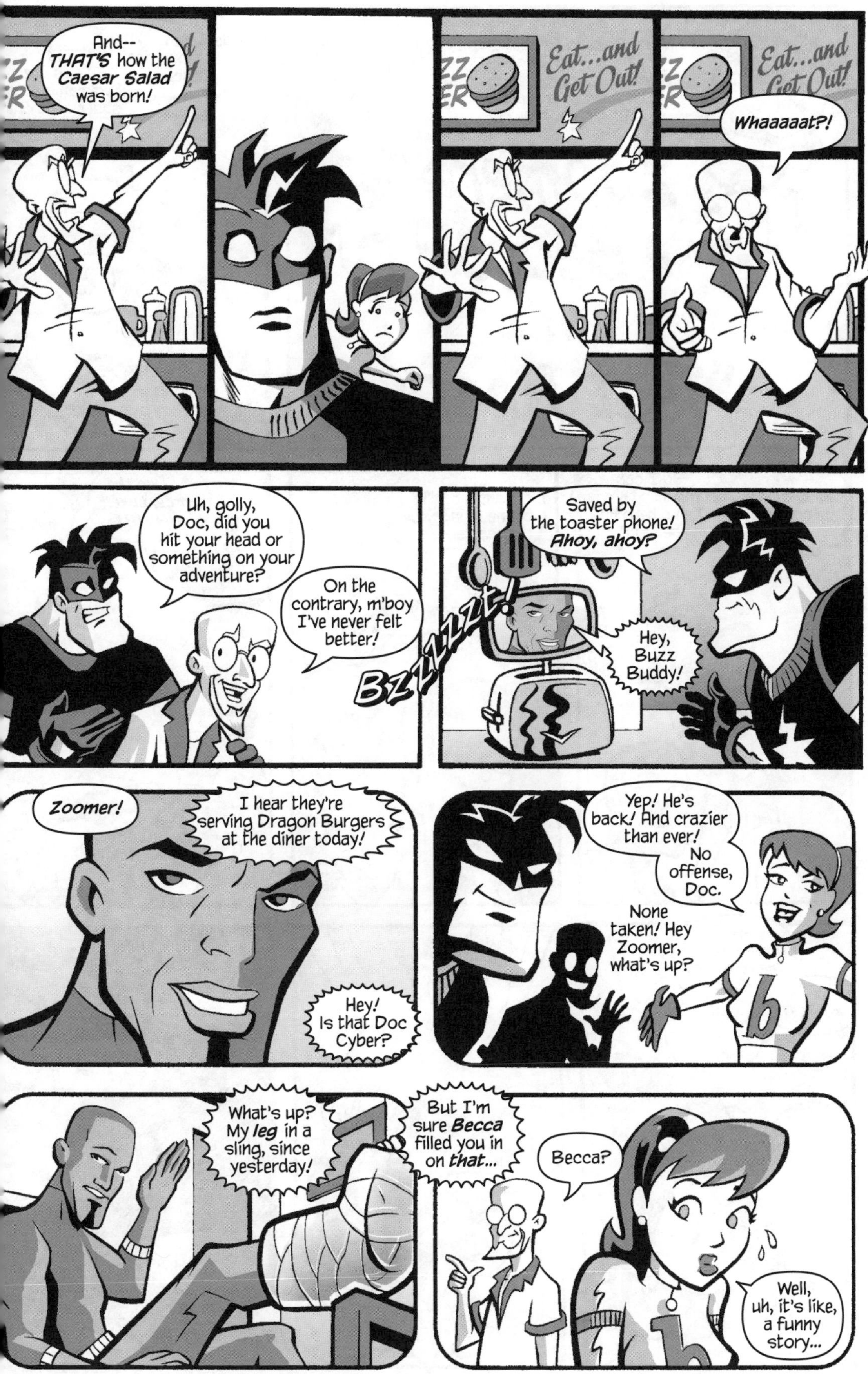
And-- THAT'S how the Caesar Salad was born!
Eat...and Get Out!
Eat...and Get Out!
Whaaaaat?!
Uh, golly, Doc, did you hit your head or something on your adventure?
On the contrary, m'boy I've never felt better!
Bzzzzzt!
Saved by the toaster phone! Ahoy, ahoy?
Hey, Buzz Buddy!
Zoomer!
I hear they're serving Dragon Burgers at the diner today!
Hey! Is that Doc Cyber?
Yep! He's back! And crazier than ever!
No offense, Doc.
None taken! Hey Zoomer, what's up?
What's up? My leg in a sling, since yesterday!
But I'm sure Becca filled you in on that...
Becca?
Well, uh, it's like, a funny story...

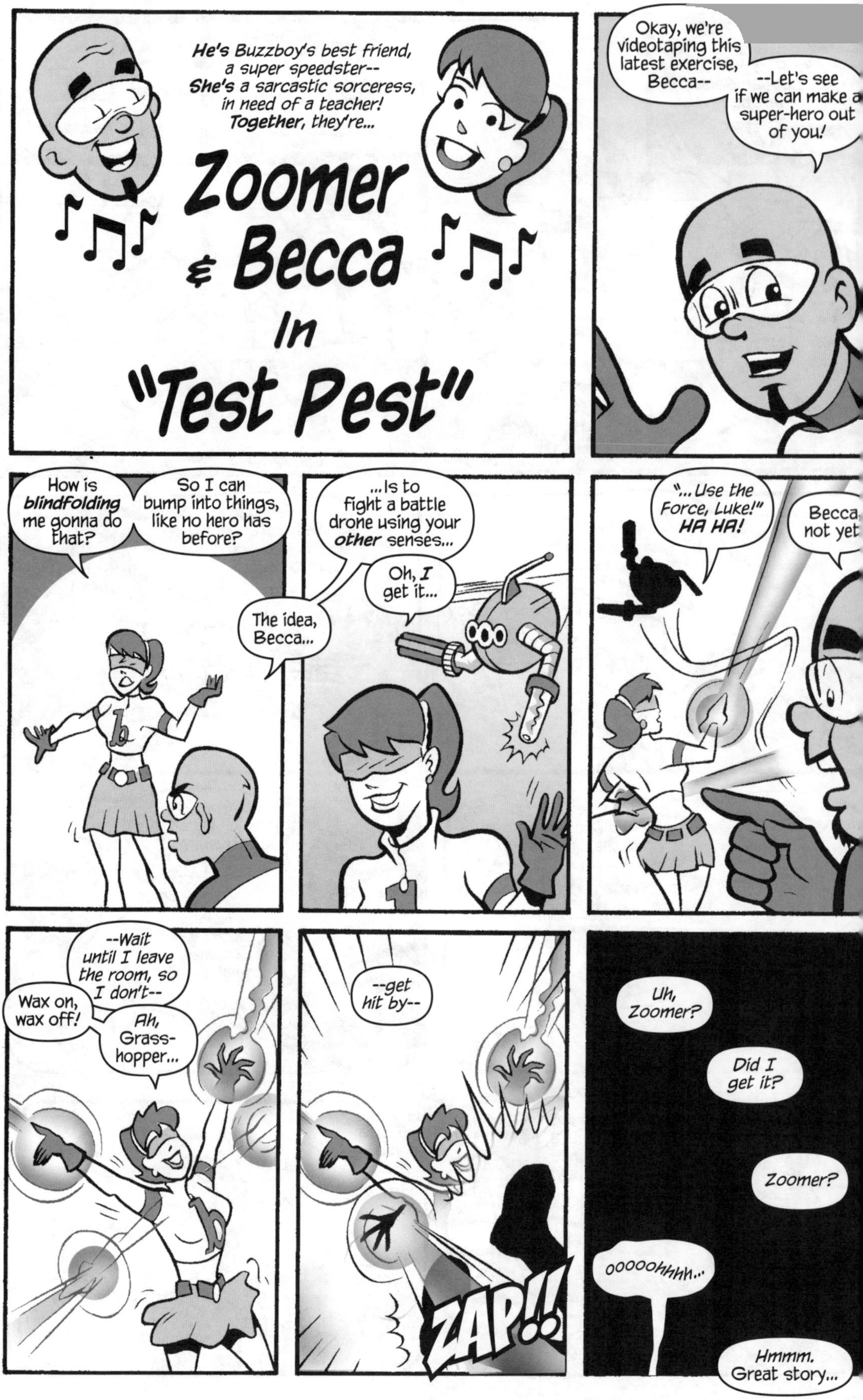

He's Buzzboy's best friend, a super speedster-- She's a sarcastic sorceress, in need of a teacher! Together, they're...
Zoomer & Becca In "Test Pest"
Okay, we're videotaping this latest exercise, Becca--
--Let's see if we can make a super-hero out of you!
How is blindfolding me gonna do that?
So I can bump into things, like no hero has before?
The idea, Becca...
...Is to fight a battle drone using your other senses...
Oh, I get it...
"...Use the Force, Luke!" HA HA!
Becca, not yet
Wax on, wax off!
--Wait until I leave the room, so I don't--
Ah, Grass-hopper...
--get hit by--
ZAP!!
Uh, Zoomer?
Did I get it?
Zoomer?
oooohhhh...
Hmmm. Great story...

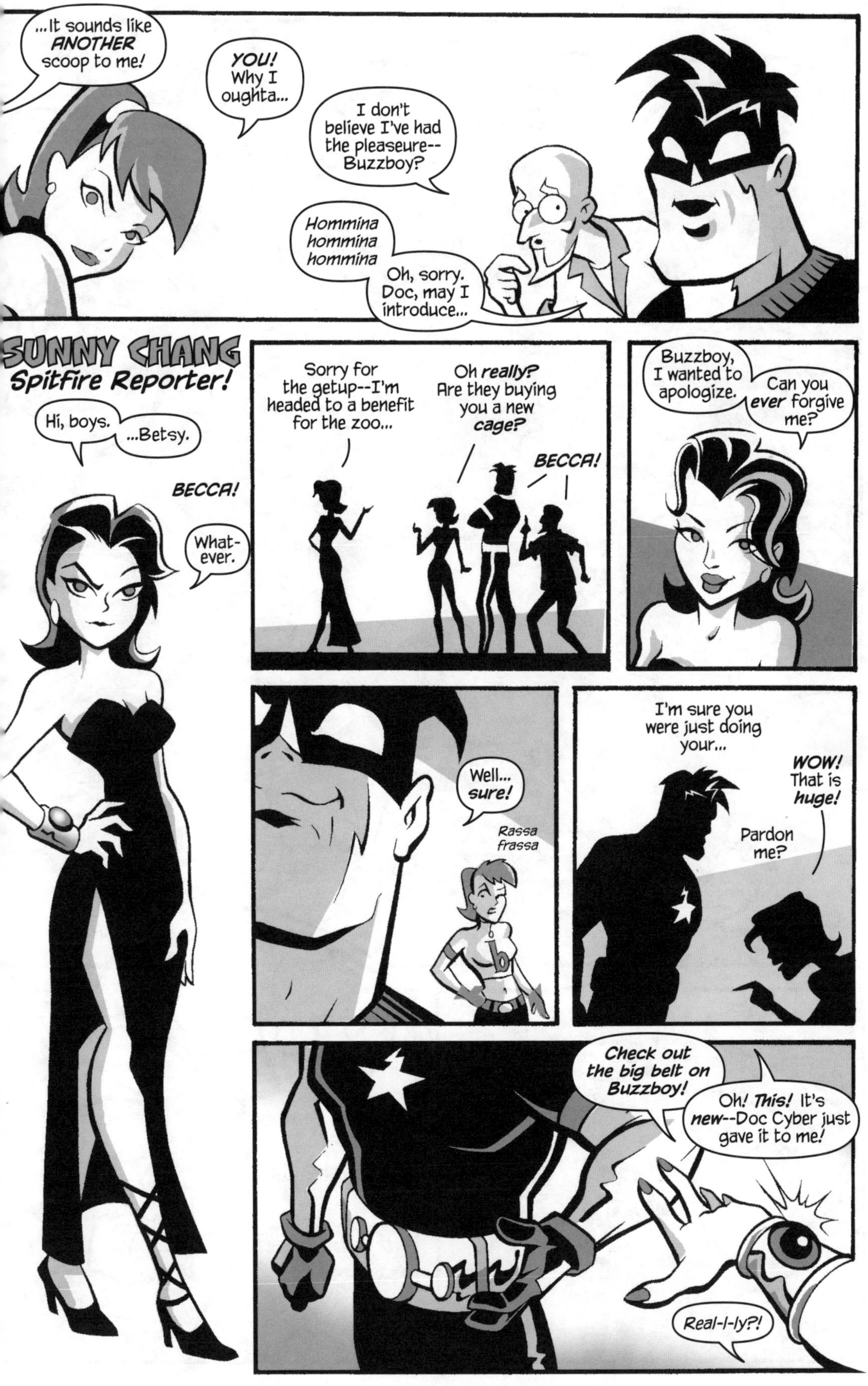

...It sounds like ANOTHER scoop to me!
YOU! Why I oughta...
I don't believe I've had the pleaseure-- Buzzboy?
Hommina hommina hommina
Oh, sorry. Doc, may I introduce...
SUNNY CHANG
Spitfire Reporter!
Hi, boys.
...Betsy.
BECCA!
What-ever.
Sorry for the getup--I'm headed to a benefit for the zoo...
Oh really? Are they buying you a new cage?
BECCA!
Buzzboy, I wanted to apologize.
Can you ever forgive me?
Well... sure!
Rassa frassa
I'm sure you were just doing your...
WOW! That is huge!
Pardon me?
Check out the big belt on Buzzboy!
Oh! This! It's new--Doc Cyber just gave it to me!
Real-l-ly?!

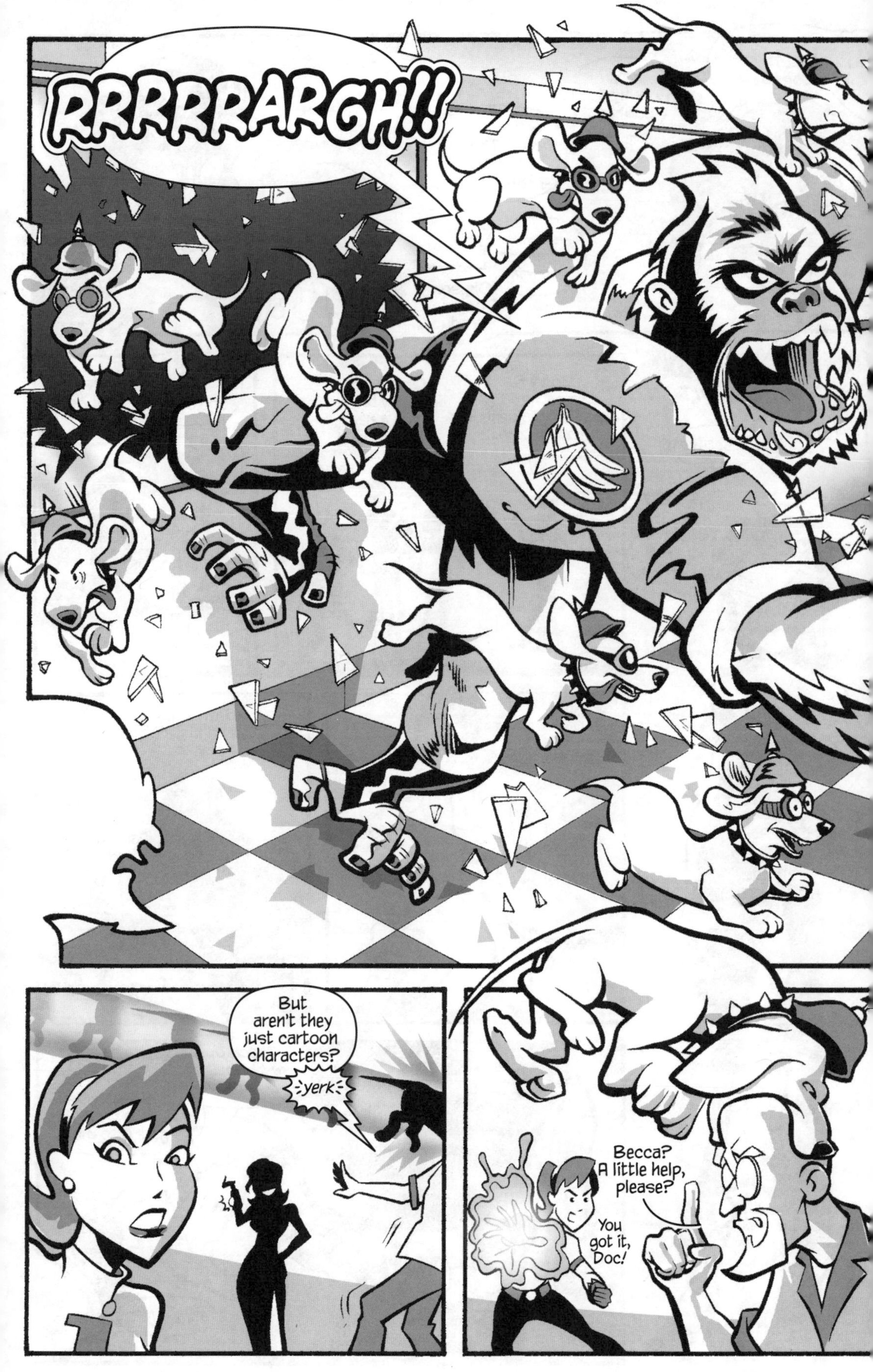
RRRRRARGH!!
But aren't they just cartoon characters?
yerk
Becca? A little help, please?
You got it, Doc!

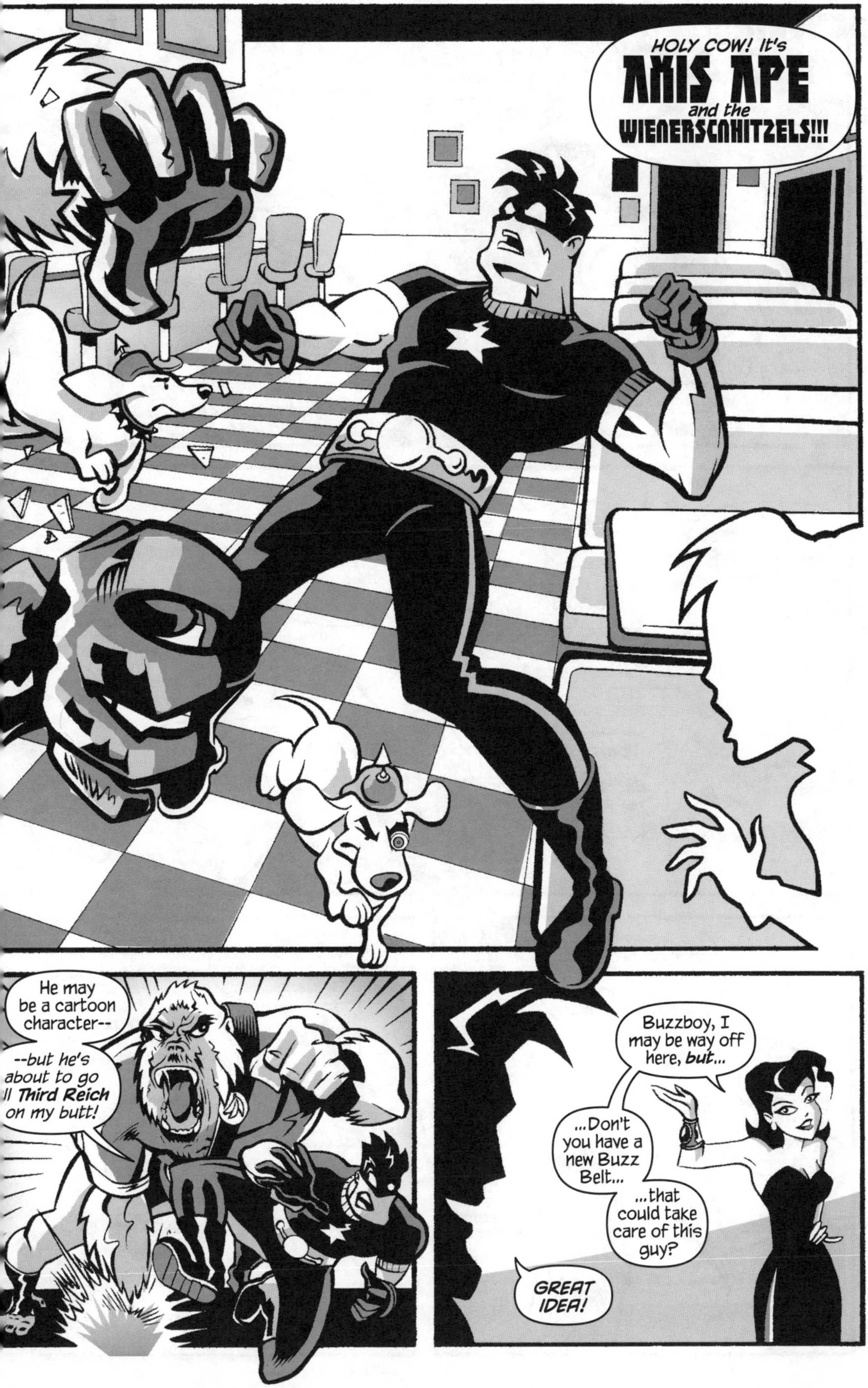
HOLY COW! It's AXIS APE and the WIENERSCHNITZELS!!!
He may be a cartoon character--
--but he's about to go ll *Third Reich* on my butt!
Buzzboy, I may be way off here, *but*...
...Don't you have a new Buzz Belt...
...that could take care of this guy?
GREAT IDEA!

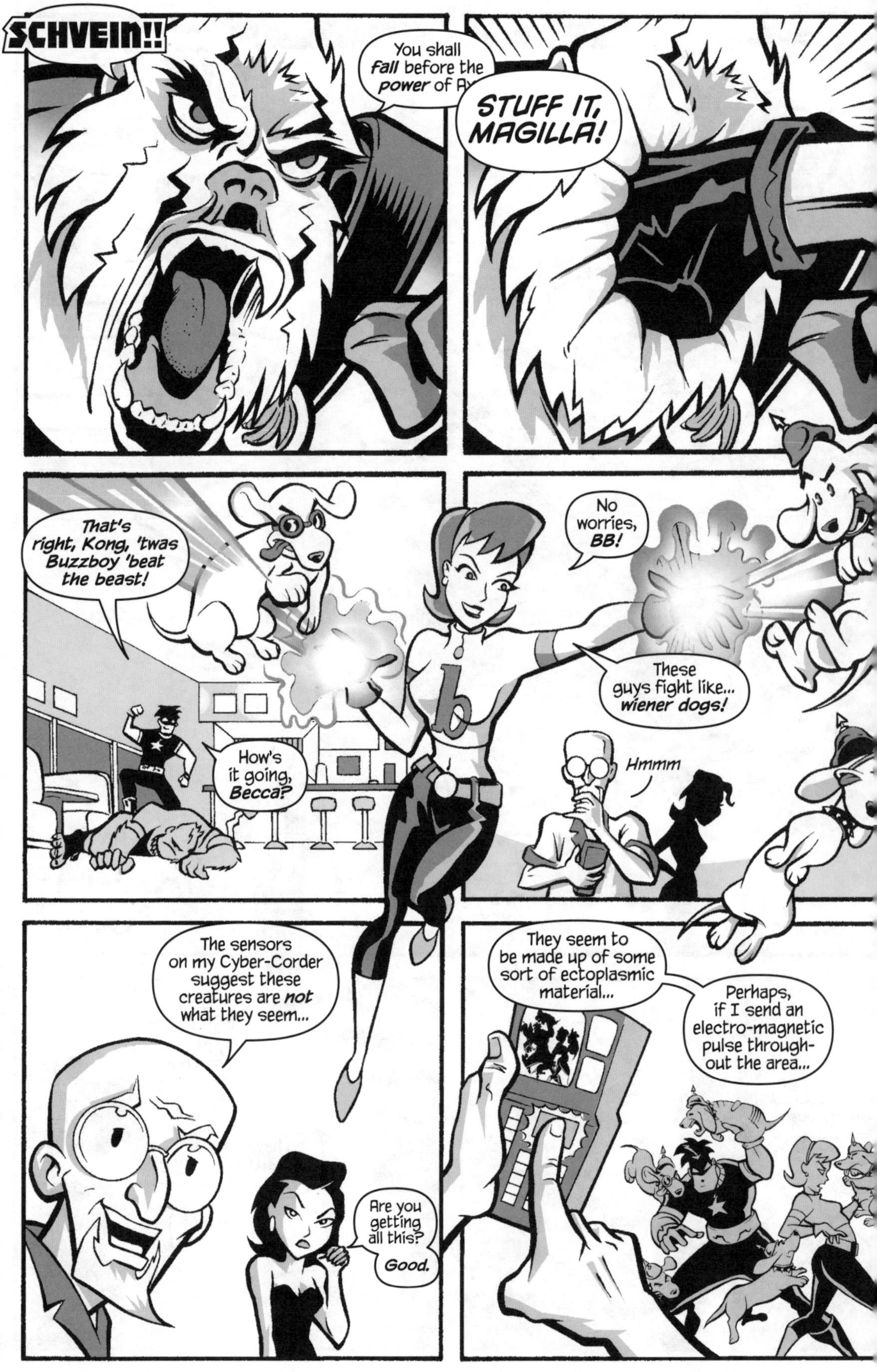
SCHVEIN!!
You shall fall before the power of A
STUFF IT, MAGILLA!
That's right, Kong, 'twas Buzzboy 'beat the beast!
How's it going, Becca?
No worries, BB!
These guys fight like... wiener dogs!
Hmmm
The sensors on my Cyber-Corder suggest these creatures are not what they seem...
Are you getting all this? Good.
They seem to be made up of some sort of ectoplasmic material...
Perhaps, if I send an electro-magnetic pulse through-out the area...

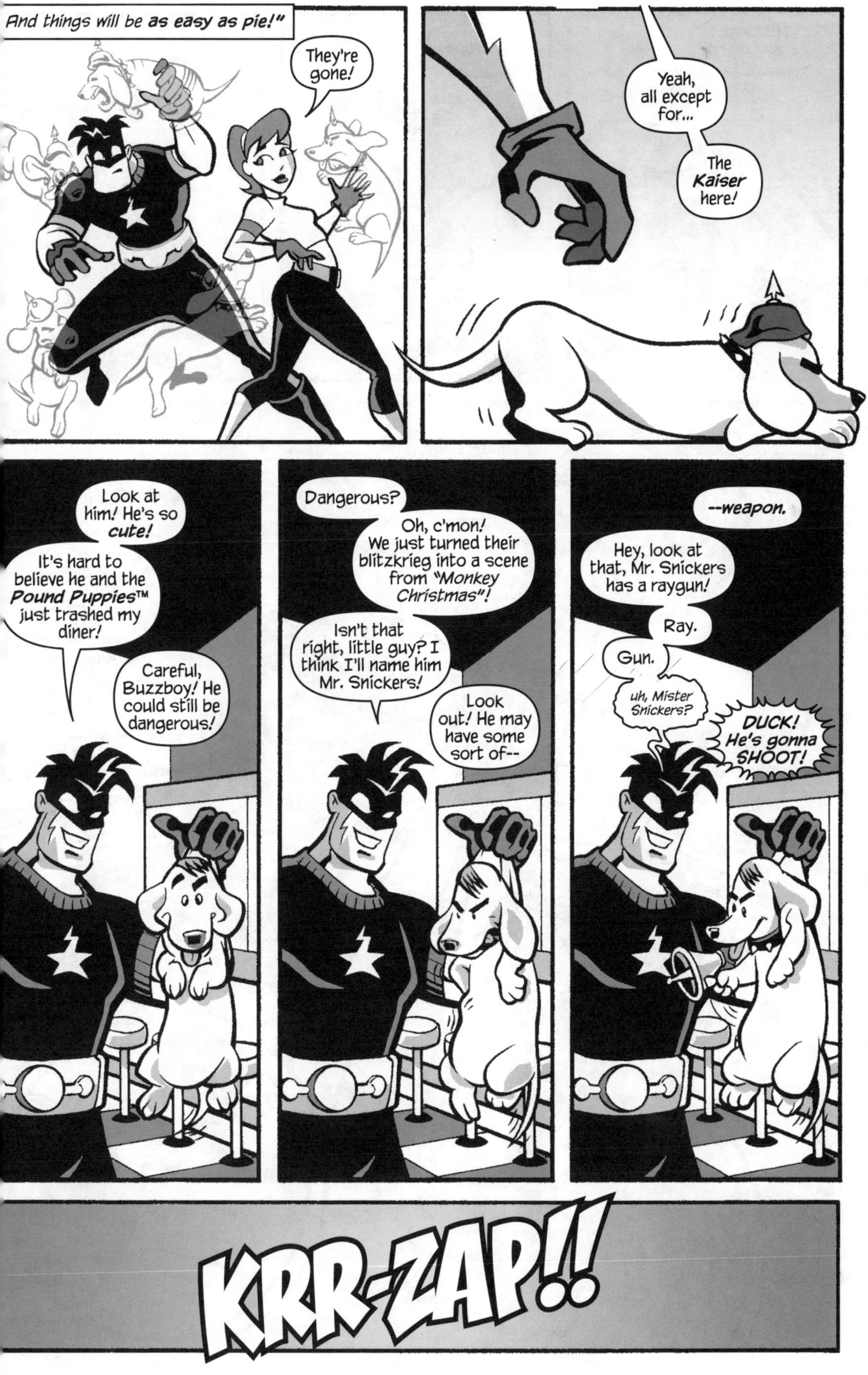

And things will be as easy as pie!"
They're gone!
Yeah, all except for...
The Kaiser here!
Look at him! He's so cute!
It's hard to believe he and the Pound Puppies™ just trashed my diner!
Careful, Buzzboy! He could still be dangerous!
Dangerous?
Oh, c'mon! We just turned their blitzkrieg into a scene from "Monkey Christmas"!
Isn't that right, little guy? I think I'll name him Mr. Snickers!
Look out! He may have some sort of--
--weapon.
Hey, look at that, Mr. Snickers has a raygun!
Ray.
Gun.
uh, Mister Snickers?
DUCK! He's gonna SHOOT!
KRR-ZAP!!

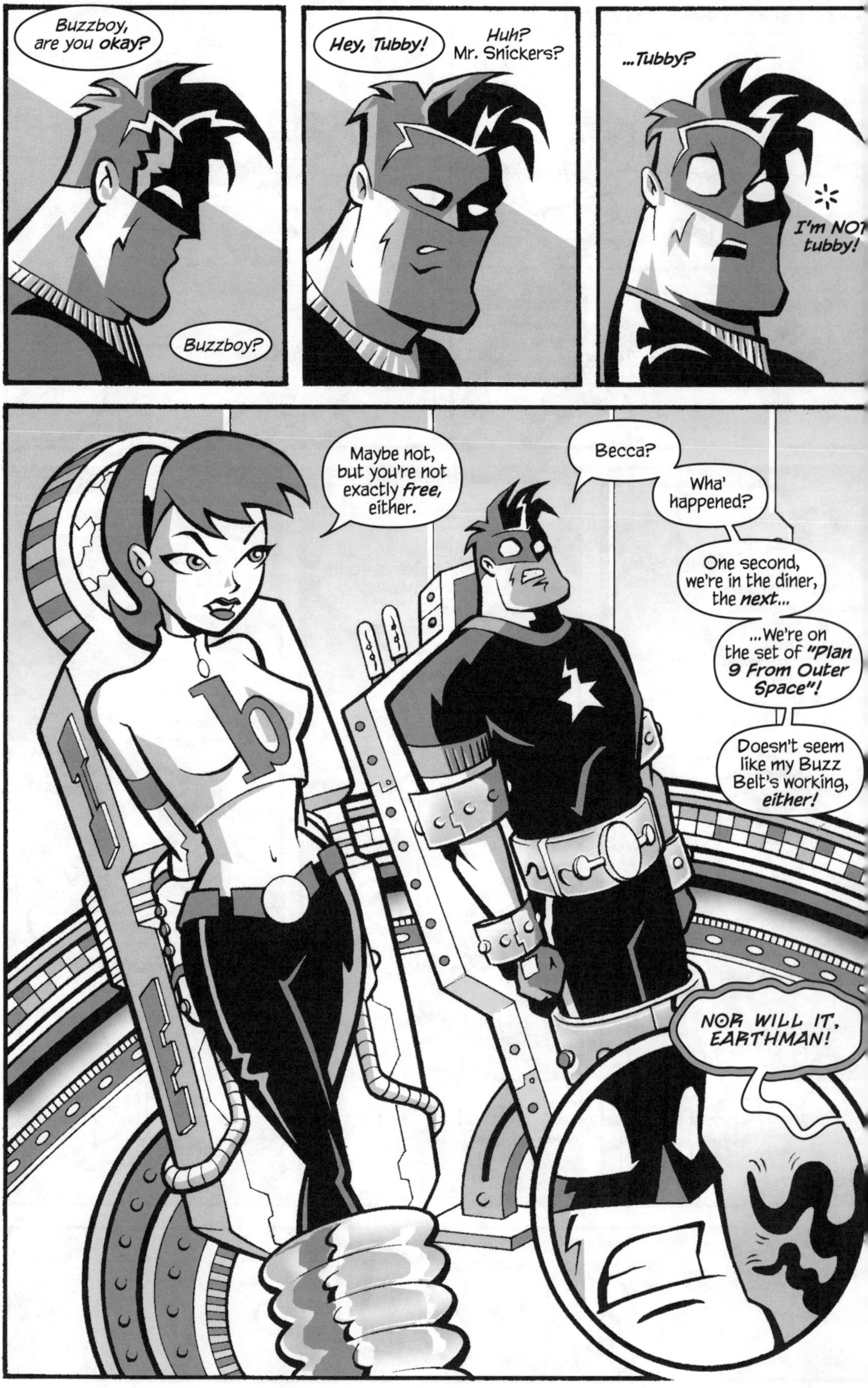

Buzzboy, are you okay?
Buzzboy?
Hey, Tubby!
Huh? Mr. Snickers?
...Tubby?
I'm NOT tubby!
Maybe not, but you're not exactly free, either.
Becca?
Wha' happened?
One second, we're in the diner, the next...
...We're on the set of "Plan 9 From Outer Space"!
Doesn't seem like my Buzz Belt's working, either!
NOR WILL IT, EARTHMAN!

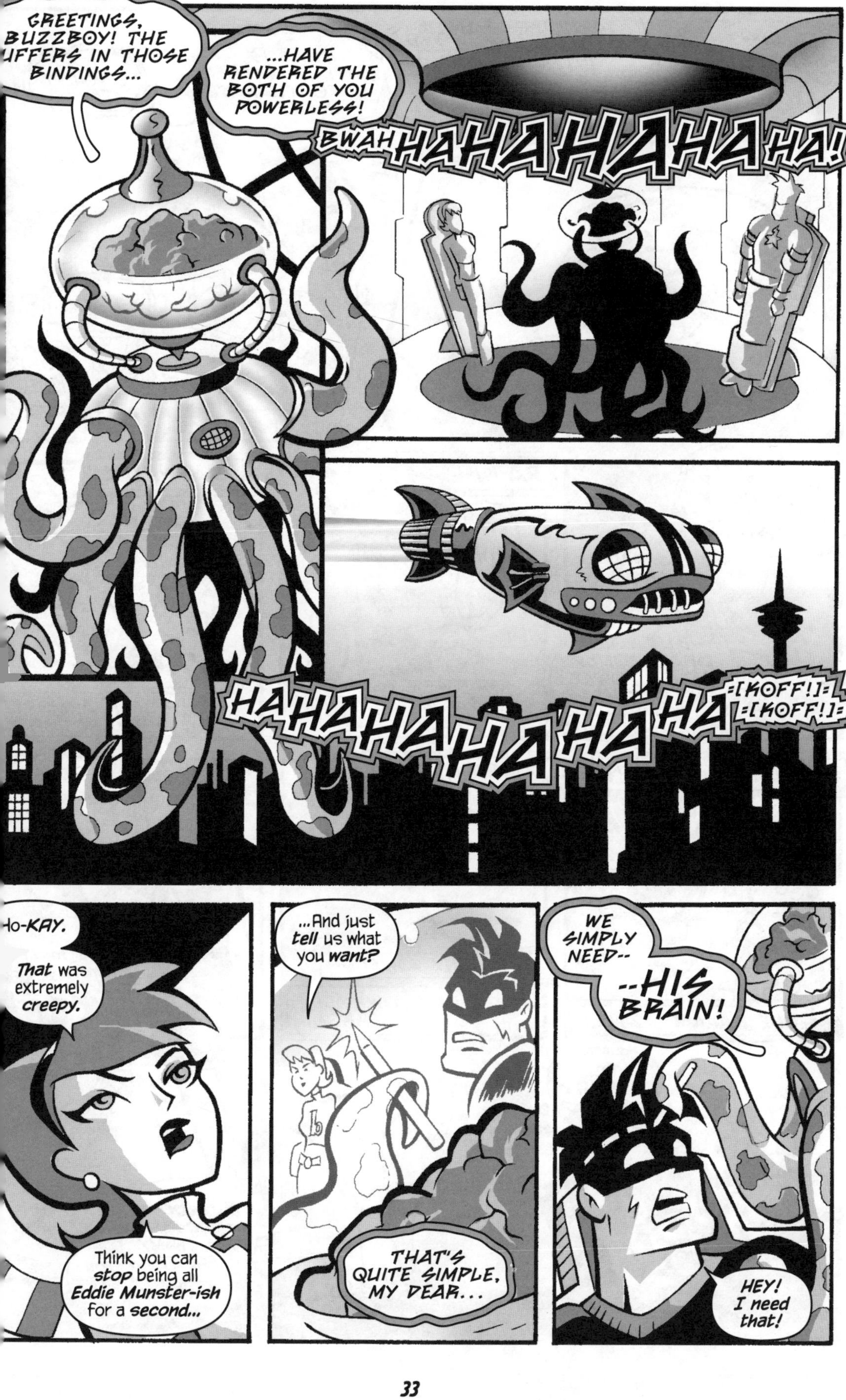
GREETINGS, BUZZBOY! THE UFFERS IN THOSE BINDINGS...
...HAVE RENDERED THE BOTH OF YOU POWERLESS!
BWAH HAHAHAHAHAHA HA!
HAHAHAHAHAHAHA =[KOFF!]= =[KOFF!]=
Ho-KAY.
That was extremely creepy.
Think you can stop being all Eddie Munster-ish for a second...
...And just tell us what you want?
THAT'S QUITE SIMPLE, MY DEAR...
WE SIMPLY NEED--
--HIS BRAIN!
HEY! I need that!

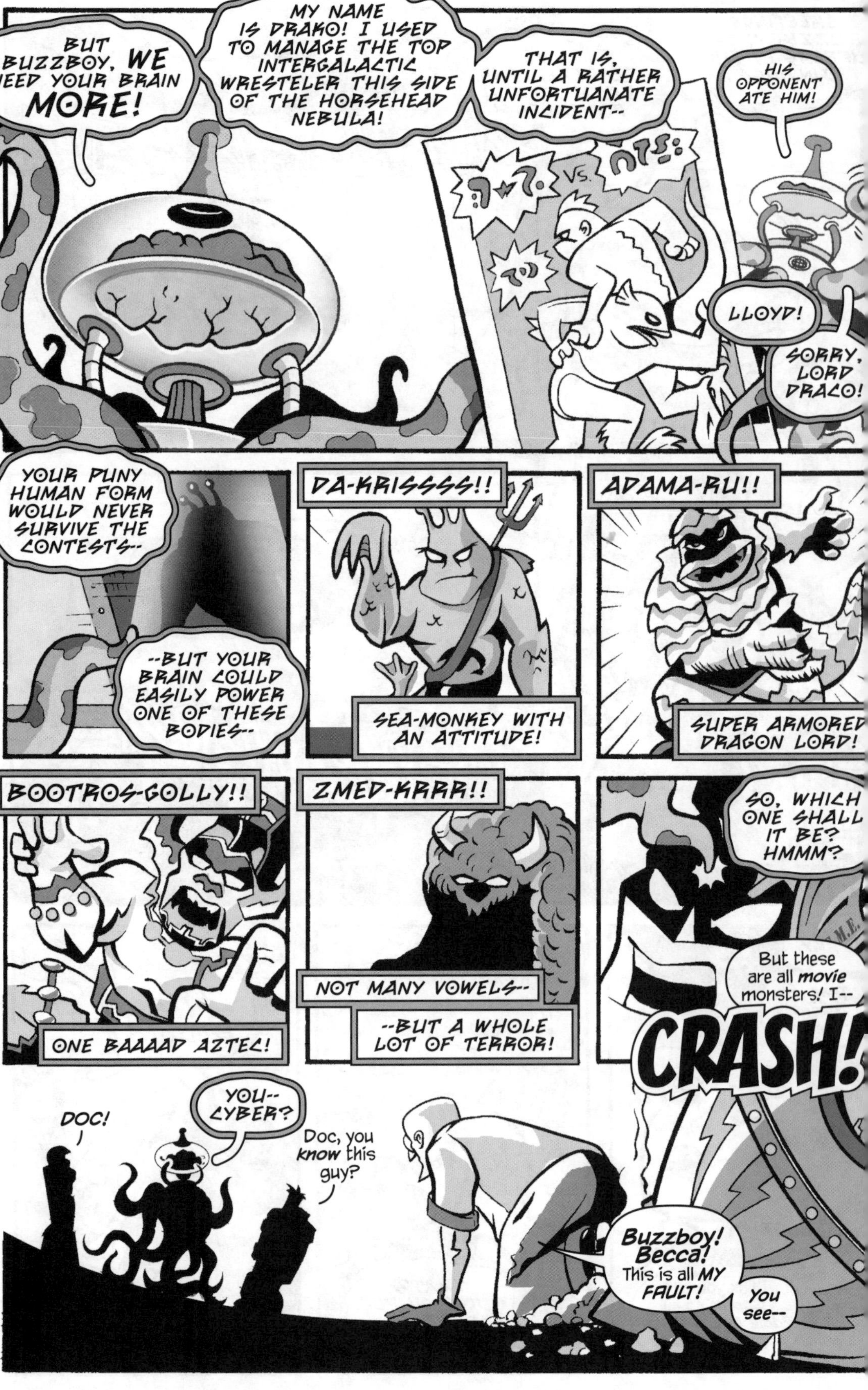

BUT BUZZBOY, WE NEED YOUR BRAIN MORE!
MY NAME IS DRAKO! I USED TO MANAGE THE TOP INTERGALACTIC WRESTELER THIS SIDE OF THE HORSEHEAD NEBULA!
THAT IS, UNTIL A RATHER UNFORTUANATE INCIDENT--
VS.
HIS OPPONENT ATE HIM!
LLOYD!
SORRY, LORD DRACO!
YOUR PUNY HUMAN FORM WOULD NEVER SURVIVE THE CONTESTS--
--BUT YOUR BRAIN COULD EASILY POWER ONE OF THESE BODIES--
DA-KRISSSSS!!
SEA-MONKEY WITH AN ATTITUDE!
ADAMA-RU!!
SUPER ARMORED DRAGON LORD!
BOOTROS-GOLLY!!
ONE BAAAAD AZTEC!
ZMED-KRRR!!
NOT MANY VOWELS--
--BUT A WHOLE LOT OF TERROR!
SO, WHICH ONE SHALL IT BE? HMMM?
But these are all *movie* monsters! I--
CRASH!
DOC!
YOU-- CYBER?
Doc, you *know* this guy?
Buzzboy! Becca! This is all *MY FAULT!*
You see--

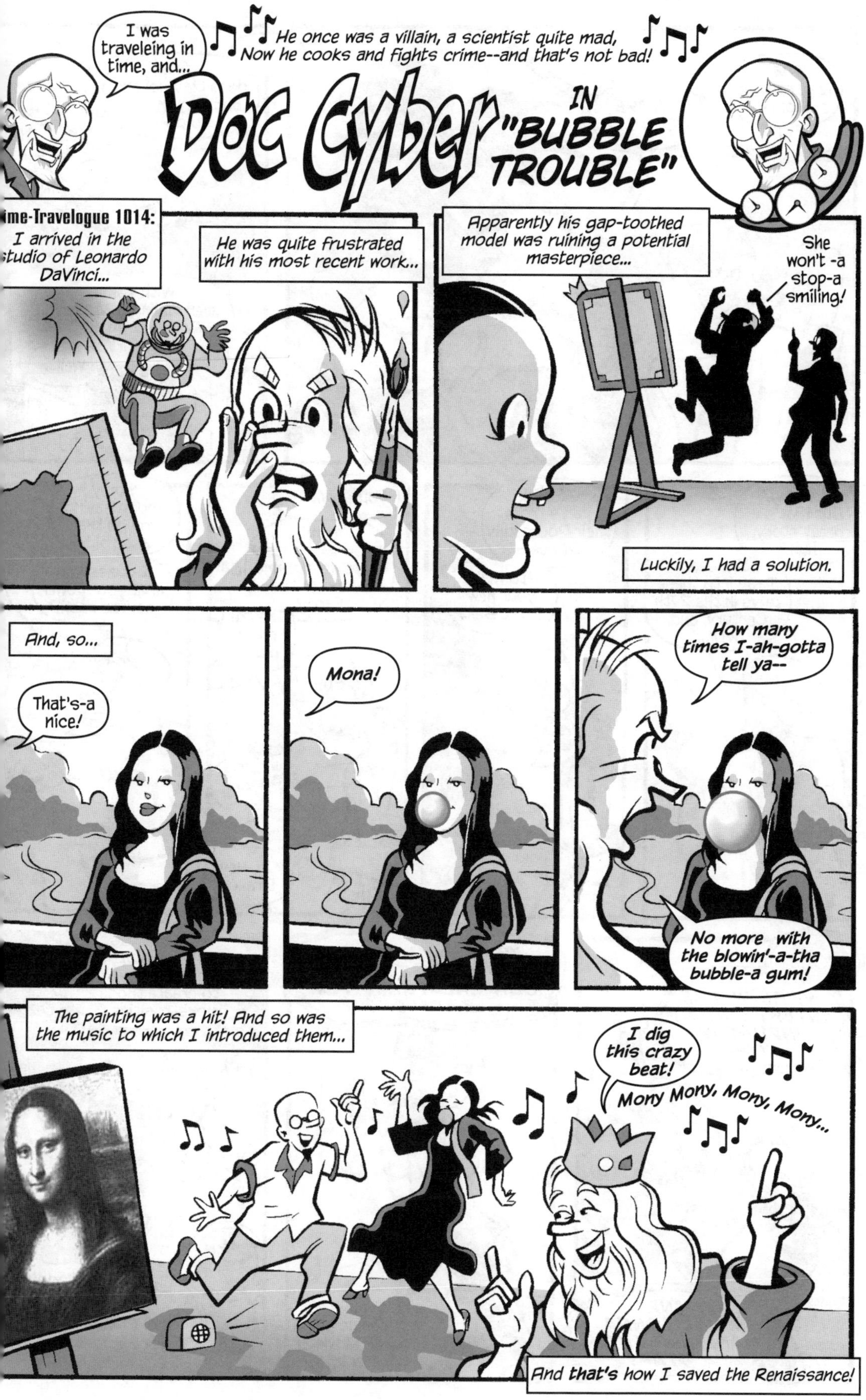

I was traveleing in time, and...
He once was a villain, a scientist quite mad, Now he cooks and fights crime--and that's not bad!
Doc Cyber in "Bubble Trouble"
ime-Travelogue 1014: I arrived in the studio of Leonardo DaVinci...
He was quite frustrated with his most recent work...
Apparently his gap-toothed model was ruining a potential masterpiece...
She won't -a stop-a smiling!
Luckily, I had a solution.
And, so...
That's-a nice!
Mona!
How many times I-ah-gotta tell ya--
No more with the blowin'-a-tha bubble-a gum!
The painting was a hit! And so was the music to which I introduced them...
I dig this crazy beat!
Mony Mony, Mony, Mony...
And that's how I saved the Renaissance!

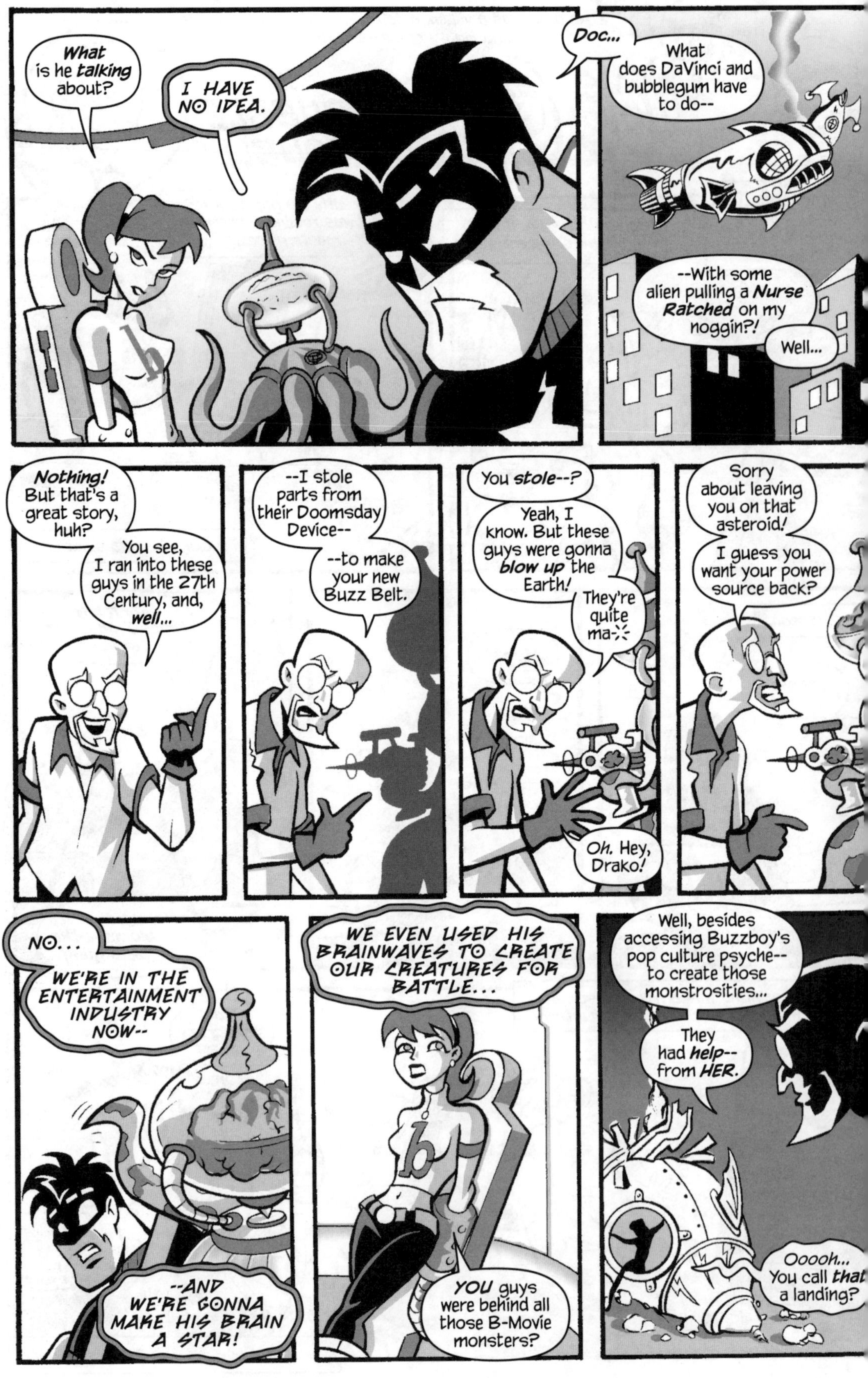

What is he talking about?
I HAVE NO IDEA.
Doc...
What does DaVinci and bubblegum have to do--
--With some alien pulling a Nurse Ratched on my noggin?!
Well...
Nothing! But that's a great story, huh?
You see, I ran into these guys in the 27th Century, and, well...
--I stole parts from their Doomsday Device--
--to make your new Buzz Belt.
You stole--?
Yeah, I know. But these guys were gonna blow up the Earth!
They're quite ma-
Oh. Hey, Drako!
Sorry about leaving you on that asteroid!
I guess you want your power source back?
NO...
WE'RE IN THE ENTERTAINMENT INDUSTRY NOW--
--AND WE'RE GONNA MAKE HIS BRAIN A STAR!
WE EVEN USED HIS BRAINWAVES TO CREATE OUR CREATURES FOR BATTLE...
YOU guys were behind all those B-Movie monsters?
Well, besides accessing Buzzboy's pop culture psyche--to create those monstrosities...
They had help--from HER.
Ooooh... You call that a landing?

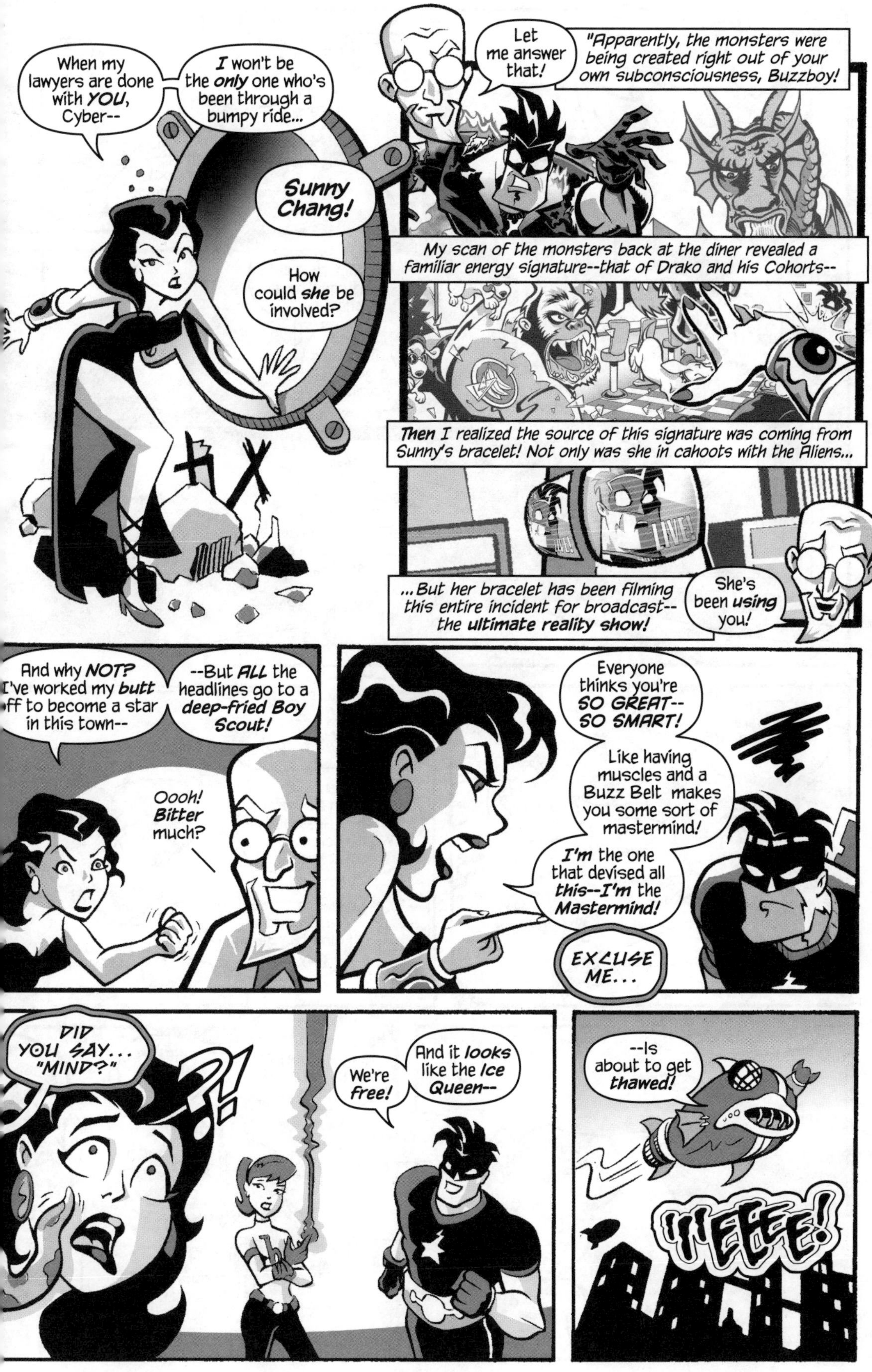

When my lawyers are done with YOU, Cyber--
I won't be the only one who's been through a bumpy ride...
Sunny Chang!
How could she be involved?
Let me answer that!
"Apparently, the monsters were being created right out of your own subconsciousness, Buzzboy!
My scan of the monsters back at the diner revealed a familiar energy signature--that of Drako and his Cohorts--
Then I realized the source of this signature was coming from Sunny's bracelet! Not only was she in cahoots with the Aliens...
LIVE!
...But her bracelet has been filming this entire incident for broadcast--the ultimate reality show!
She's been using you!
And why NOT? I've worked my butt off to become a star in this town--
--But ALL the headlines go to a deep-fried Boy Scout!
Oooh! Bitter much?
Everyone thinks you're SO GREAT--SO SMART!
Like having muscles and a Buzz Belt makes you some sort of mastermind!
I'm the one that devised all this--I'm the Mastermind!
EXCUSE ME...
DID YOU SAY... "MIND?"
?!
We're free!
And it looks like the Ice Queen--
--Is about to get thawed!
WEEEE!

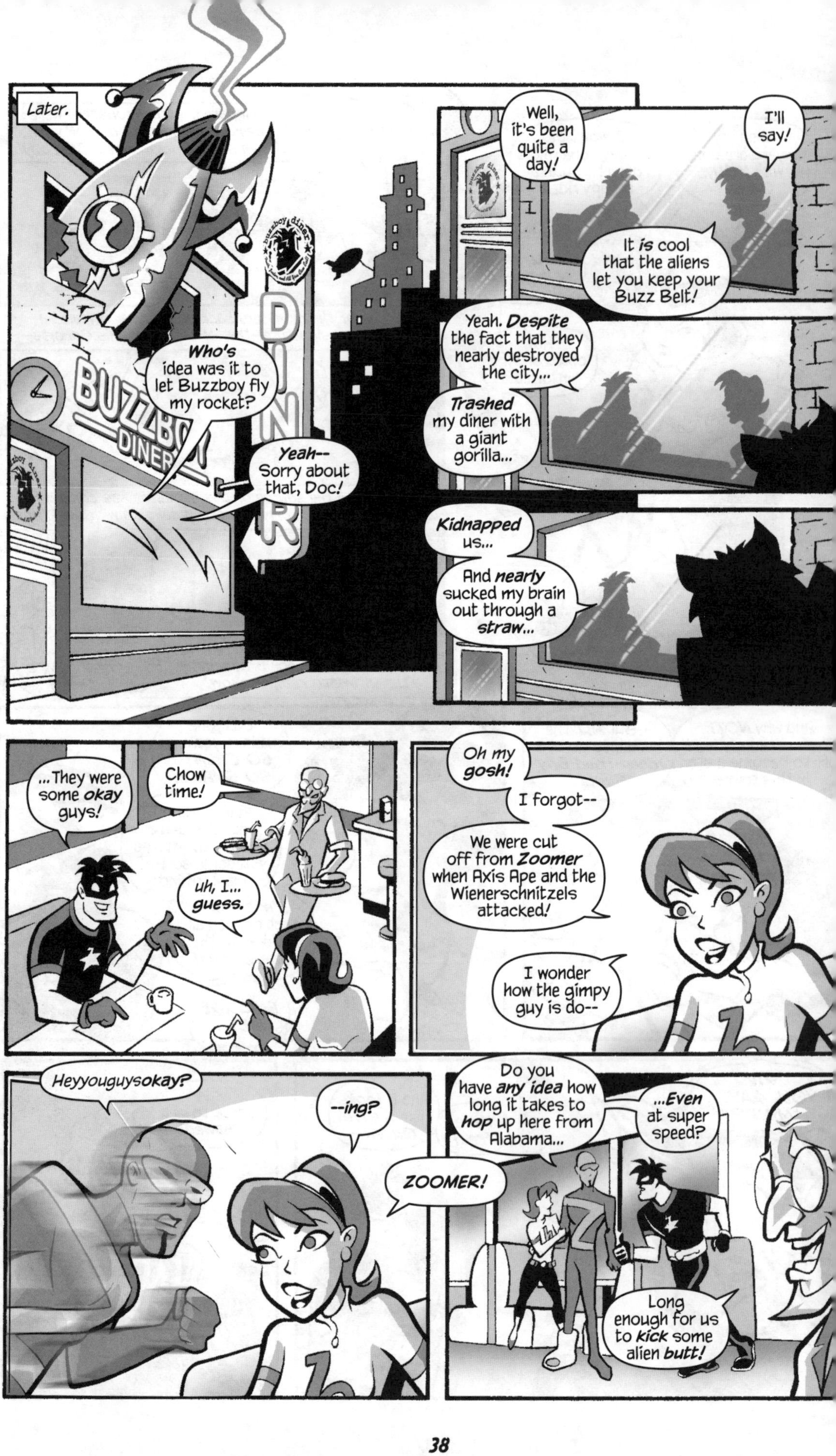
Later.
BUZZBOY DINER
DINER
Who's idea was it to let Buzzboy fly my rocket?
Yeah-- Sorry about that, Doc!
Well, it's been quite a day!
I'll say!
It *is* cool that the aliens let you keep your Buzz Belt!
Yeah. *Despite* the fact that they nearly destroyed the city...
Trashed my diner with a giant gorilla...
Kidnapped us...
And *nearly* sucked my brain out through a *straw*...
...They were some *okay* guys!
Chow time!
uh, I... *guess.*
Oh my *gosh!*
I forgot--
We were cut off from *Zoomer* when Axis Ape and the Wienerschnitzels attacked!
I wonder how the gimpy guy is do--
Heyyouguys*okay?*
--ing?
ZOOMER!
Do you have *any idea* how long it takes to *hop* up here from Alabama...
...Even at super speed?
Long enough for us to *kick* some alien *butt!*

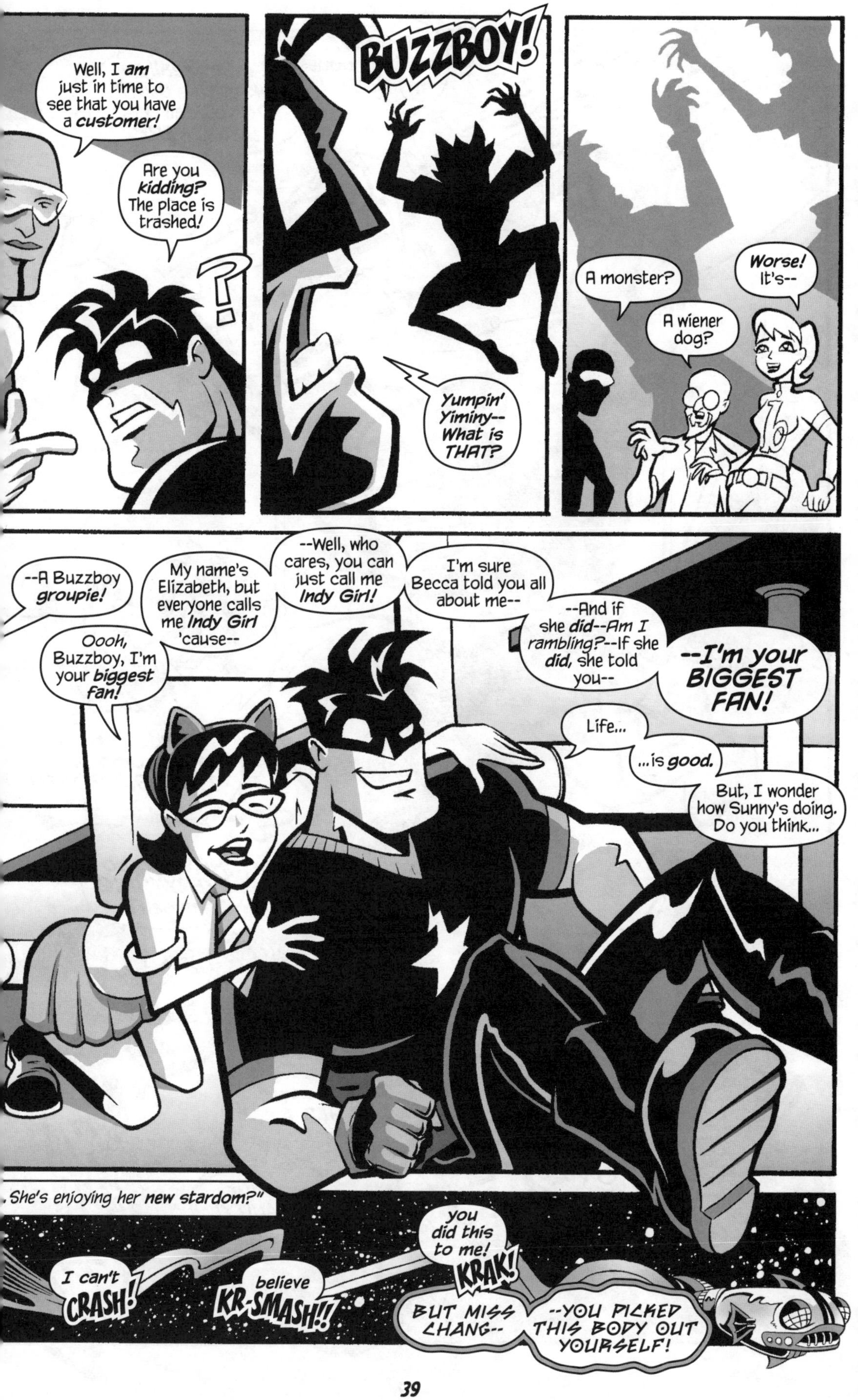

Well, I am just in time to see that you have a customer!
Are you kidding? The place is trashed!
?
BUZZBOY!
Yumpin' Yiminy-- What is THAT?
A monster?
A wiener dog?
Worse! It's--
--A Buzzboy groupie!
Oooh, Buzzboy, I'm your biggest fan!
My name's Elizabeth, but everyone calls me Indy Girl 'cause--
--Well, who cares, you can just call me Indy Girl!
I'm sure Becca told you all about me--
--And if she did--Am I rambling?--If she did, she told you--
--I'm your BIGGEST FAN!
Life...
...is good.
But, I wonder how Sunny's doing. Do you think...
...She's enjoying her new stardom?"
I can't
CRASH!
believe
KR-SMASH!!
you did this to me!
KRAK!
BUT MISS CHANG--
--YOU PICKED THIS BODY OUT YOURSELF!

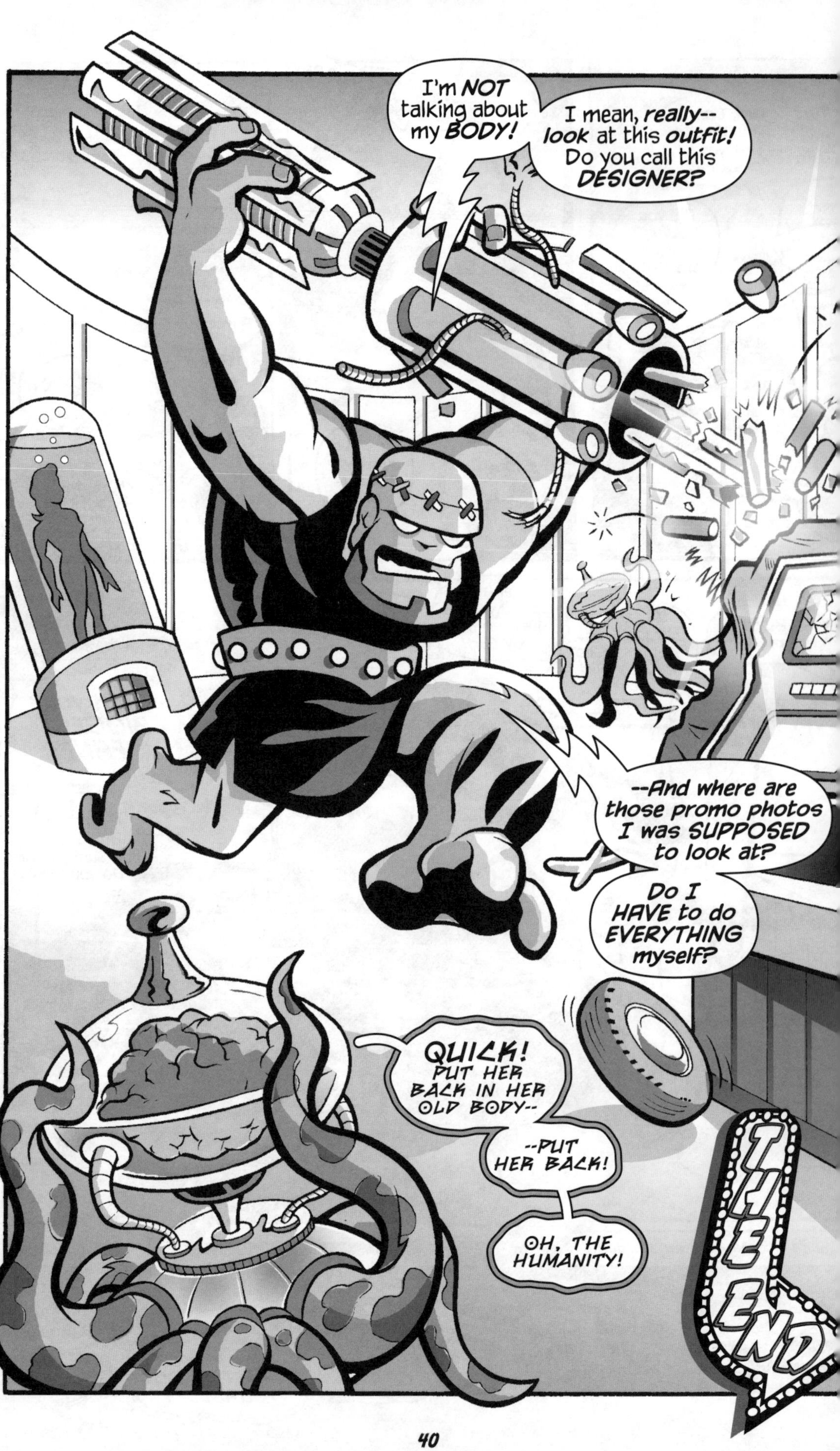
I'm NOT talking about my BODY!
I mean, really-- look at this outfit! Do you call this DESIGNER?
--And where are those promo photos I was SUPPOSED to look at?
Do I HAVE to do EVERYTHING myself?
QUICK! PUT HER BACK IN HER OLD BODY--
--PUT HER BACK!
OH, THE HUMANITY!
THE END

GET THE SCOOP ON THOSE BOISTEROUS BEHEMOTHS BATTLING BUZZBOY! IT'S TIME FOR...

DOC CYBER'S MONSTER HANDBOOK!

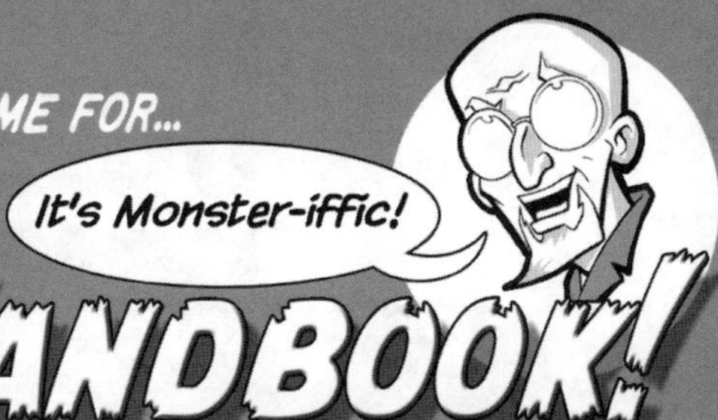
It's Monster-iffic!

THE ALIENS

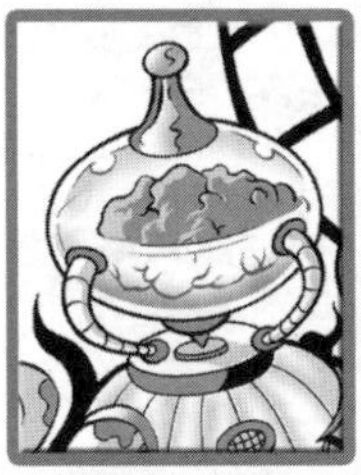

These crafty creatures from the future accessed Buzzboy's memories of old B-movie monsters, to create their own creatures, shown here. They did this to test his abilities, and terrorize the Earth. Very dangerous--Avoid!

Monster Design: Neil Vokes

YING! YANG! YOON!

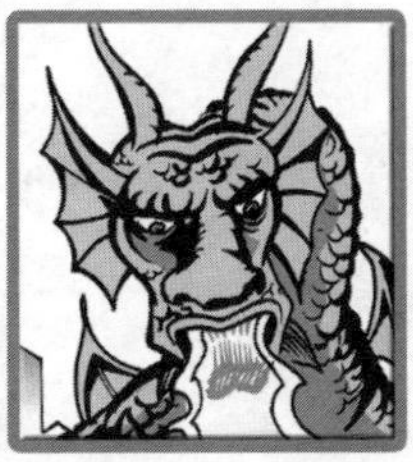

The first of the monsters created by the Aliens, Ying! Yang! Yoon! is obviously taken from Buzzboy's fond memories of the 60's era works of comics greats Stan Lee, Jack Kirby, and Dick Ayers.

Monster Design: No comment. It's a parody, so don't sue me! - JG

AXIS APE & THE WIENERSCHNITZELS

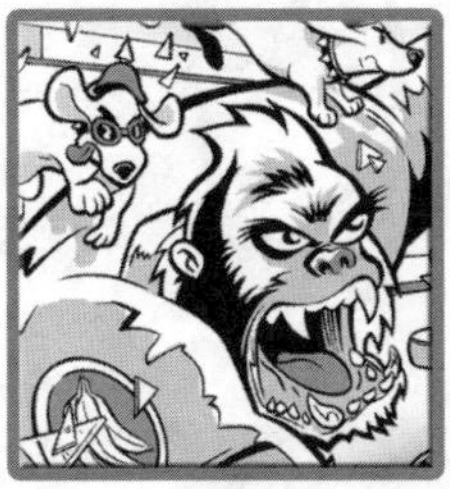

Axis Ape and the Wienerschnitzels were cartoon parodies of the Allies' enemies in Word War II - defeated every kiddie matinee by Oswald the Lucky Rabbit, and Portia Pigg, from Reggie Rooney's "Rooney Toons" cartoons.

Monster Design: Axis Ape: John Shine & Chris Green
Wienerschnitzels: John Gallagher, w/ thanks to Frank Cho

DA-KRISSSS

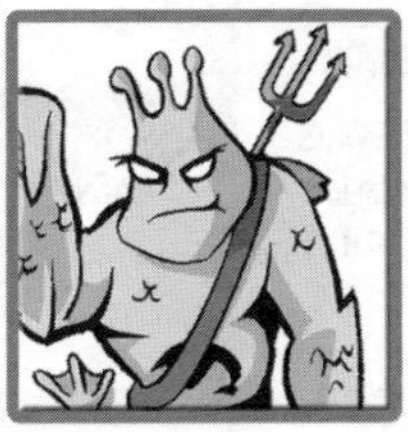

Quite simply, Buzzboy has a strange fear of Sea Monkeys, those mysterious sea creatures the whole family can have fun with. The aliens somehow tapped into this. Thank heavens they never found out about BB's fear of clowns!

Monster Design: Gallagher, named by the author's nephews, Dan and Christian Gallagher.

ADAMA-RU

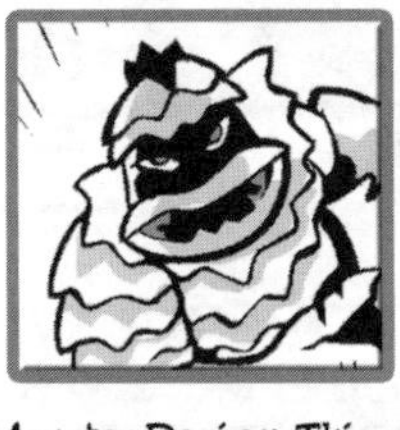

Man in suit! Man in suit! Looking like a creature from the infamous Godzilla movies, Adama-Ru is a fire-breathing, rubbery, bad guy!

Monster Design: This monster was designed from head to tail by Adam Ruby, age 6, another cool nephew of the author.

BOOTROS-GOLLY

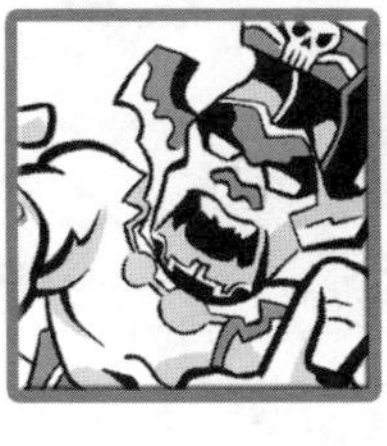

When he was twelve, Buzzboy snuck into an early screening of "Aztec Women on the Moon"--and his memories of this creature lived on, until the aliens sucked his image from BB's brain.

Monster Design: Ronn Sutton

ZMED-KRRR

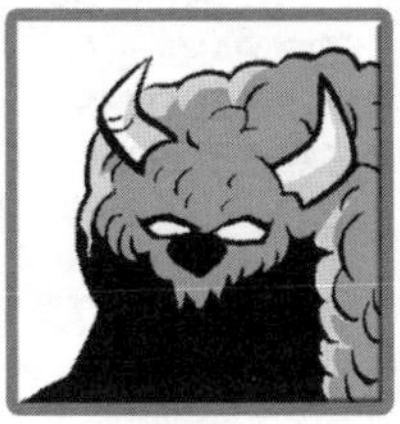

This creature was created from Buzzboy's memories of comics legend (and Spider-Man co-creator) Steve Ditko's muck-covered, lumpy alien creatures from the comics of the 60's. The name seems to come from an old "TJ Hooker" TV show actor.

Monster Design: Again, no comment-- it's a tribute!

INDY GIRL

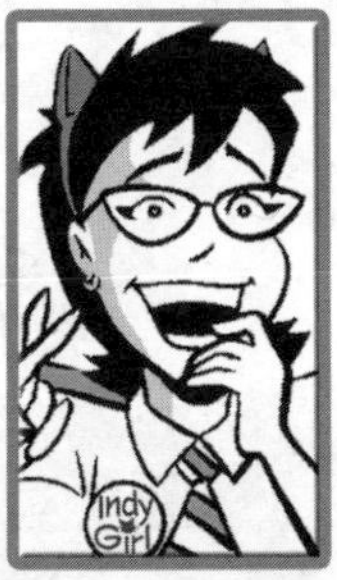
Indy Girl

Not really a monster, but a horiffically big fan of Buzzboy, and Becca's best friend.

Monster Design: Monstrously good at selling comics, the real Indy Girl, Elizabeth Gordon, is a friend of the author, and manager of Big Planet Comics in Vienna, VA! Thanks, Indy Girl!

buzzography

BUZZBOY

REAL NAME: TOMMY PAINE

STATS: A FORMER TEEN SUPER SIDEKICK, BUZZBOY HAS GROWN UP TO FIGHT FOR THE SAFETY OF *NEW PARADISE METROGROVE.* POWERED BY HIS MYSTERIOUS BUZZBELT, BB HAS MADE A NAME FOR HIMSELF AS *"THE WORLD'S MOST UPBEAT SUPER HERO."* HE CURRENTLY HANGS OUT AT HIS OWN *BUZZBOY DINER.*

1ST APPEARANCE: BUZZBOY #1 COMIC BOOK

BECCA

REAL NAME: BECCA SMITH

STATS: BECCA SMITH WAS BORN WITH THE MAGICAL POWERS TO BEND REALITY, AS WELL AS THE POWER OF ESP. SHE IS A REALIST, AND OFTEN LEADS BUZZBOY AND CYBER TO THINK OUT THEIR ACTIONS BEFORE SIMPLY CHARGING INTO A DANGEROUS SITUATION. SHE IS WELL KNOWN FOR HER WIT AND SARCASM.

1ST APPEARANCE: BUZZBOY #1 COMIC BOOK

DOC CYBER

REAL NAME: DR. JAMES BARTHOLOMEW CYBER

STATS: DOC CYBER WAS A RUTHLESS SUPER VILLAIN, FAMOUS FOR HIS MAD SCIENTIST INVENTIONS. ONE DAY THIS SUPER GENIUS GOT BORED, AND GAVE UP BEING EVIL FOR BAKING! NOW HE AIDS BUZZBOY IN HIS FIGHT AGAINST CRIME!

1ST APPEARANCE: BUZZBOY #1 COMIC BOOK

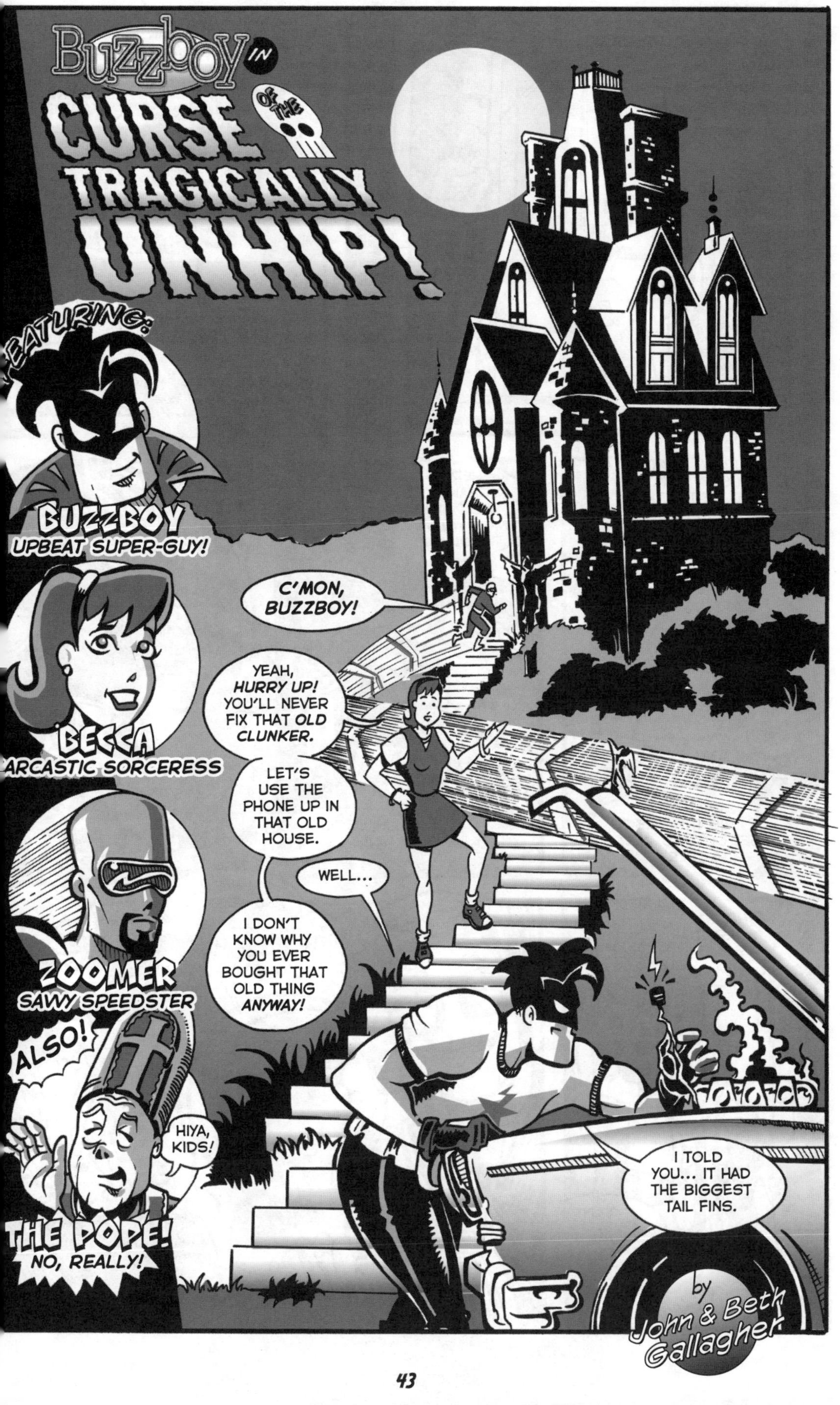

Buzzboy in
CURSE OF THE TRAGICALLY UNHIP!
FEATURING:
BUZZBOY
UPBEAT SUPER-GUY!
BECCA
ARCASTIC SORCERESS
ZOOMER
SAVVY SPEEDSTER
ALSO!
HIYA, KIDS!
THE POPE!
NO, REALLY!
C'MON, BUZZBOY!
YEAH, HURRY UP! YOU'LL NEVER FIX THAT OLD CLUNKER.
LET'S USE THE PHONE UP IN THAT OLD HOUSE.
WELL...
I DON'T KNOW WHY YOU EVER BOUGHT THAT OLD THING ANYWAY!
I TOLD YOU... IT HAD THE BIGGEST TAIL FINS.
by John & Beth Gallagher

WHAT KEPT YOU?
VERY FUNNY. HEY, THIS PLACE IS SPOOKY...
1303
OH, PLEASE!
COULDN'T WE JUST USE YOUR MAGIC TO FIX THE CAR? THIS PLACE GIVES ME THE CREEPS!
YOU'RE AFRAID?!
UMM...
THE GUY WHO EATS POP ROCKS WITH COCA COLA?
Y'KNOW, THAT'S JUST A RUMOR ABOUT THAT KID BLOWING UP!
KNOCK KNOCK
THE IDEA OF THIS TRIP WAS TO GET OUT AND MEET PEOPLE...
HERE'S A CHANCE TO MEET SOME NICE, NORMAL FOLKS!
KNOCK
UH, BECCA...
HELLO! SORRY TO SCARE YOU!
I THOUGHT YOU WERE JEHOVAH'S WITNESSES...
I'M WALT! AND WE'RE...
The Pattersons!
WANT A COOKIE?

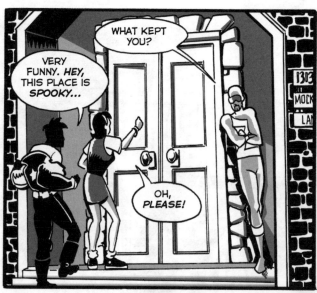

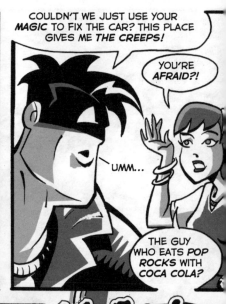

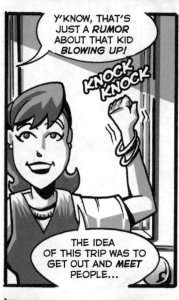

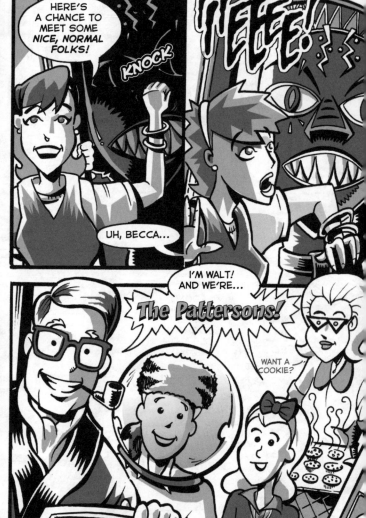

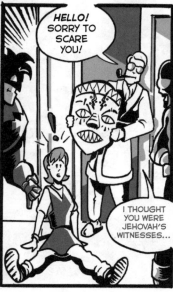

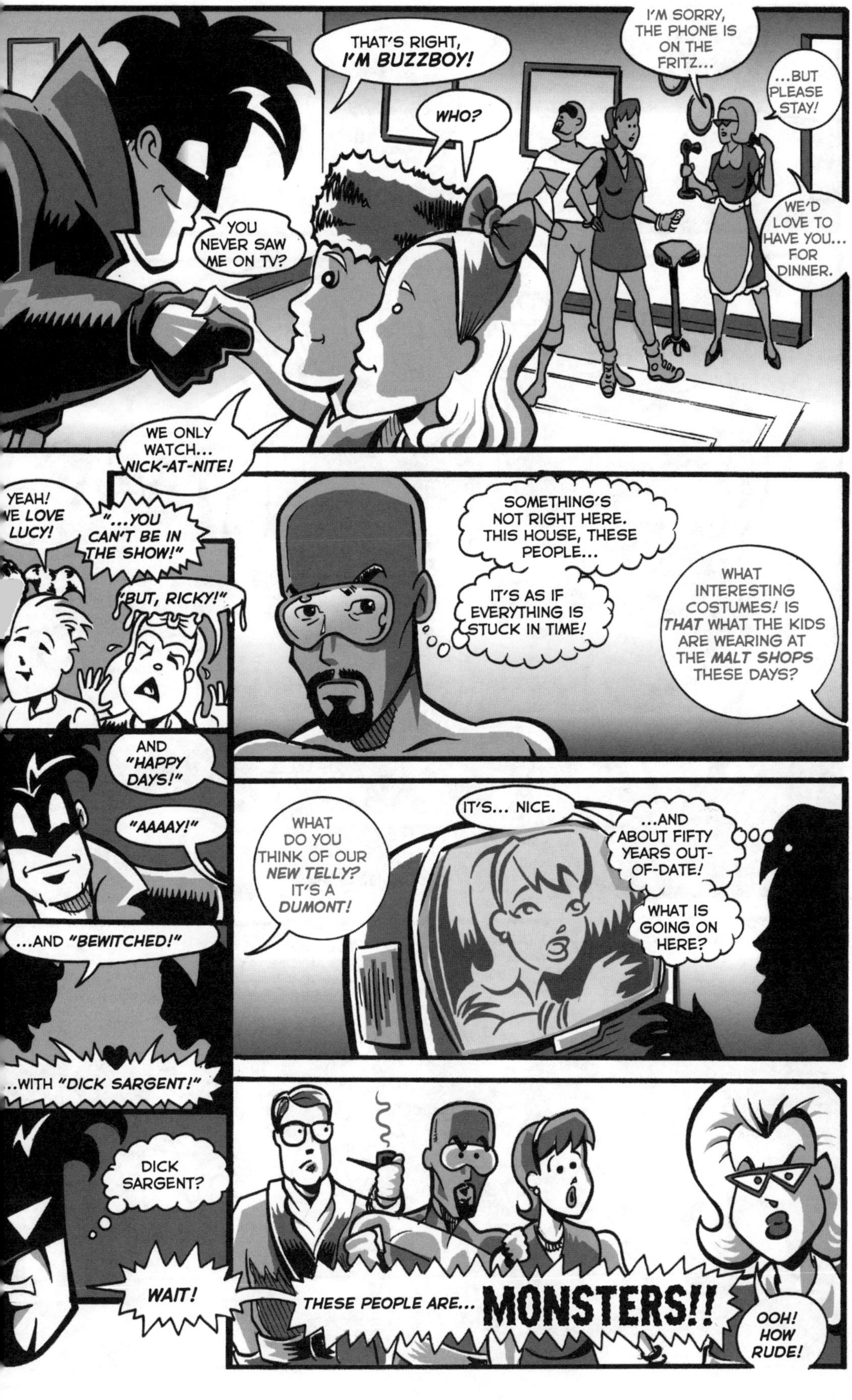
THAT'S RIGHT, *I'M BUZZBOY!*
WHO?
YOU NEVER SAW ME ON TV?
I'M SORRY, THE PHONE IS ON THE FRITZ...
...BUT PLEASE STAY!
WE'D LOVE TO HAVE YOU... FOR DINNER.
WE ONLY WATCH... *NICK-AT-NITE!*
YEAH! E LOVE LUCY!
"...YOU CAN'T BE IN THE SHOW!"
"BUT, RICKY!"
SOMETHING'S NOT RIGHT HERE. THIS HOUSE, THESE PEOPLE...
IT'S AS IF EVERYTHING IS STUCK IN TIME!
WHAT INTERESTING COSTUMES! IS *THAT* WHAT THE KIDS ARE WEARING AT THE *MALT SHOPS* THESE DAYS?
AND *"HAPPY DAYS!"*
"AAAAY!"
...AND *"BEWITCHED!"*
...WITH *"DICK SARGENT!"*
WHAT DO YOU THINK OF OUR *NEW TELLY?* IT'S A *DUMONT!*
IT'S... NICE.
...AND ABOUT FIFTY YEARS OUT-OF-DATE!
WHAT IS GOING ON HERE?
DICK SARGENT?
WAIT!
THESE PEOPLE ARE... MONSTERS!!
OOH! HOW RUDE!

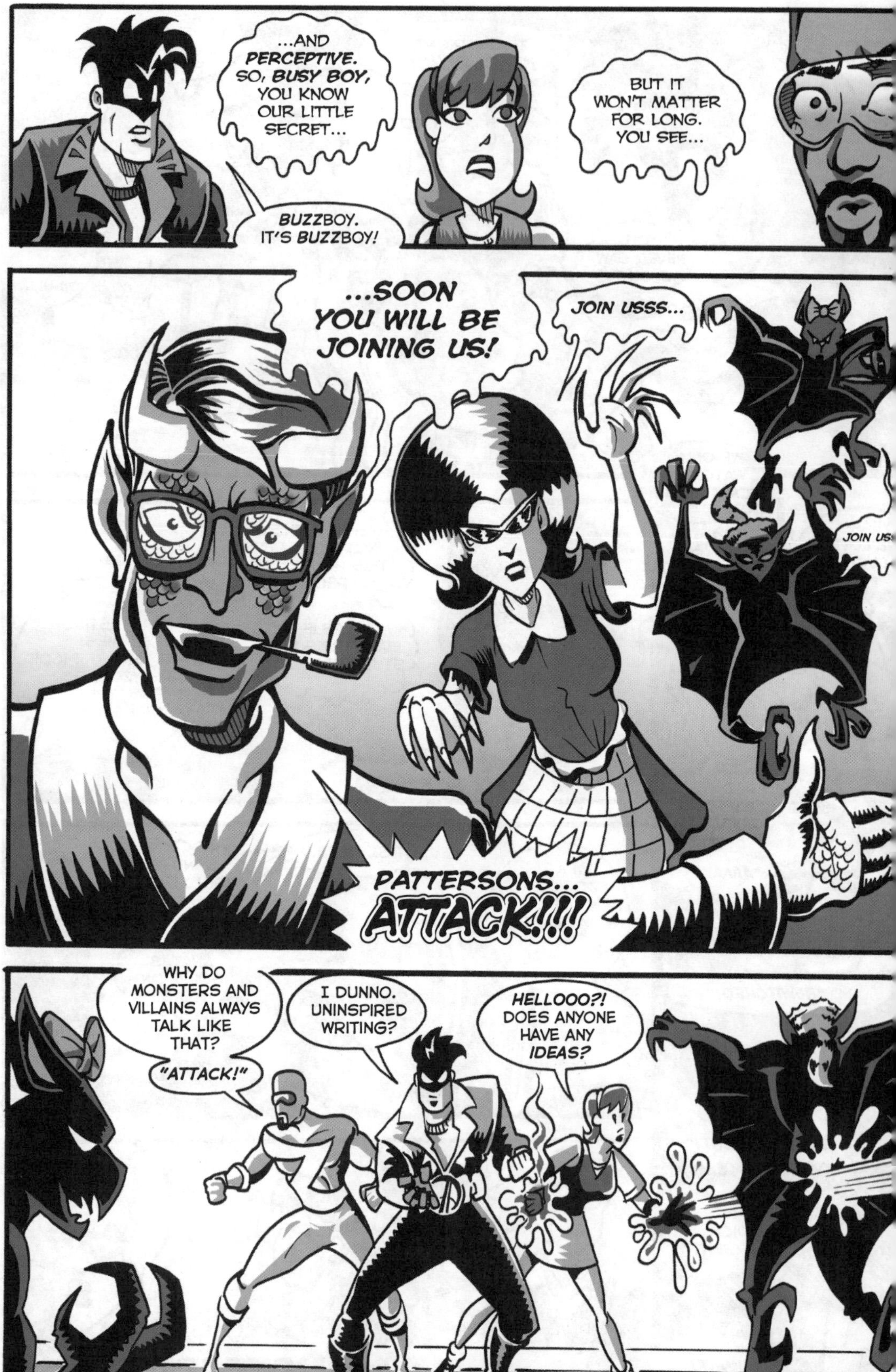
...AND PERCEPTIVE. SO, BUSY BOY, YOU KNOW OUR LITTLE SECRET...
BUZZBOY. IT'S BUZZBOY!
BUT IT WON'T MATTER FOR LONG. YOU SEE...
...SOON YOU WILL BE JOINING US!
JOIN USSS...
PATTERSONS... ATTACK!!!
WHY DO MONSTERS AND VILLAINS ALWAYS TALK LIKE THAT?
"ATTACK!"
I DUNNO. UNINSPIRED WRITING?
HELLOOO?! DOES ANYONE HAVE ANY IDEAS?

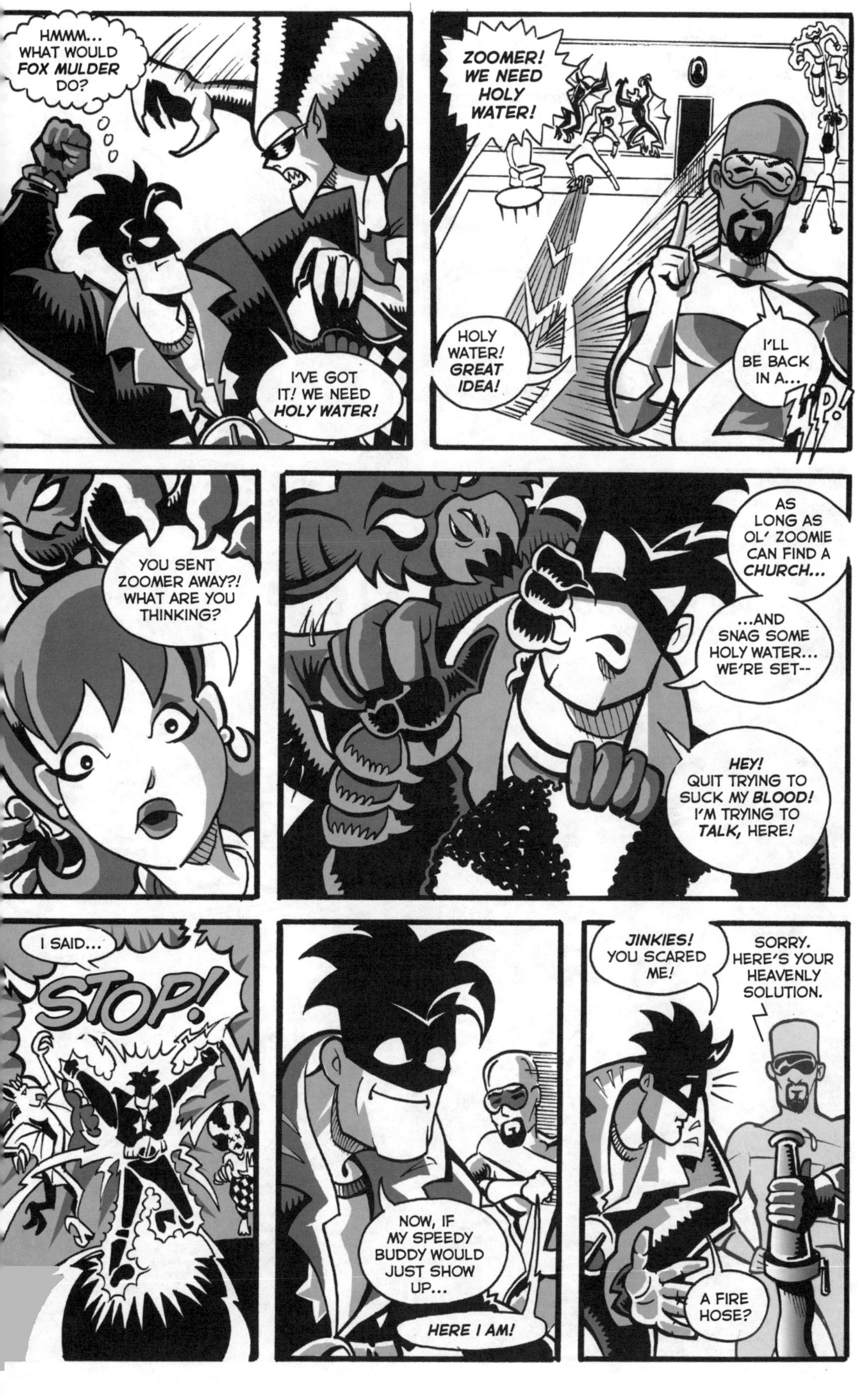
HMMM... WHAT WOULD FOX MULDER DO?
I'VE GOT IT! WE NEED HOLY WATER!
ZOOMER! WE NEED HOLY WATER!
HOLY WATER! GREAT IDEA!
I'LL BE BACK IN A...
ZIP!
YOU SENT ZOOMER AWAY?! WHAT ARE YOU THINKING?
AS LONG AS OL' ZOOMIE CAN FIND A CHURCH...
...AND SNAG SOME HOLY WATER... WE'RE SET--
HEY! QUIT TRYING TO SUCK MY BLOOD! I'M TRYING TO TALK, HERE!
I SAID...
STOP!
NOW, IF MY SPEEDY BUDDY WOULD JUST SHOW UP...
HERE I AM!
JINKIES! YOU SCARED ME!
SORRY. HERE'S YOUR HEAVENLY SOLUTION.
A FIRE HOSE?

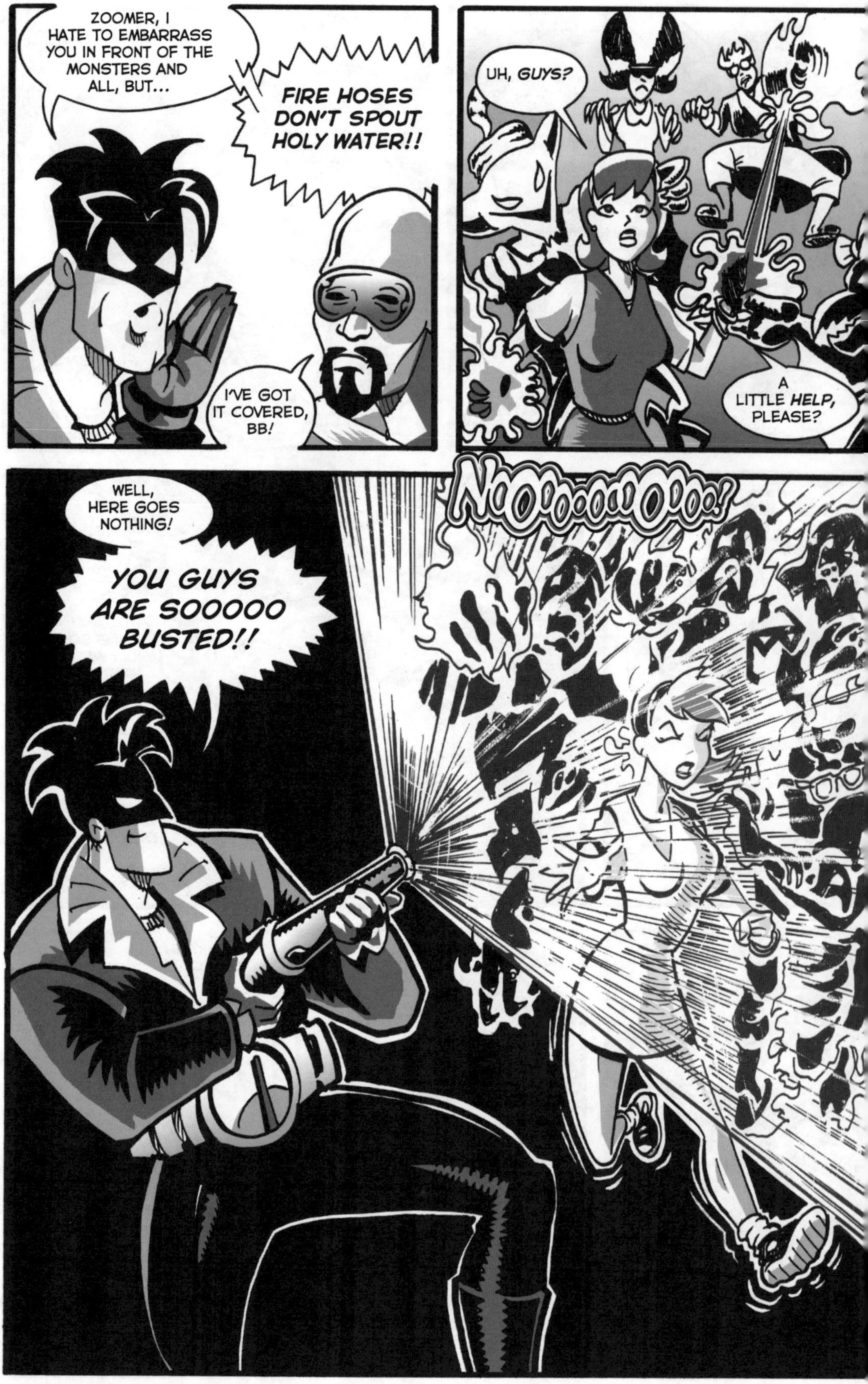

ZOOMER, I HATE TO EMBARRASS YOU IN FRONT OF THE MONSTERS AND ALL, BUT...
FIRE HOSES DON'T SPOUT HOLY WATER!!
I'VE GOT IT COVERED, BB!
UH, GUYS?
A LITTLE HELP, PLEASE?
WELL, HERE GOES NOTHING!
YOU GUYS ARE SOOOOO BUSTED!!

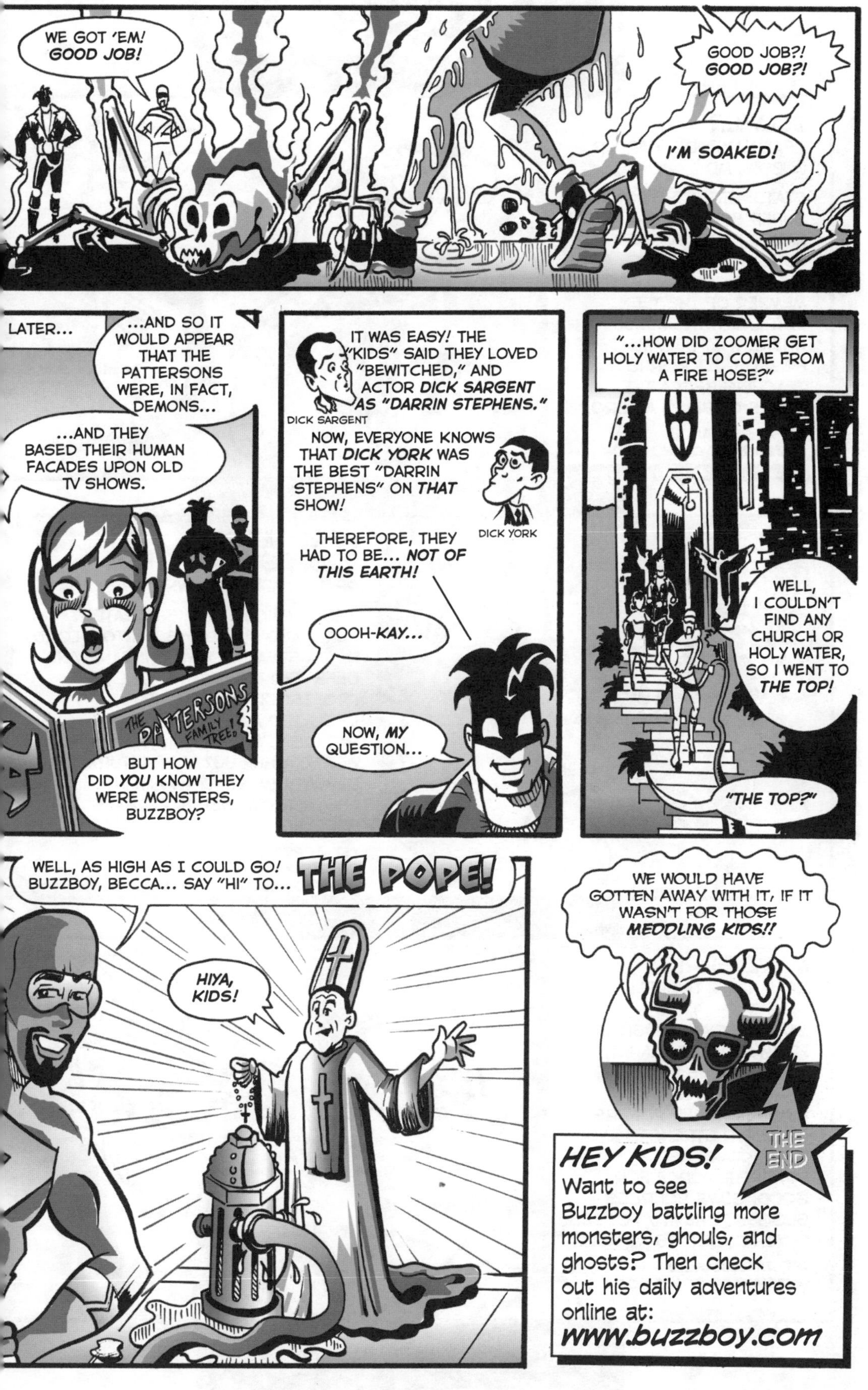

WE GOT 'EM! GOOD JOB!
GOOD JOB?! GOOD JOB?!
I'M SOAKED!
LATER...
...AND SO IT WOULD APPEAR THAT THE PATTERSONS WERE, IN FACT, DEMONS...
...AND THEY BASED THEIR HUMAN FACADES UPON OLD TV SHOWS.
THE PATTERSONS FAMILY TREE!
BUT HOW DID YOU KNOW THEY WERE MONSTERS, BUZZBOY?
IT WAS EASY! THE "KIDS" SAID THEY LOVED "BEWITCHED," AND ACTOR DICK SARGENT AS "DARRIN STEPHENS."
DICK SARGENT
NOW, EVERYONE KNOWS THAT DICK YORK WAS THE BEST "DARRIN STEPHENS" ON THAT SHOW!
DICK YORK
THEREFORE, THEY HAD TO BE... NOT OF THIS EARTH!
OOOH-KAY...
NOW, MY QUESTION...
"...HOW DID ZOOMER GET HOLY WATER TO COME FROM A FIRE HOSE?"
WELL, I COULDN'T FIND ANY CHURCH OR HOLY WATER, SO I WENT TO THE TOP!
"THE TOP?"
WELL, AS HIGH AS I COULD GO! BUZZBOY, BECCA... SAY "HI" TO... THE POPE!
HIYA, KIDS!
WE WOULD HAVE GOTTEN AWAY WITH IT, IF IT WASN'T FOR THOSE MEDDLING KIDS!!
THE END
HEY KIDS!
Want to see Buzzboy battling more monsters, ghouls, and ghosts? Then check out his daily adventures online at:
www.buzzboy.com

buzzography

ZOOMER

REAL NAME: DR. CARTER DUBOIS, MD

STATS: GIVEN THE POWER OF SUPER SPEED BY THE HERO NAMED XLR8, ZOOMER FOUGHT FOR JUSTICE AS HIS SIDEKICK, AND WAS A MEMBER OF THE TEEN EXTREME WITH BUZZBOY, WHERE THEY BECAME BEST FRIENDS. ZOOMER IS TEACHING BECCA THE ROPES OF BEING A HERO.

1ST APPEARANCE: BUZZBOY #2 COMIC BOOK

LORD ULTRA/ PROFESSOR SCHISM

REAL NAME: UNKNOWN

STATS: ONCE EARTH'S GREATEST HERO, AND BUZZBOY'S MENTOR, LORD ULTRA SEEMINGLY WENT INSANE, AND DEFEATED EARTH'S HEROES AS PROFESSOR SCHISM. HE HAD DECLARED MARTIAL LAW IN NEW PARADISE, WITH HIS SIGHTS ON THE WORLD, WHEN BUZZBOY RETURNED TO DEFEAT HIM, SENDING HIM INTO ANOTHER DIMENSION, PERHAPS FOREVER.

1ST APPEARANCE: BUZZBOY #1 COMIC BOOK

MARZ GRRL

REAL NAME: UNSPELLABLE

STATS: STRANGE VISITOR FROM ANOTHER PLANET, MARZ GRRL IS FROM THE MARS OF A PARALLEL DIMENSION. HER POWERS OF SUPER STRENGTH AND FLIGHT MAKE HER A POWERFUL FORCE FOR GOOD. SOME SOURCES SUGGEST SHE MAY POSSESS PSYCHIC ABILITIES AS WELL.

1ST APPEARANCE: BUZZBOY #4 COMIC BOOK

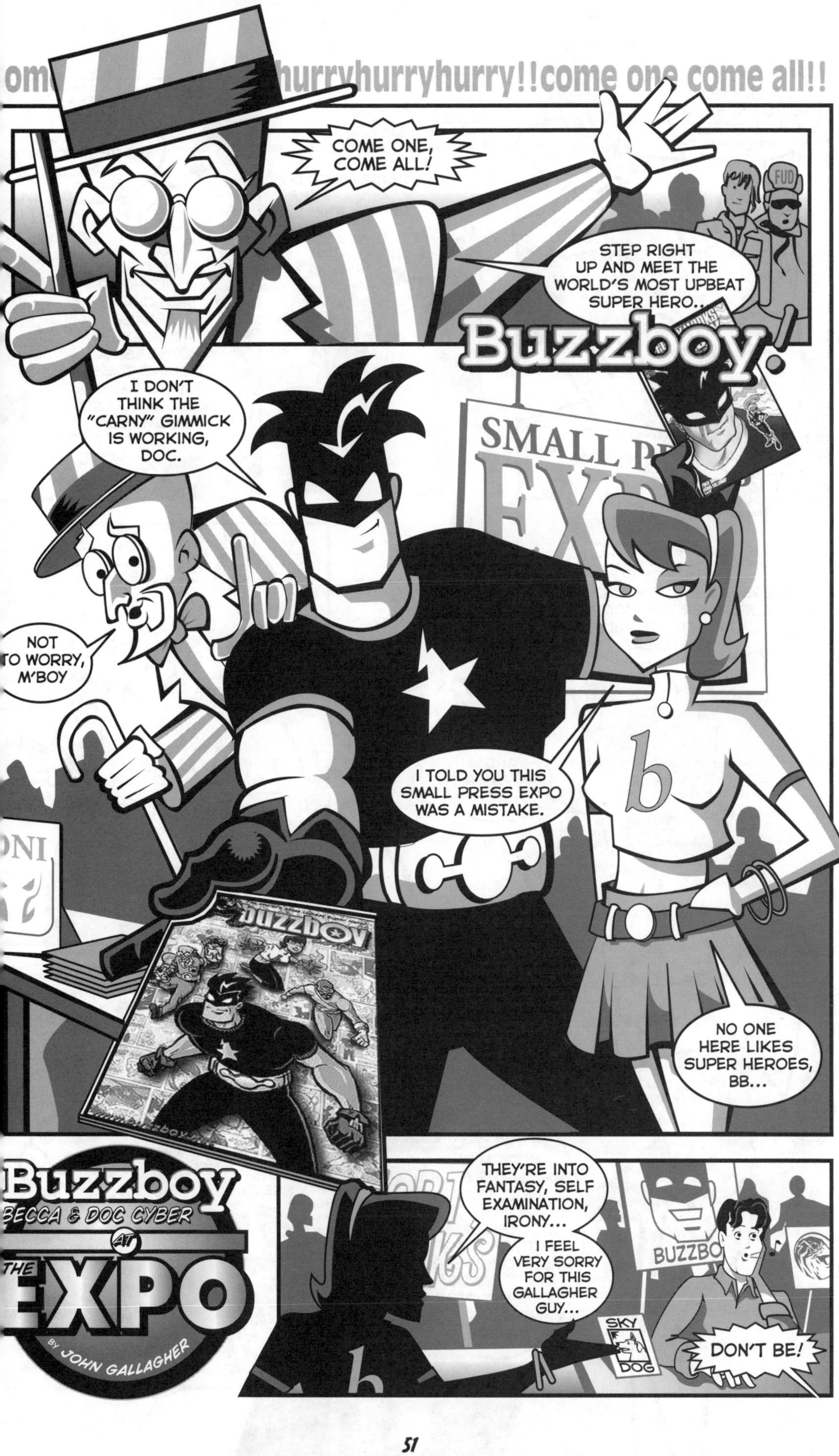
om hurryhurryhurry!!come one come all!!
COME ONE, COME ALL!
STEP RIGHT UP AND MEET THE WORLD'S MOST UPBEAT SUPER HERO...
Buzzboy!
I DON'T THINK THE "CARNY" GIMMICK IS WORKING, DOC.
NOT TO WORRY, M'BOY
I TOLD YOU THIS SMALL PRESS EXPO WAS A MISTAKE.
NO ONE HERE LIKES SUPER HEROES, BB...
Buzzboy
BECCA & DOC CYBER
AT
THE EXPO
BY JOHN GALLAGHER
THEY'RE INTO FANTASY, SELF EXAMINATION, IRONY...
I FEEL VERY SORRY FOR THIS GALLAGHER GUY...
SKY DOG
DON'T BE!

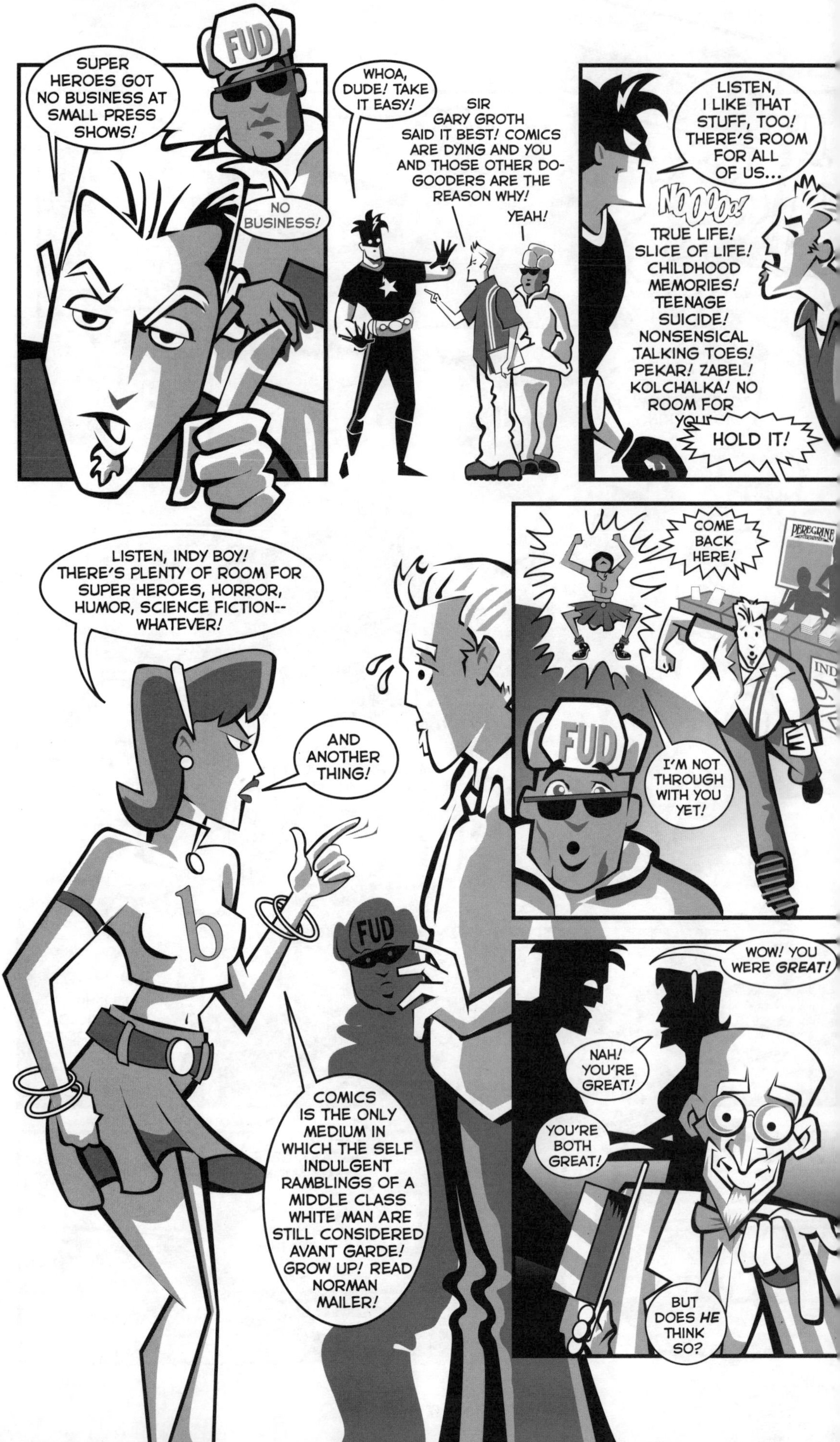
SUPER HEROES GOT NO BUSINESS AT SMALL PRESS SHOWS!
FUD
NO BUSINESS!
WHOA, DUDE! TAKE IT EASY!
SIR GARY GROTH SAID IT BEST! COMICS ARE DYING AND YOU AND THOSE OTHER DO-GOODERS ARE THE REASON WHY!
YEAH!
LISTEN, I LIKE THAT STUFF, TOO! THERE'S ROOM FOR ALL OF US...
NOOOOO!
TRUE LIFE! SLICE OF LIFE! CHILDHOOD MEMORIES! TEENAGE SUICIDE! NONSENSICAL TALKING TOES! PEKAR! ZABEL! KOLCHALKA! NO ROOM FOR YO
HOLD IT!
LISTEN, INDY BOY! THERE'S PLENTY OF ROOM FOR SUPER HEROES, HORROR, HUMOR, SCIENCE FICTION--WHATEVER!
AND ANOTHER THING!
b
FUD
COMICS IS THE ONLY MEDIUM IN WHICH THE SELF INDULGENT RAMBLINGS OF A MIDDLE CLASS WHITE MAN ARE STILL CONSIDERED AVANT GARDE! GROW UP! READ NORMAN MAILER!
COME BACK HERE!
PEREGRINE
FUD
I'M NOT THROUGH WITH YOU YET!
WOW! YOU WERE *GREAT!*
NAH! YOU'RE GREAT!
YOU'RE BOTH GREAT!
BUT DOES *HE* THINK SO?

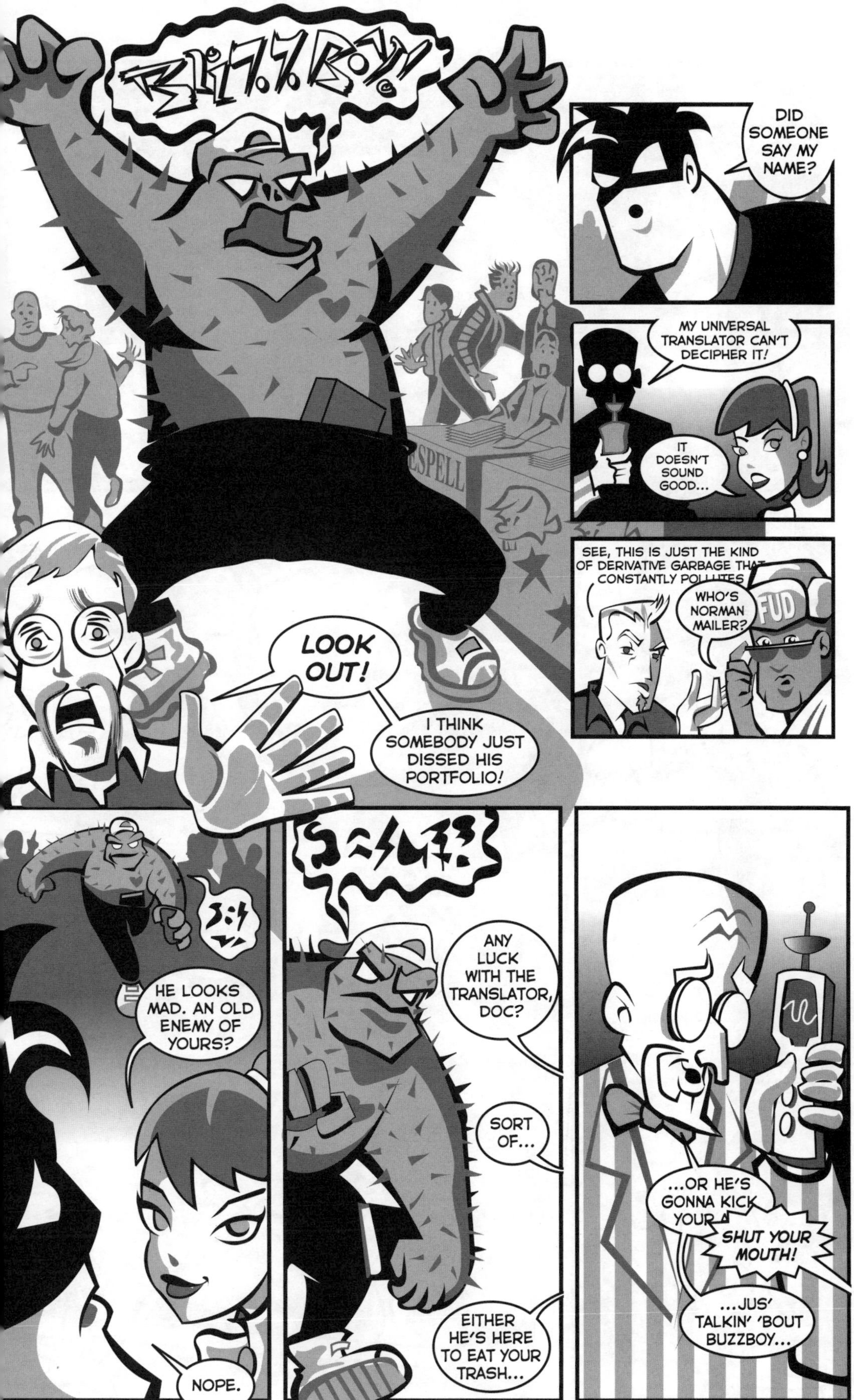
DID SOMEONE SAY MY NAME?
MY UNIVERSAL TRANSLATOR CAN'T DECIPHER IT!
IT DOESN'T SOUND GOOD...
SEE, THIS IS JUST THE KIND OF DERIVATIVE GARBAGE THAT CONSTANTLY POLLUTES
WHO'S NORMAN MAILER?
FUD
LOOK OUT!
I THINK SOMEBODY JUST DISSED HIS PORTFOLIO!
HE LOOKS MAD. AN OLD ENEMY OF YOURS?
NOPE.
ANY LUCK WITH THE TRANSLATOR, DOC?
SORT OF...
EITHER HE'S HERE TO EAT YOUR TRASH...
...OR HE'S GONNA KICK YOUR A
SHUT YOUR MOUTH!
...JUS' TALKIN' 'BOUT BUZZBOY...

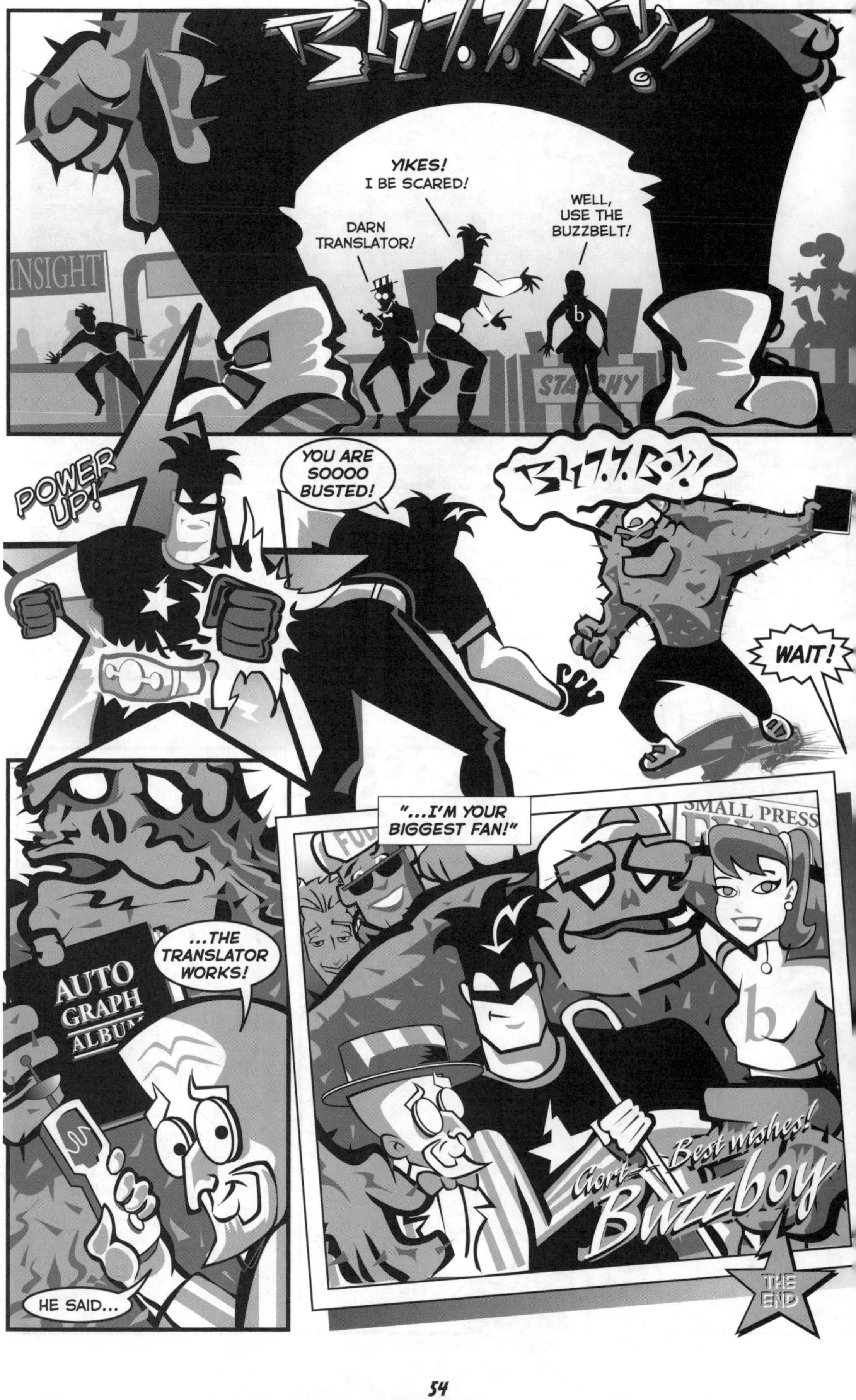
BUZZBOY!
DARN TRANSLATOR!
YIKES! I BE SCARED!
WELL, USE THE BUZZBELT!
INSIGHT
POWER UP!
YOU ARE SOOOO BUSTED!
BUZZBOY!
WAIT!
AUTO GRAPH ALBUM
...THE TRANSLATOR WORKS!
HE SAID...
"...I'M YOUR BIGGEST FAN!"
SMALL PRESS
Gort—Best wishes!
Buzzboy
THE END

buzzography

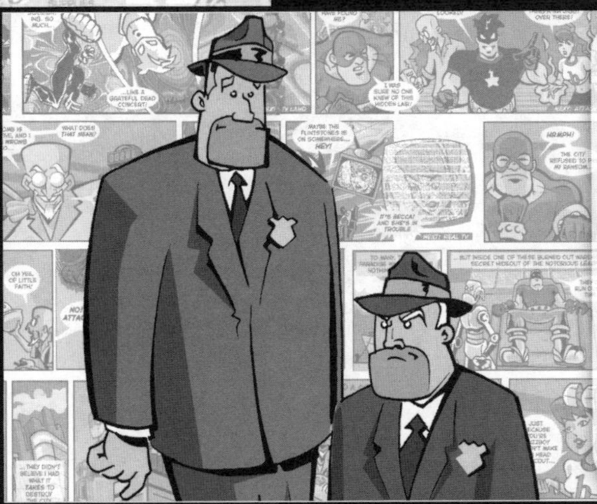

BIG DITTY & LITTLE DITTY

STATS: A FATHER/SON TEAM OF DETECTIVES, OF VARYING HEIGHTS. BIG DITTY WAS BROUGHT INTO NEW PARADISE AS CHIEF INSPECTOR, IN CHARGE OF REVAMPING THE NPPD AFTER LORD ULTRA'S DEFEAT. HE CARES LITTLE FOR SUPER HEROES, ESPECIALLY BUZZBOY. LITTLE DITTY, A GENTLE, WHISPERING GIANT, WORSHIPS BUZZBOY LIKE A ROCK STAR.

1ST APPEARANCES:
BIG DITTY: "40 WINKS/BUZZBOY" COMIC
LITTLE DITTY: COMING SOON!

LAWBREAKER

REAL NAME: UNKNOWN

STATS: NO ONE IS SURE WHERE THIS MONSTER CAME FROM, BUT WHENEVER HE APPEARS, SOMETHING IS GOING TO GET BROKEN! BUZZBOY HAS BEEN PUMMELED REPEATEDLY BY THIS BLUE BEHEMOTH, YET LAWBREAKER IS ALMOST CHILDLIKE IN HIS DEMEANOR.

1ST APPEARANCE:
BUZZBOY: SHORT CUTS

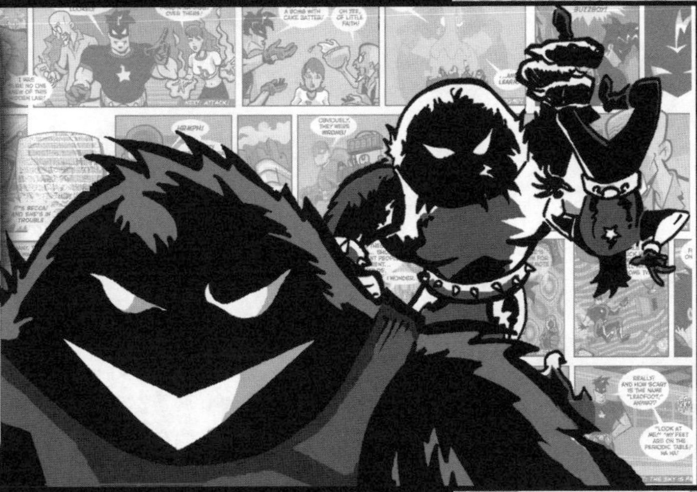

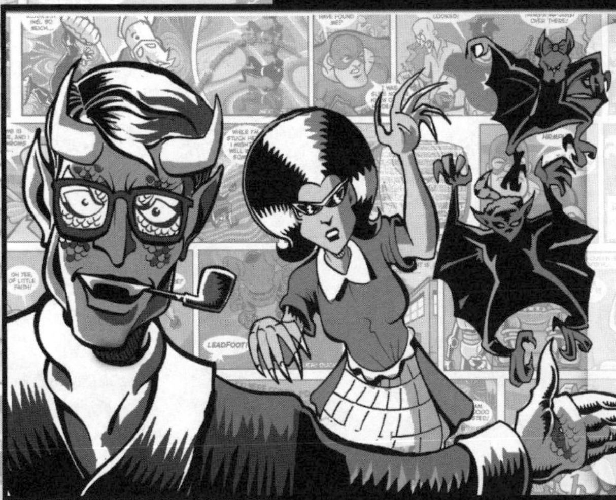

THE PATTERSONS

STATS: A KINDLY FAMILY OF MONSTERS, WHO DISGUISE THEMSELVES AS A HUMAN FAMILY, BASED ON OLD TV SHOWS SUCH AS "LEAVE IT TO BEAVER" AND "FATHER KNOWS BEST." THEY LURE THEIR VICTIMS INTO THEIR HOME, OFFERING KINDNESS, COOKIES, AND MILK--BUT IN THE END, *IT'S THE VISITOR THEY HAVE FOR DINNER!*

1ST APPEARANCE:
SON OF RAMPAGE, JUNE 1998
APPEARING IN "BUZZBOY: SHORT CUTS," ON SALE NOW!

SECOND★COURSE

"We are the music makers,
and we are the dreamers
of dreams."
- Willy Wonka
Willy Wonka and the
Chocalate Factory

DREAMS

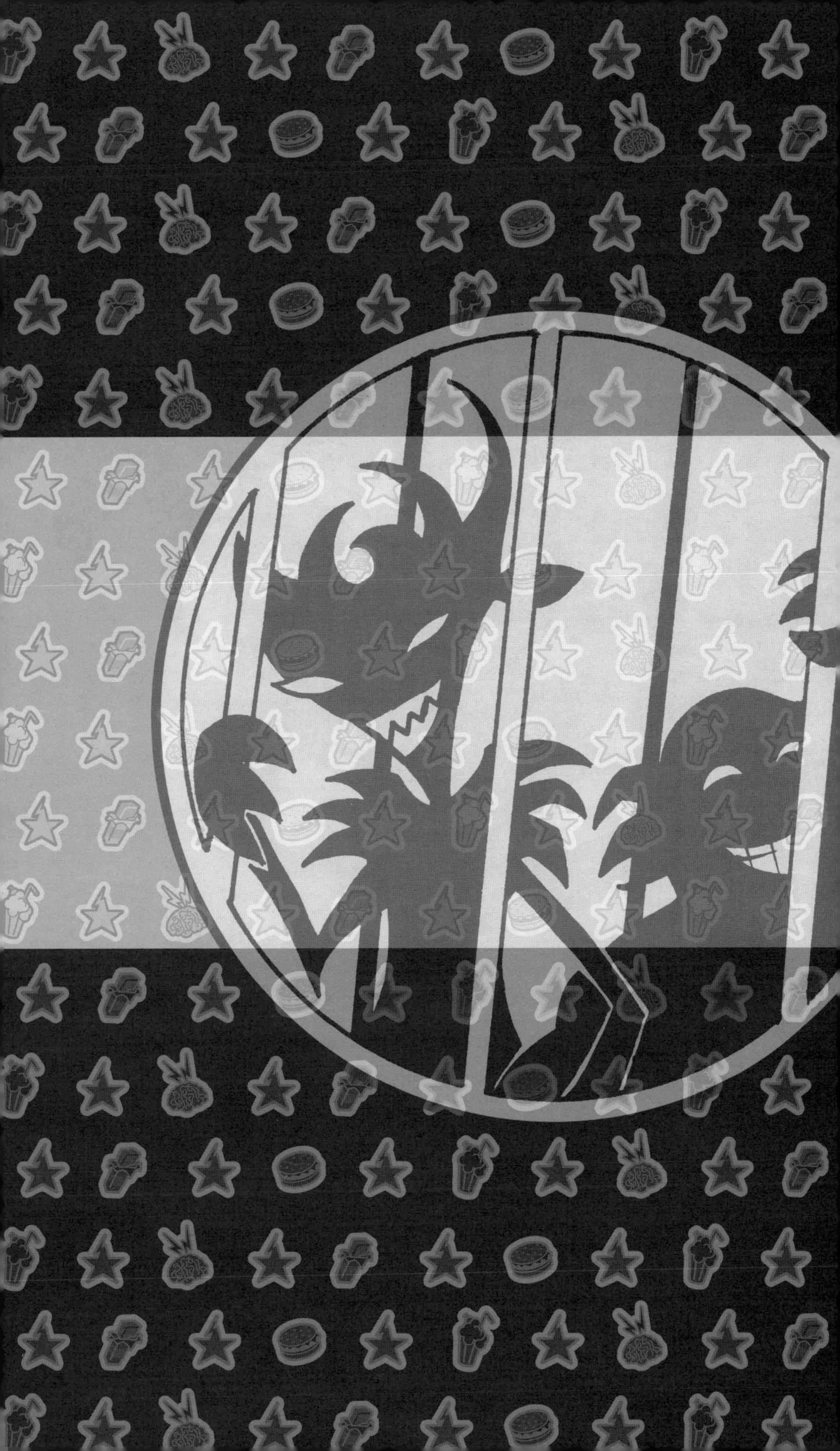

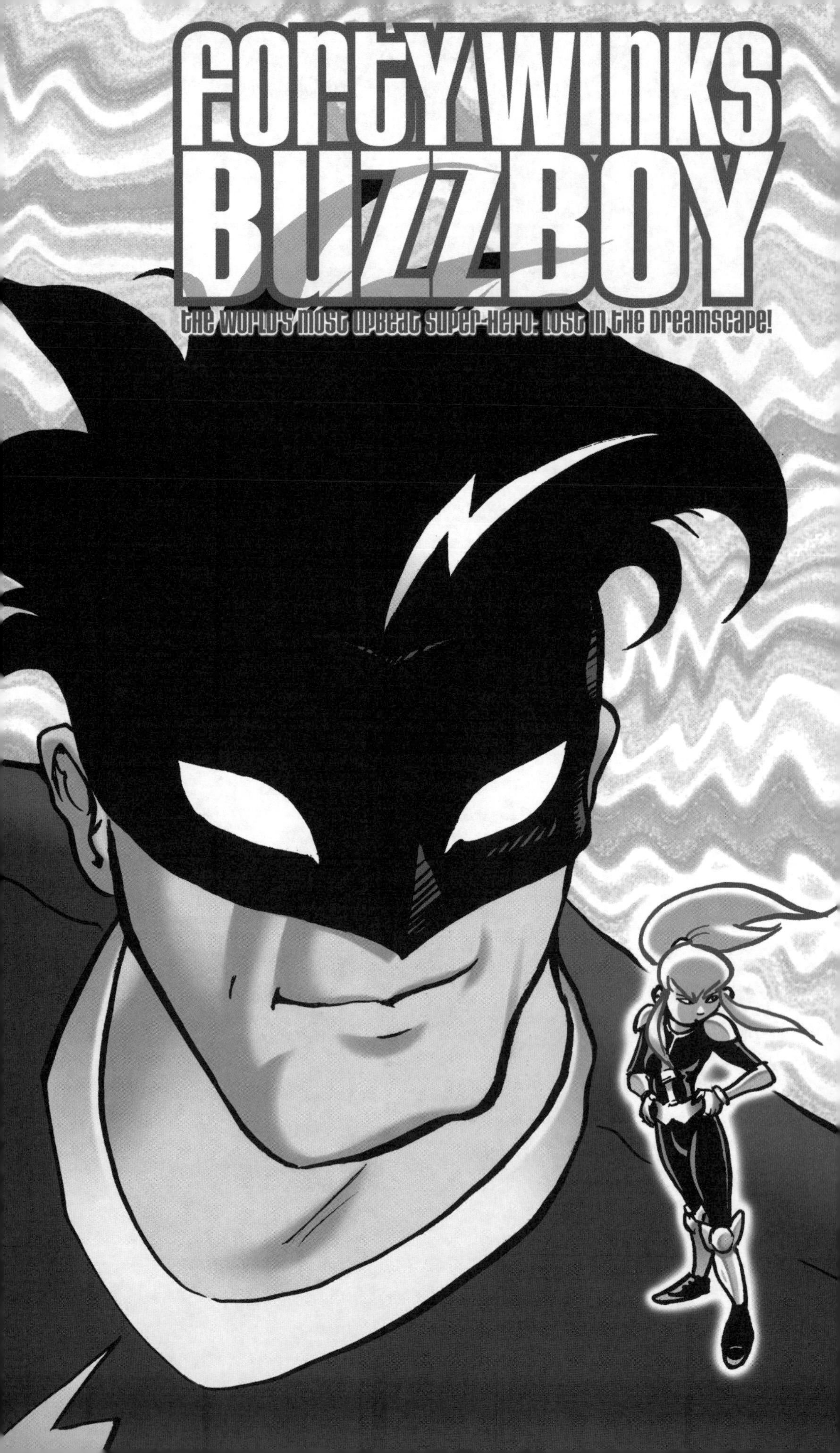
FORTY WINKS
BUZZBOY
THE WORLD'S MOST UPBEAT SUPER-HERO: LOST IN THE DREAMSCAPE!

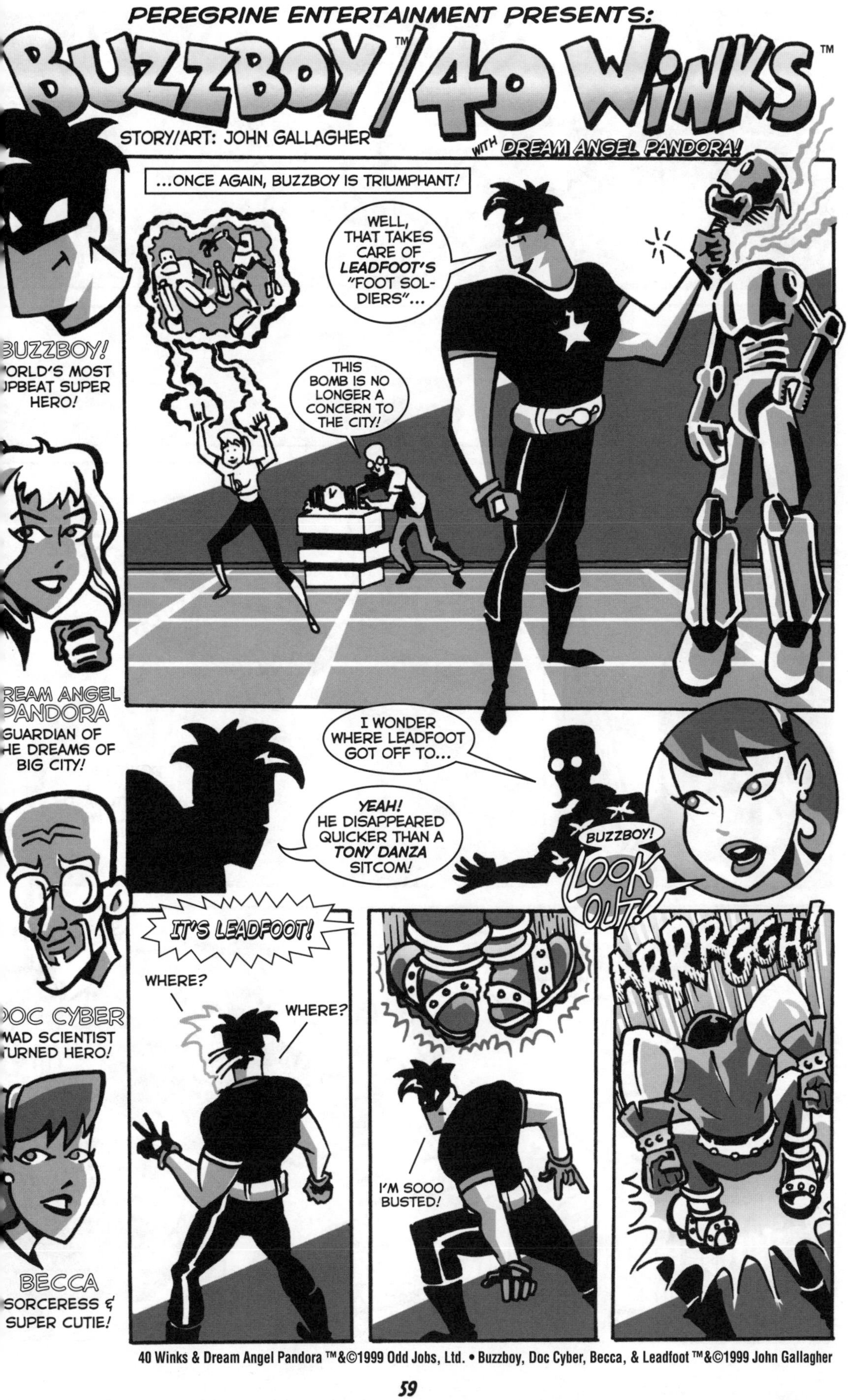
PEREGRINE ENTERTAINMENT PRESENTS:
BUZZBOY™/40 WINKS™
STORY/ART: JOHN GALLAGHER
WITH DREAM ANGEL PANDORA!
BUZZBOY! ORLD'S MOST PBEAT SUPER HERO!
REAM ANGEL PANDORA GUARDIAN OF HE DREAMS OF BIG CITY!
OC CYBER MAD SCIENTIST URNED HERO!
BECCA SORCERESS & SUPER CUTIE!
...ONCE AGAIN, BUZZBOY IS TRIUMPHANT!
WELL, THAT TAKES CARE OF LEADFOOT'S "FOOT SOL-DIERS"...
THIS BOMB IS NO LONGER A CONCERN TO THE CITY!
I WONDER WHERE LEADFOOT GOT OFF TO...
YEAH! HE DISAPPEARED QUICKER THAN A TONY DANZA SITCOM!
BUZZBOY! LOOK OUT!
IT'S LEADFOOT!
WHERE?
WHERE?
I'M SOOO BUSTED!
ARRRGGH!

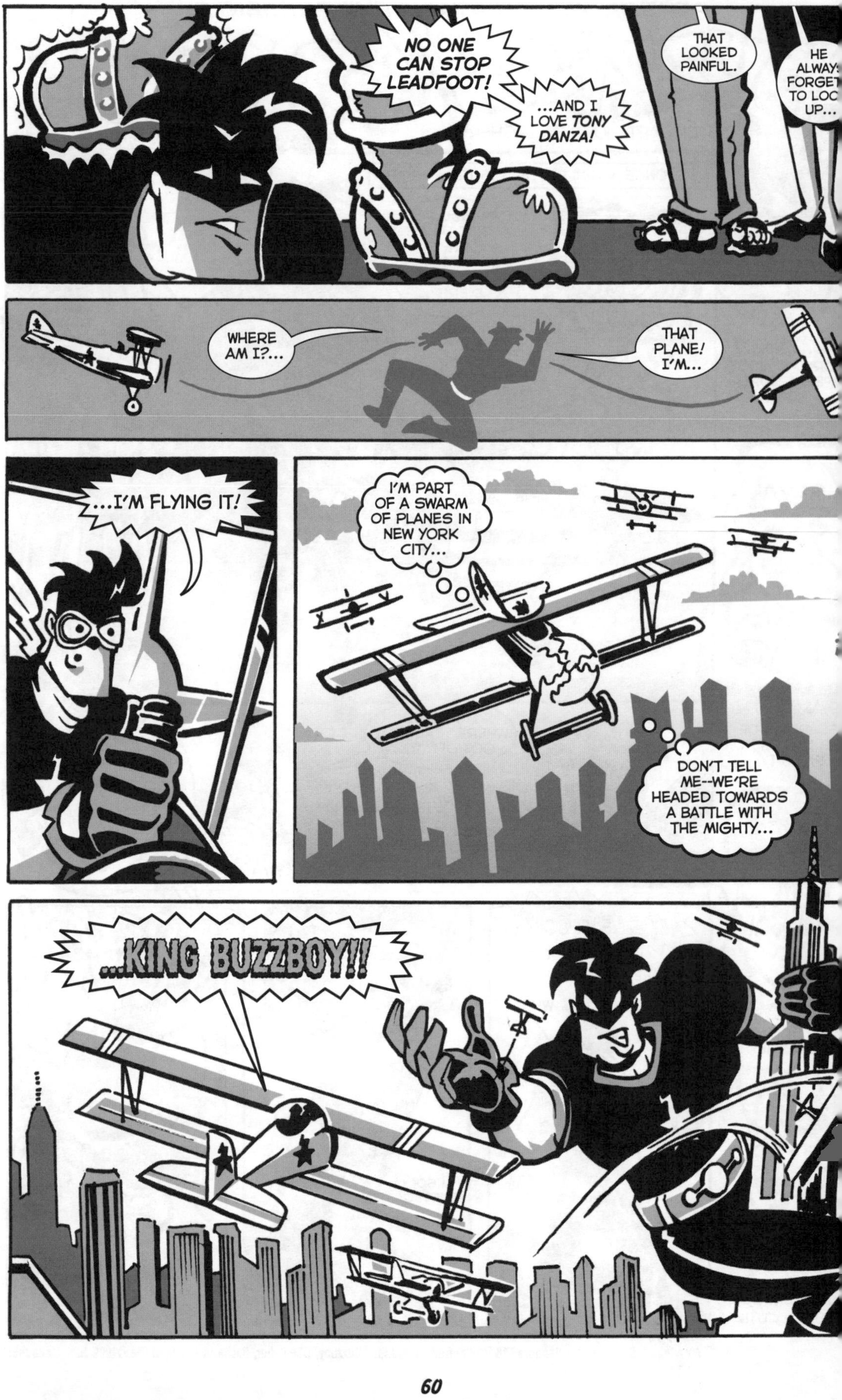
NO ONE CAN STOP LEADFOOT!
...AND I LOVE TONY DANZA!
THAT LOOKED PAINFUL.
HE ALWAY FORGET TO LOC UP...
WHERE AM I?...
THAT PLANE! I'M...
...I'M FLYING IT!
I'M PART OF A SWARM OF PLANES IN NEW YORK CITY...
DON'T TELL ME--WE'RE HEADED TOWARDS A BATTLE WITH THE MIGHTY...
...KING BUZZBOY!!

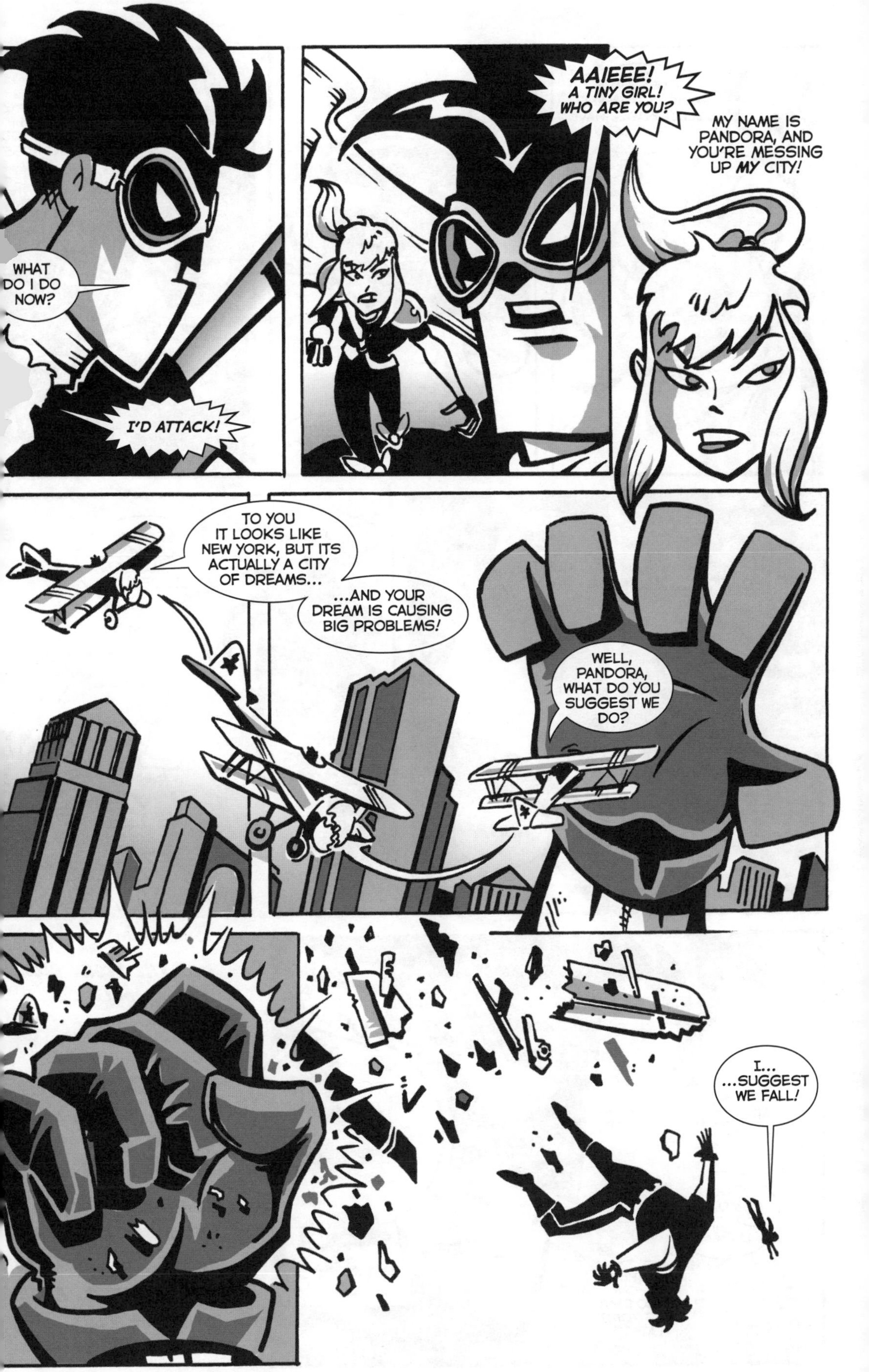
WHAT DO I DO NOW?
I'D ATTACK!
AAIEEE! A TINY GIRL! WHO ARE YOU?
MY NAME IS PANDORA, AND YOU'RE MESSING UP MY CITY!
TO YOU IT LOOKS LIKE NEW YORK, BUT ITS ACTUALLY A CITY OF DREAMS...
...AND YOUR DREAM IS CAUSING BIG PROBLEMS!
WELL, PANDORA, WHAT DO YOU SUGGEST WE DO?
I... ...SUGGEST WE FALL!

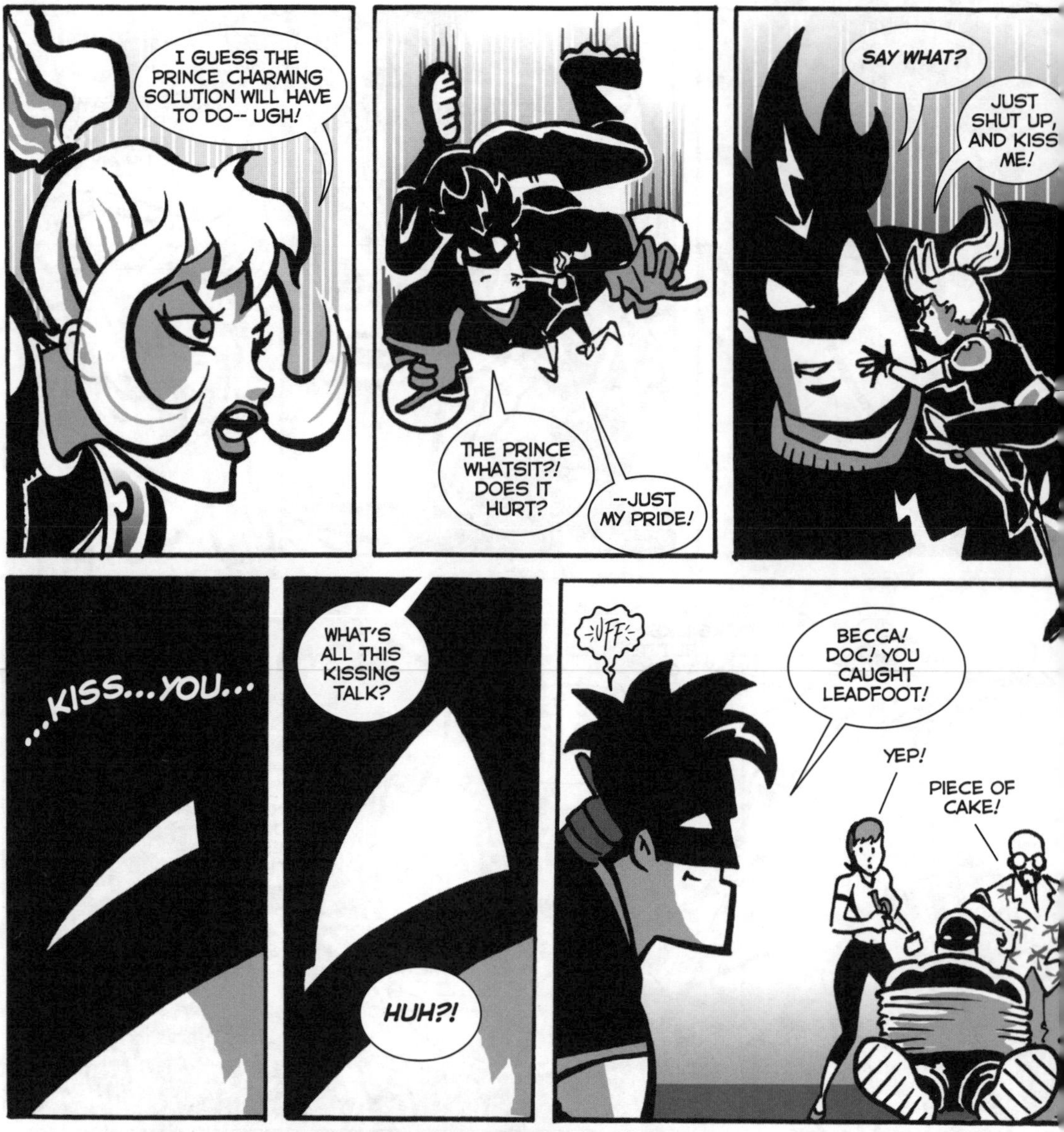
I GUESS THE PRINCE CHARMING SOLUTION WILL HAVE TO DO-- UGH!
THE PRINCE WHATSIT?! DOES IT HURT?
--JUST MY PRIDE!
SAY WHAT?
JUST SHUT UP, AND KISS ME!
...KISS...YOU...
WHAT'S ALL THIS KISSING TALK?
HUH?!
UFF
BECCA! DOC! YOU CAUGHT LEADFOOT!
YEP!
PIECE OF CAKE!

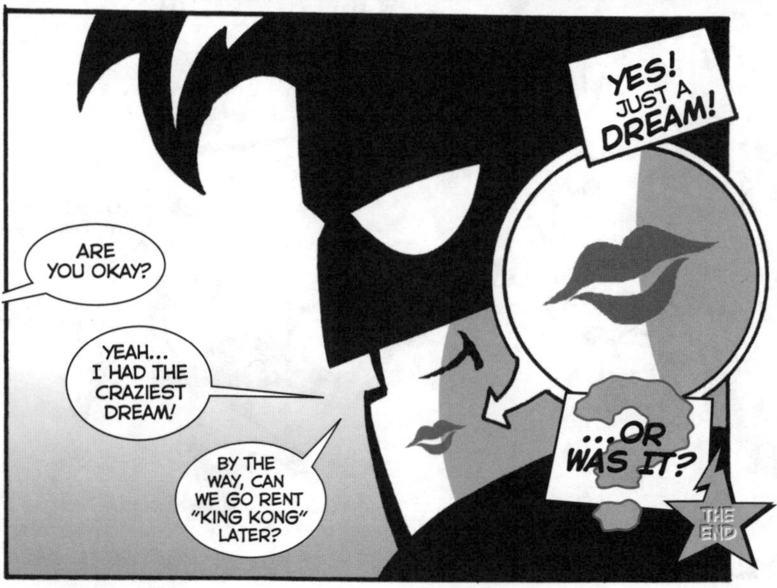
YES! JUST A DREAM!
ARE YOU OKAY?
YEAH... I HAD THE CRAZIEST DREAM!
BY THE WAY, CAN WE GO RENT "KING KONG" LATER?
...OR WAS IT?
THE END

BUT THE STORY DIDN'T END THERE!

FOR, A SHORT TIME LATER, BUZZBOY AND DREAM ANGEL PANDORA MET UP AGAIN...

SUNNY CHANG HAD RETURNED FROM SPACE HER BRAIN SAFELY IN HER OLD BODY, AS OUR STORY UNFOLDS...

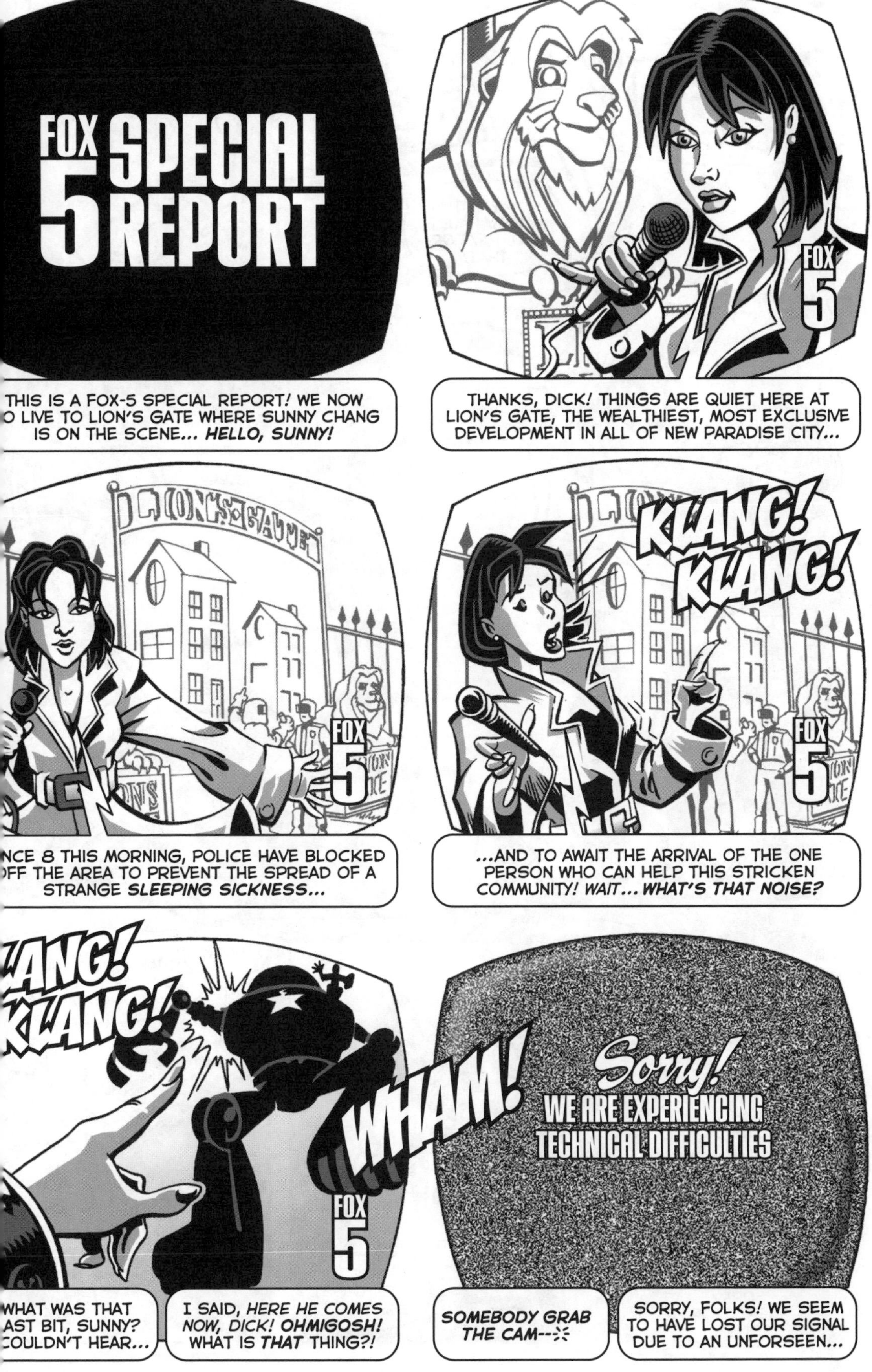
FOX 5 SPECIAL REPORT
THIS IS A FOX-5 SPECIAL REPORT! WE NOW O LIVE TO LION'S GATE WHERE SUNNY CHANG IS ON THE SCENE... HELLO, SUNNY!
FOX 5
THANKS, DICK! THINGS ARE QUIET HERE AT LION'S GATE, THE WEALTHIEST, MOST EXCLUSIVE DEVELOPMENT IN ALL OF NEW PARADISE CITY...
LION'S GATE
FOX 5
NCE 8 THIS MORNING, POLICE HAVE BLOCKED FF THE AREA TO PREVENT THE SPREAD OF A STRANGE SLEEPING SICKNESS...
KLANG! KLANG!
FOX 5
...AND TO AWAIT THE ARRIVAL OF THE ONE PERSON WHO CAN HELP THIS STRICKEN COMMUNITY! WAIT... WHAT'S THAT NOISE?
ANG! KLANG!
FOX 5
WHAT WAS THAT AST BIT, SUNNY? COULDN'T HEAR...
I SAID, HERE HE COMES NOW, DICK! OHMIGOSH! WHAT IS THAT THING?!
WHAM!
Sorry!
WE ARE EXPERIENCING TECHNICAL DIFFICULTIES
SOMEBODY GRAB THE CAM--
SORRY, FOLKS! WE SEEM TO HAVE LOST OUR SIGNAL DUE TO AN UNFORSEEN...

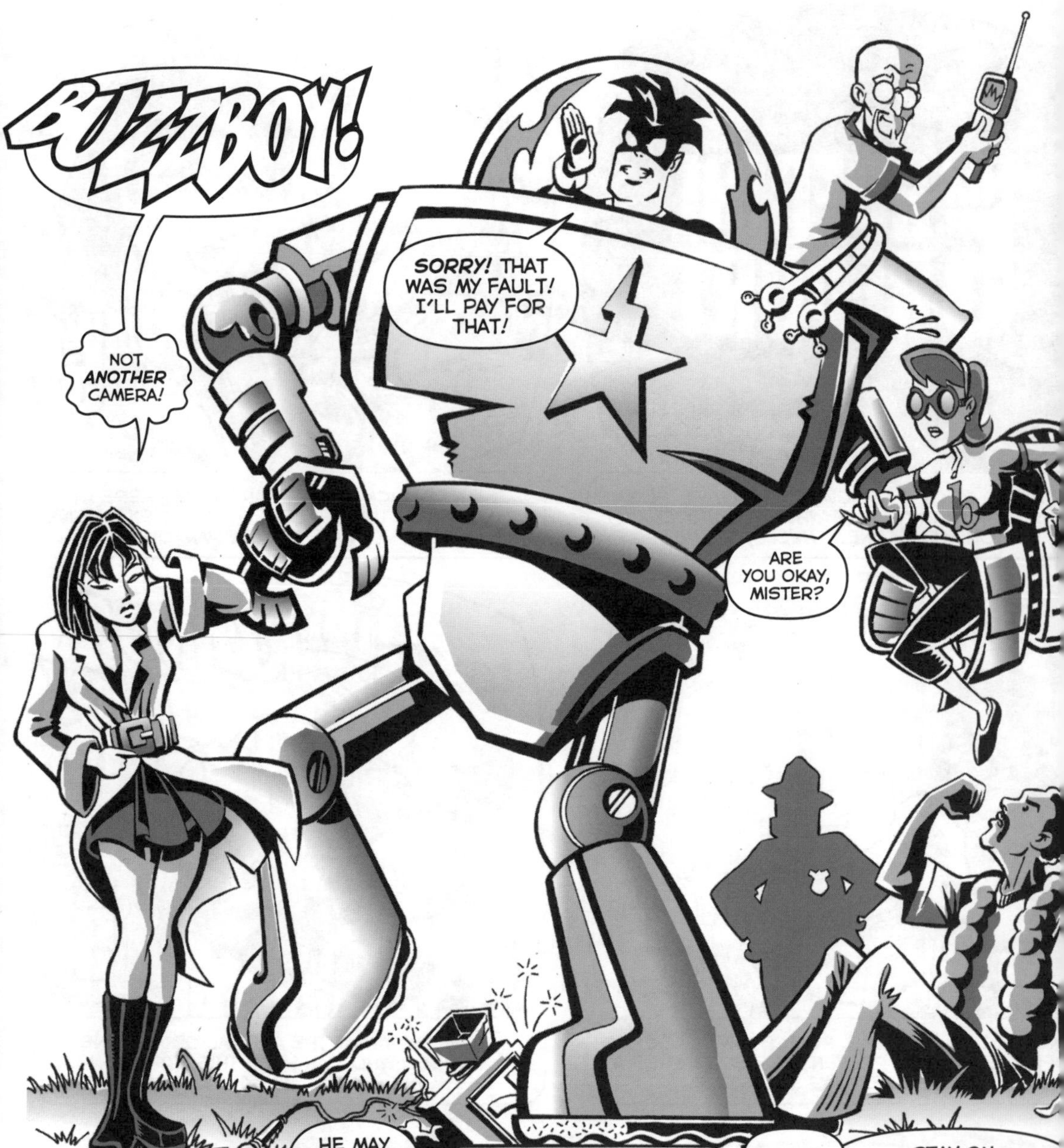
BUZZBOY!
NOT *ANOTHER* CAMERA!
SORRY! THAT WAS MY FAULT! I'LL PAY FOR THAT!
ARE YOU OKAY, MISTER?

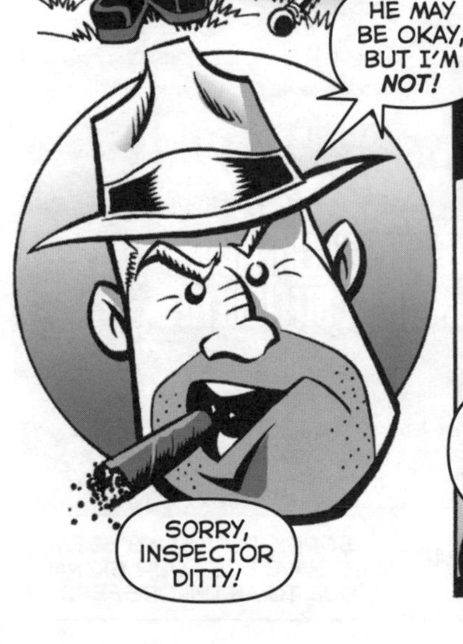
HE MAY BE OKAY, BUT I'M ***NOT!***
SORRY, INSPECTOR DITTY!

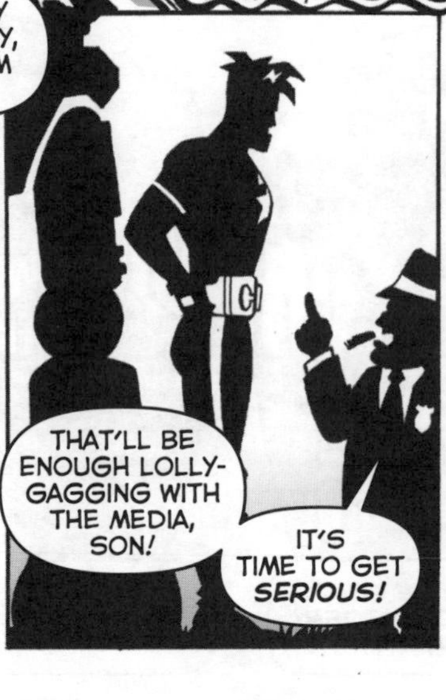
THAT'LL BE ENOUGH LOLLY-GAGGING WITH THE MEDIA, SON!
IT'S TIME TO GET ***SERIOUS!***

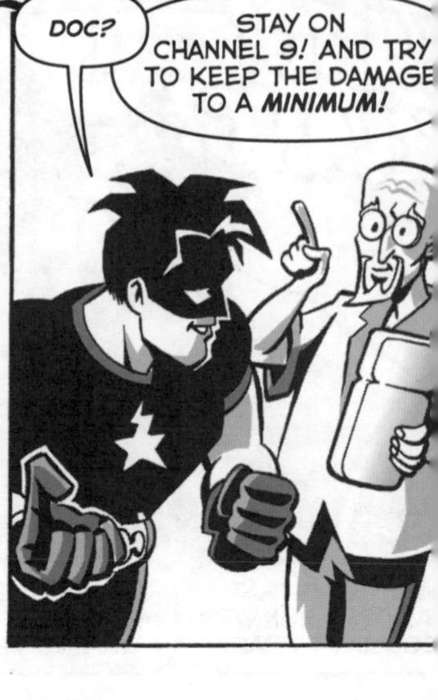
DOC?
STAY ON CHANNEL 9! AND TRY TO KEEP THE DAMAGE TO A ***MINIMUM!***

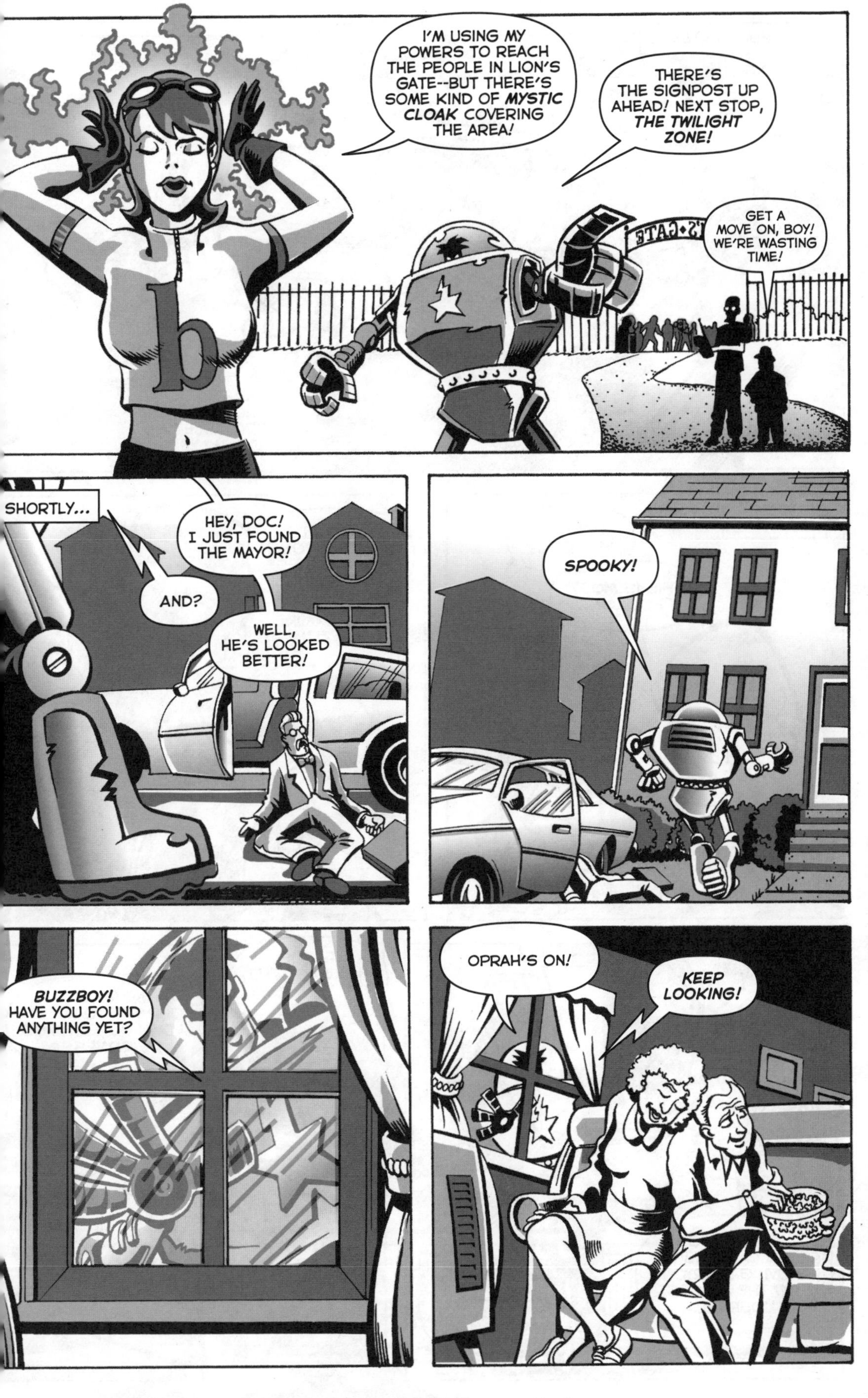
I'M USING MY POWERS TO REACH THE PEOPLE IN LION'S GATE--BUT THERE'S SOME KIND OF MYSTIC CLOAK COVERING THE AREA!
THERE'S THE SIGNPOST UP AHEAD! NEXT STOP, THE TWILIGHT ZONE!
GET A MOVE ON, BOY! WE'RE WASTING TIME!
SHORTLY...
HEY, DOC! I JUST FOUND THE MAYOR!
AND?
WELL, HE'S LOOKED BETTER!
SPOOKY!
BUZZBOY! HAVE YOU FOUND ANYTHING YET?
OPRAH'S ON!
KEEP LOOKING!

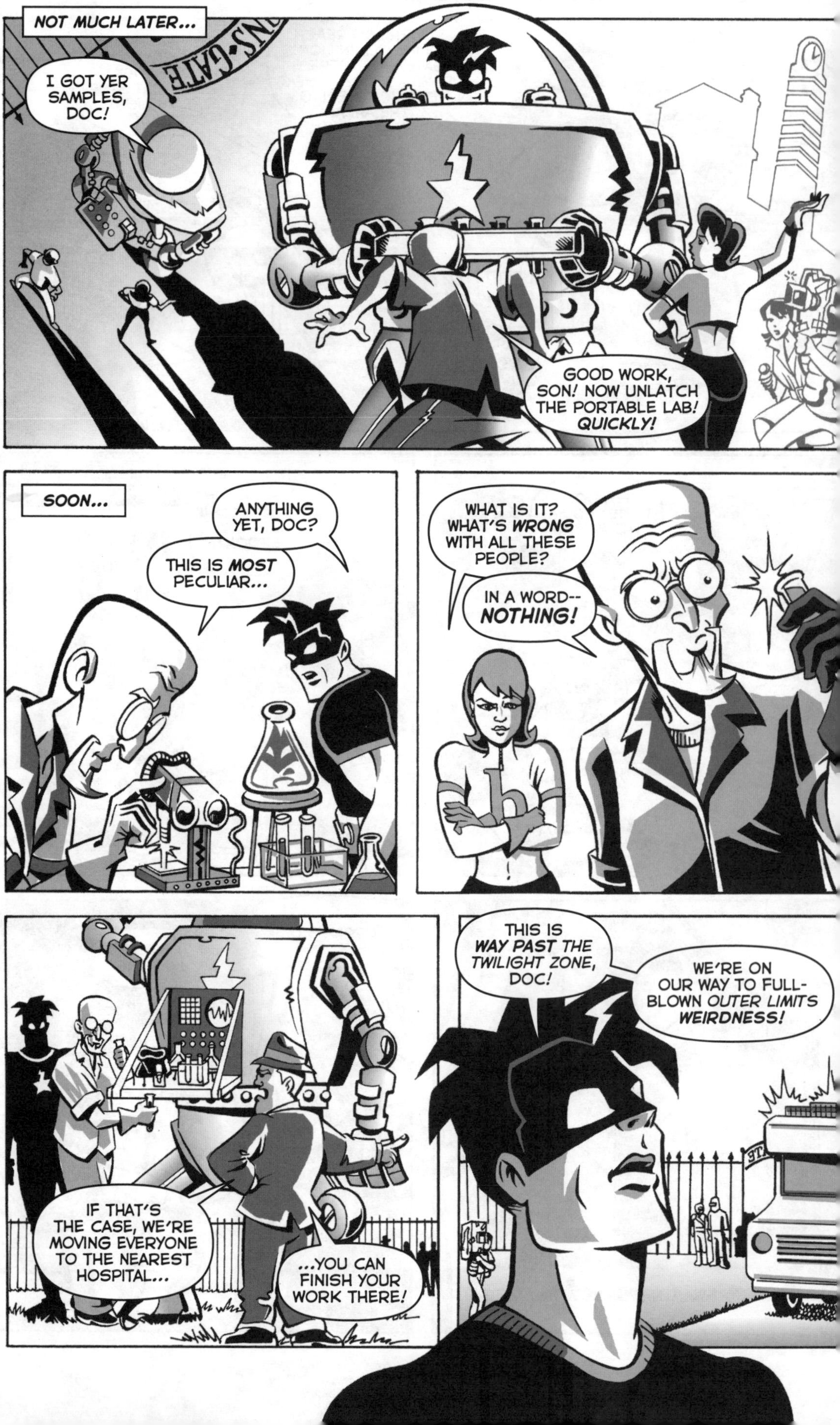
NOT MUCH LATER...
I GOT YER SAMPLES, DOC!
GOOD WORK, SON! NOW UNLATCH THE PORTABLE LAB! *QUICKLY!*
SOON...
ANYTHING YET, DOC?
THIS IS ***MOST*** PECULIAR...
WHAT IS IT? WHAT'S ***WRONG*** WITH ALL THESE PEOPLE?
IN A WORD-- ***NOTHING!***
IF THAT'S THE CASE, WE'RE MOVING EVERYONE TO THE NEAREST HOSPITAL...
...YOU CAN FINISH YOUR WORK THERE!
THIS IS ***WAY PAST*** THE *TWILIGHT ZONE,* DOC!
WE'RE ON OUR WAY TO FULL-BLOWN *OUTER LIMITS* ***WEIRDNESS!***

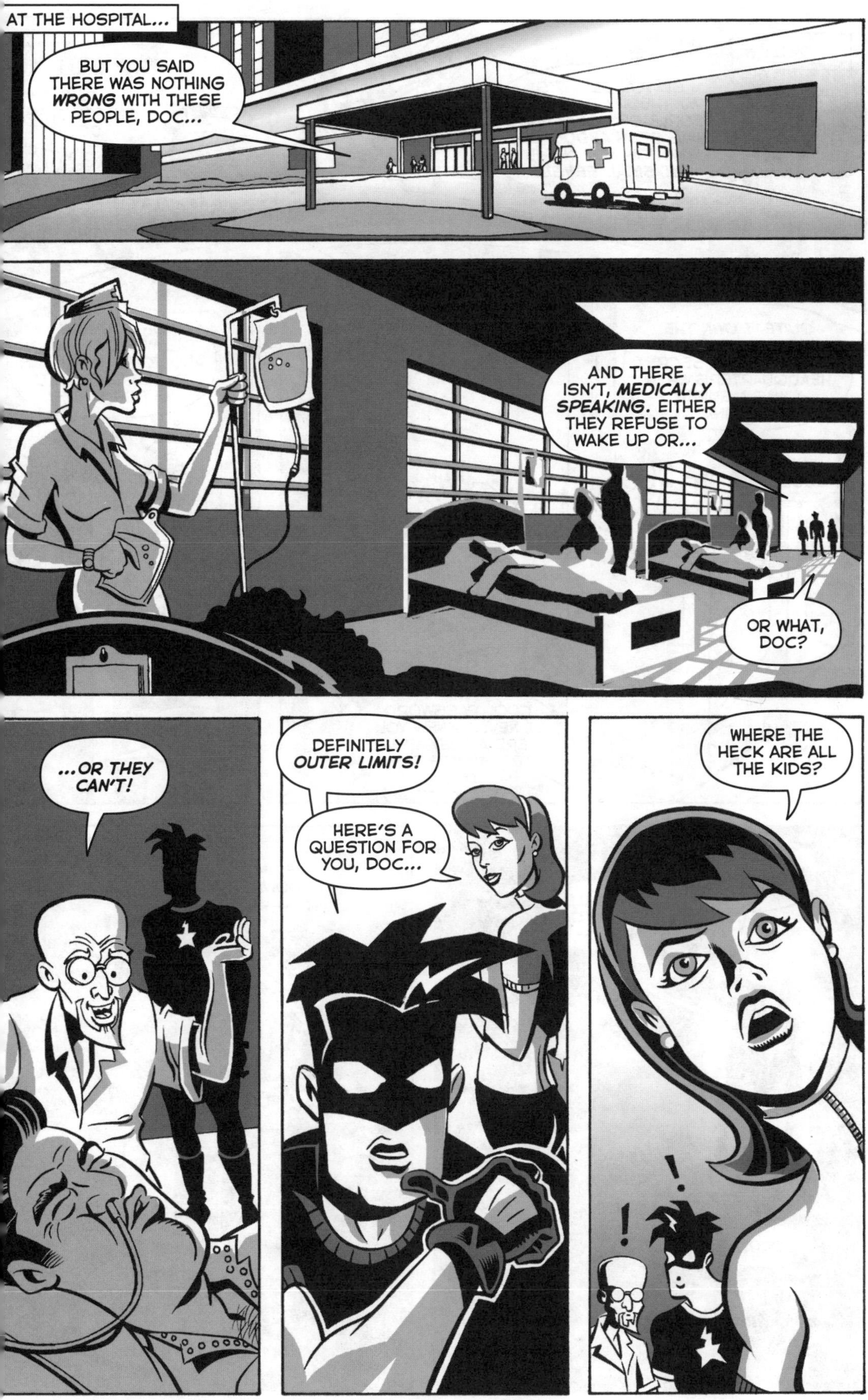
AT THE HOSPITAL...
BUT YOU SAID THERE WAS NOTHING *WRONG* WITH THESE PEOPLE, DOC...
AND THERE ISN'T, *MEDICALLY SPEAKING*. EITHER THEY REFUSE TO WAKE UP OR...
OR WHAT, DOC?
...OR THEY CAN'T!
DEFINITELY *OUTER LIMITS!*
HERE'S A QUESTION FOR YOU, DOC...
WHERE THE HECK ARE ALL THE KIDS?
!
!

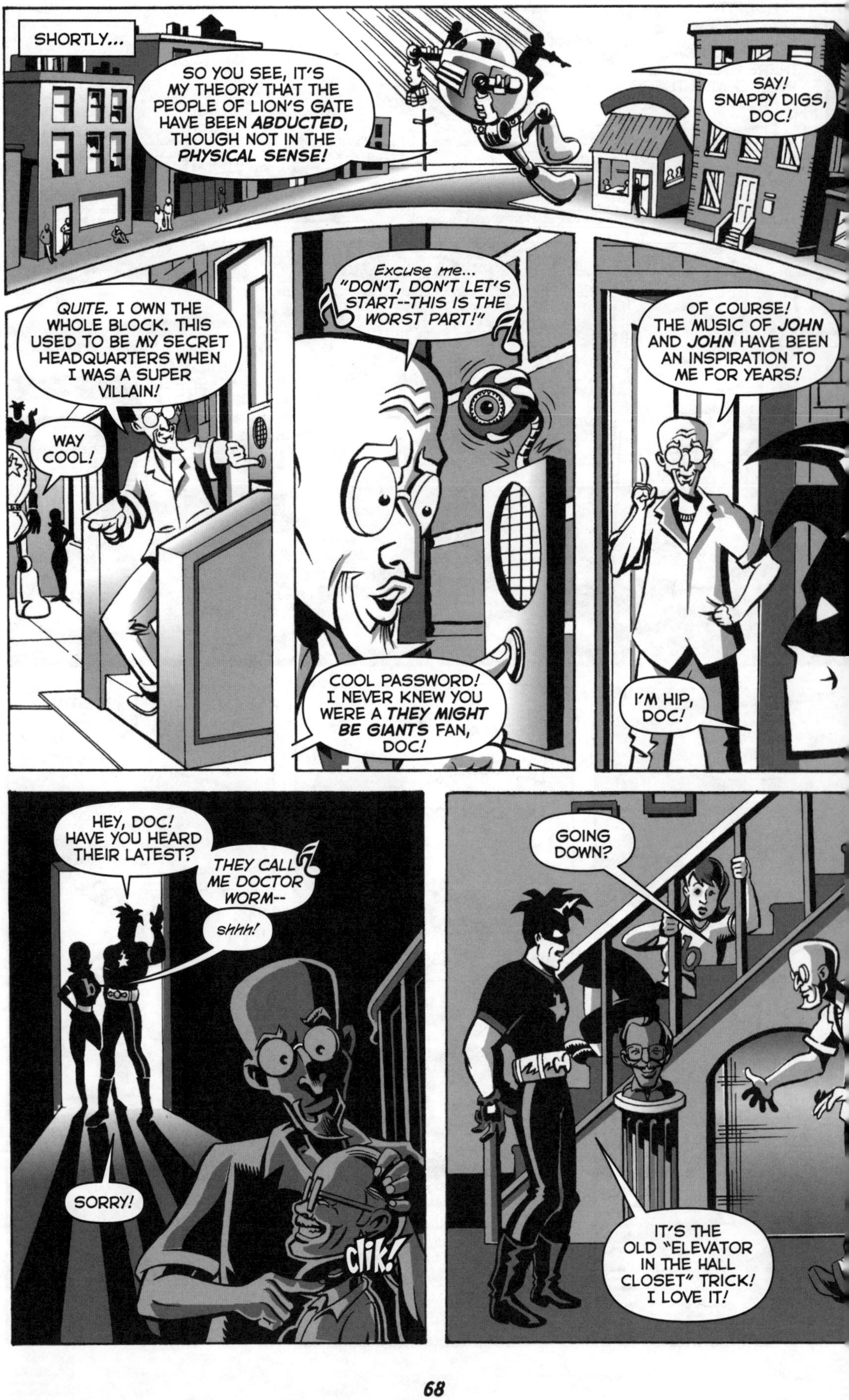
SHORTLY...
SO YOU SEE, IT'S MY THEORY THAT THE PEOPLE OF LION'S GATE HAVE BEEN ABDUCTED, THOUGH NOT IN THE PHYSICAL SENSE!
SAY! SNAPPY DIGS, DOC!
QUITE. I OWN THE WHOLE BLOCK. THIS USED TO BE MY SECRET HEADQUARTERS WHEN I WAS A SUPER VILLAIN!
WAY COOL!
Excuse me... "DON'T, DON'T LET'S START--THIS IS THE WORST PART!"
COOL PASSWORD! I NEVER KNEW YOU WERE A THEY MIGHT BE GIANTS FAN, DOC!
OF COURSE! THE MUSIC OF JOHN AND JOHN HAVE BEEN AN INSPIRATION TO ME FOR YEARS!
I'M HIP, DOC!
HEY, DOC! HAVE YOU HEARD THEIR LATEST?
THEY CALL ME DOCTOR WORM--
shhh!
SORRY!
CLIK!
GOING DOWN?
IT'S THE OLD "ELEVATOR IN THE HALL CLOSET" TRICK! I LOVE IT!

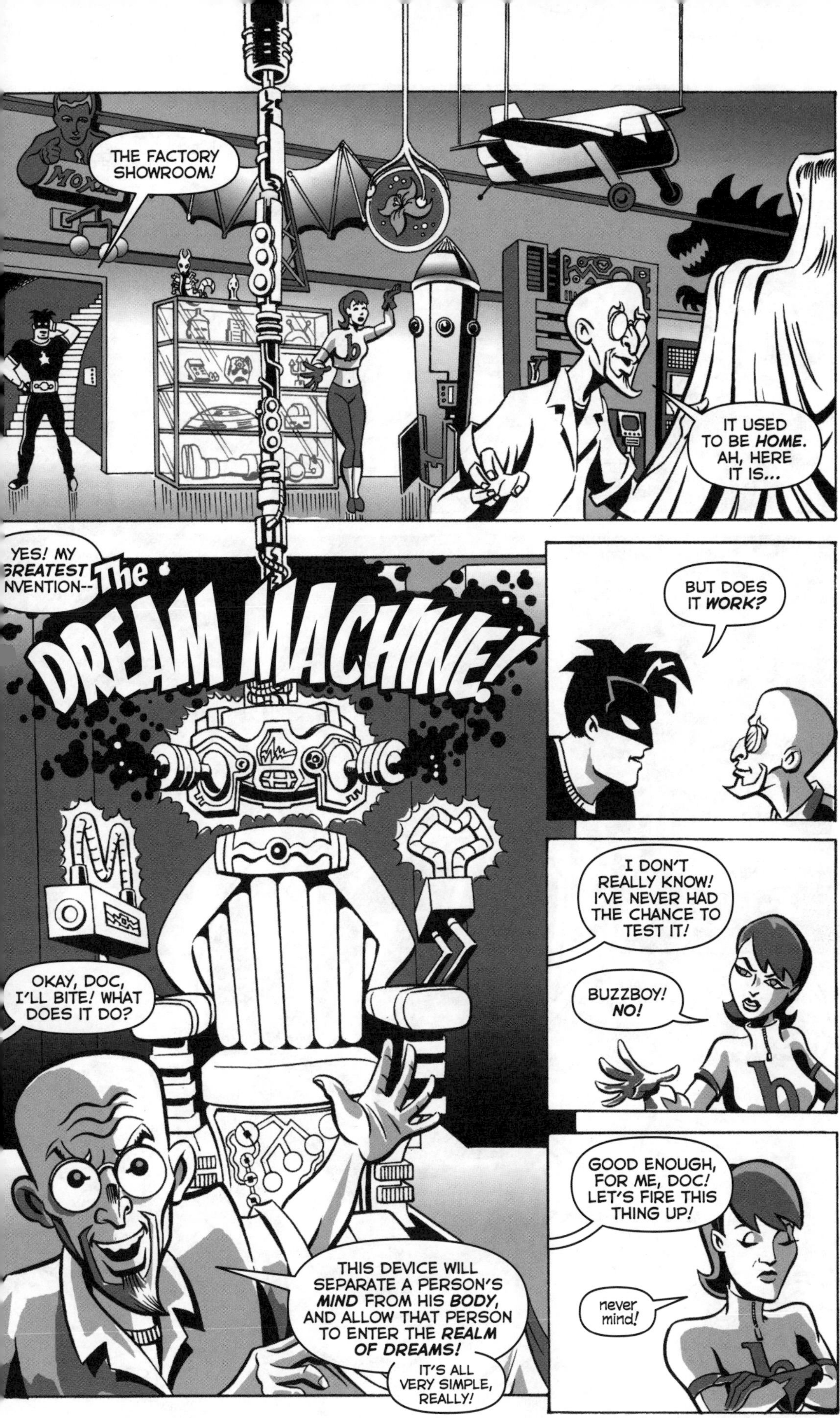
THE FACTORY SHOWROOM!
IT USED TO BE *HOME.* AH, HERE IT IS...
YES! MY *GREATEST* INVENTION--
The DREAM MACHINE!
OKAY, DOC, I'LL BITE! WHAT DOES IT DO?
THIS DEVICE WILL SEPARATE A PERSON'S *MIND* FROM HIS *BODY,* AND ALLOW THAT PERSON TO ENTER THE *REALM OF DREAMS!*
IT'S ALL VERY SIMPLE, REALLY!
BUT DOES IT *WORK?*
I DON'T REALLY KNOW! I'VE NEVER HAD THE CHANCE TO TEST IT!
BUZZBOY! *NO!*
GOOD ENOUGH, FOR ME, DOC! LET'S FIRE THIS THING UP!
never mind!

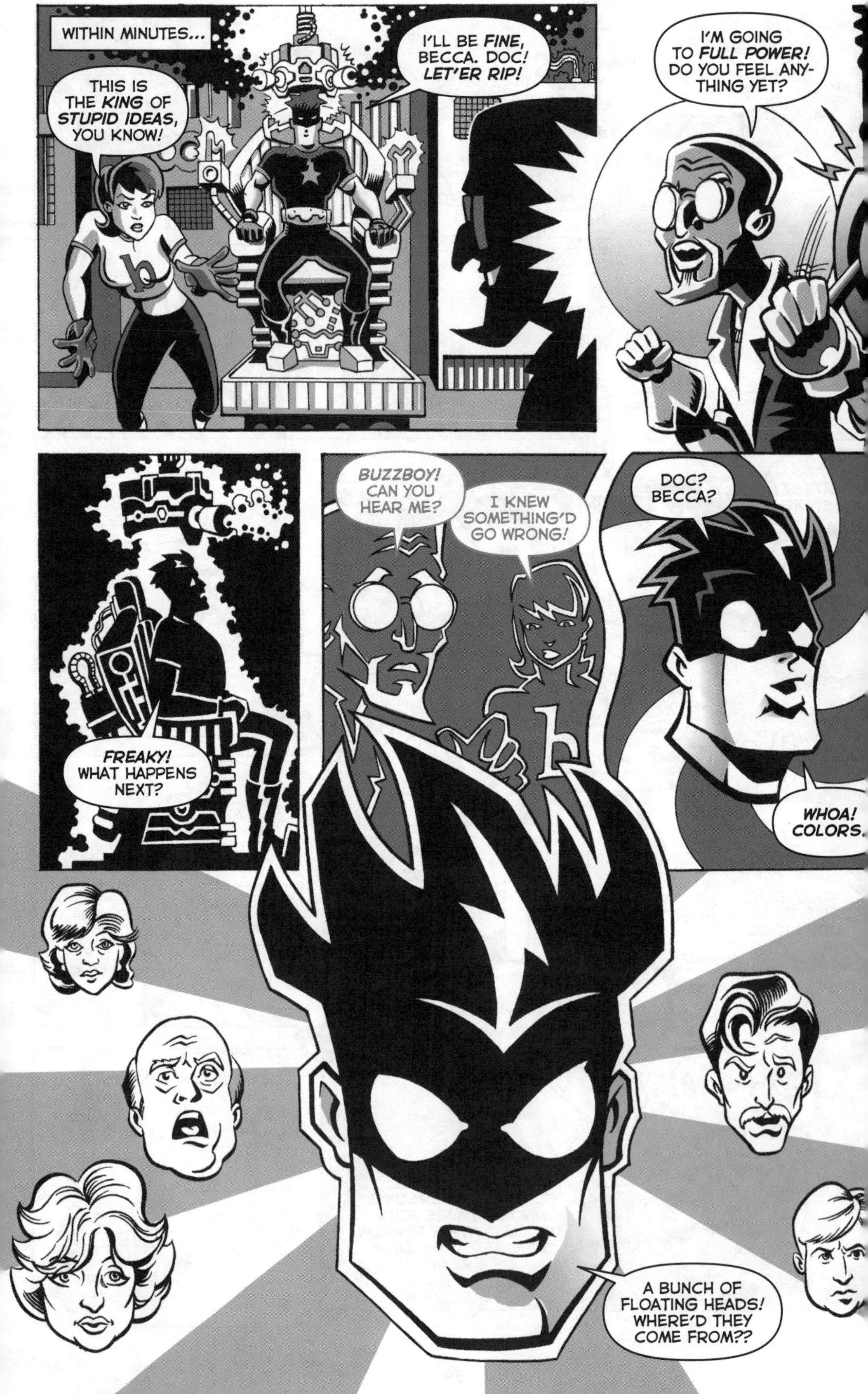

WITHIN MINUTES...
THIS IS THE KING OF STUPID IDEAS, YOU KNOW!
I'LL BE FINE, BECCA. DOC! LET'ER RIP!
I'M GOING TO FULL POWER! DO YOU FEEL ANYTHING YET?
FREAKY! WHAT HAPPENS NEXT?
BUZZBOY! CAN YOU HEAR ME?
I KNEW SOMETHING'D GO WRONG!
DOC? BECCA?
WHOA! COLORS.
A BUNCH OF FLOATING HEADS! WHERE'D THEY COME FROM??

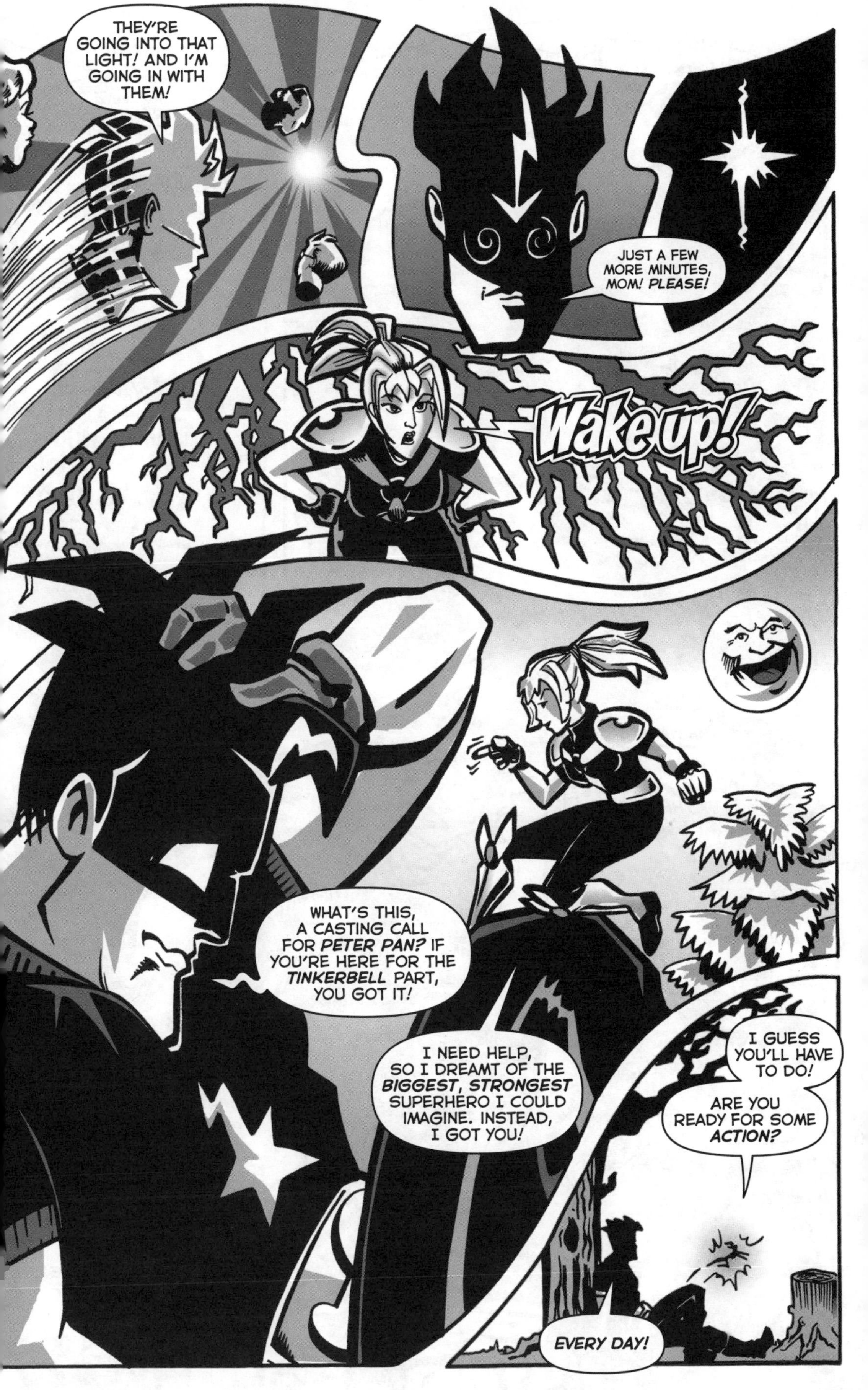
THEY'RE GOING INTO THAT LIGHT! AND I'M GOING IN WITH THEM!
JUST A FEW MORE MINUTES, MOM! PLEASE!
Wake up!
WHAT'S THIS, A CASTING CALL FOR PETER PAN? IF YOU'RE HERE FOR THE TINKERBELL PART, YOU GOT IT!
I NEED HELP, SO I DREAMT OF THE BIGGEST, STRONGEST SUPERHERO I COULD IMAGINE. INSTEAD, I GOT YOU!
I GUESS YOU'LL HAVE TO DO!
ARE YOU READY FOR SOME ACTION?
EVERY DAY!

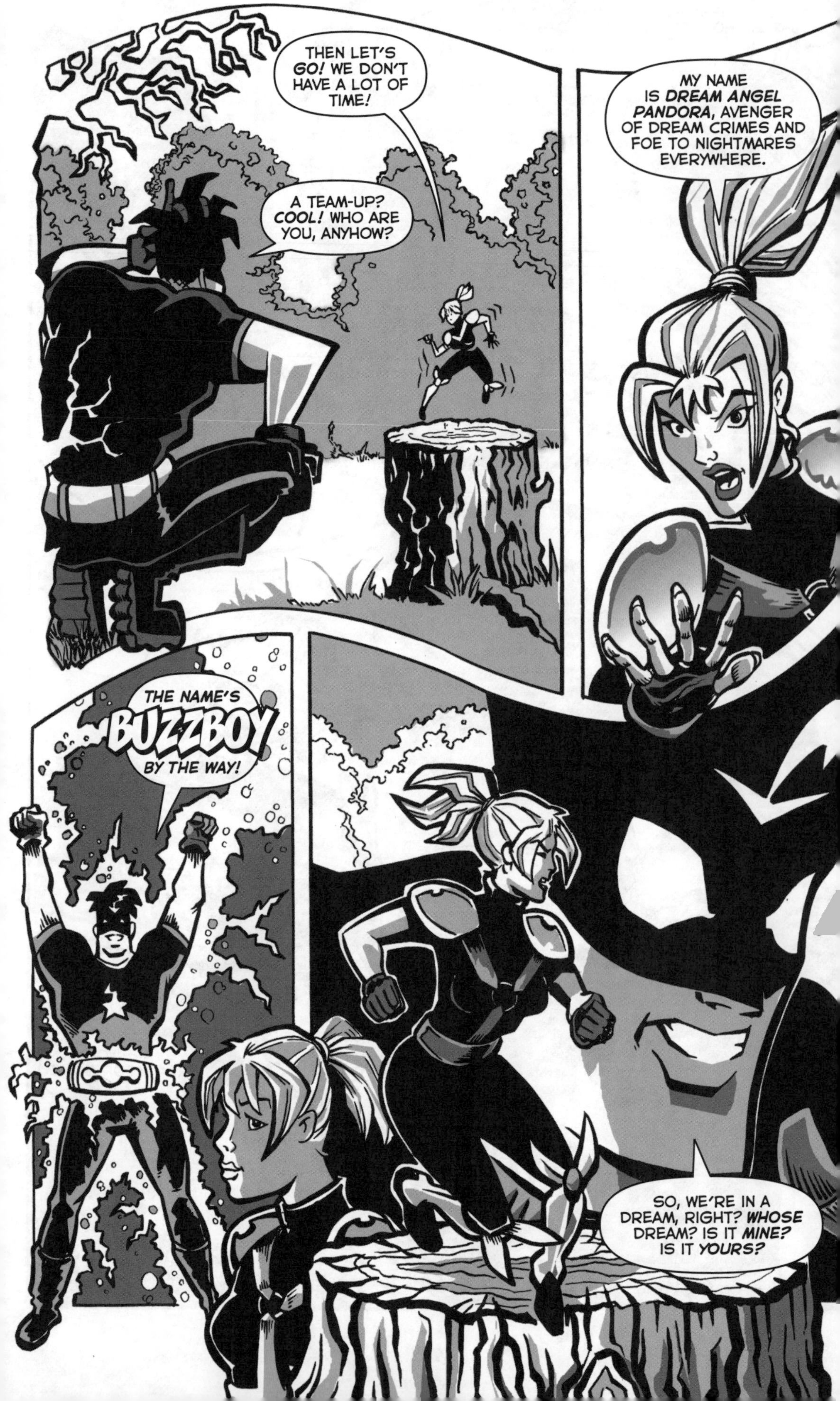
A TEAM-UP? COOL! WHO ARE YOU, ANYHOW?
THEN LET'S GO! WE DON'T HAVE A LOT OF TIME!
MY NAME IS DREAM ANGEL PANDORA, AVENGER OF DREAM CRIMES AND FOE TO NIGHTMARES EVERYWHERE.
THE NAME'S BUZZBOY BY THE WAY!
SO, WE'RE IN A DREAM, RIGHT? WHOSE DREAM? IS IT MINE? IS IT YOURS?

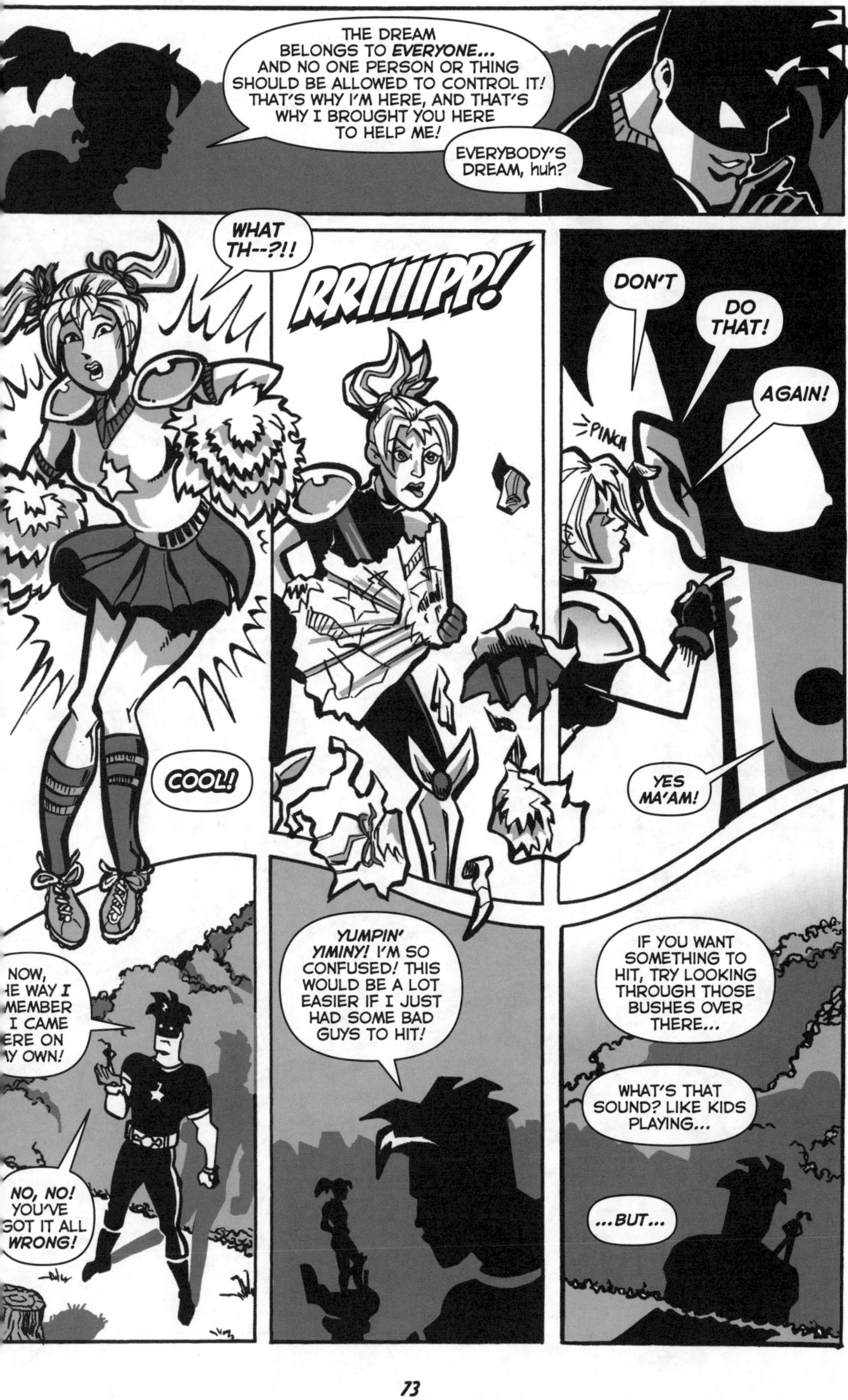
THE DREAM BELONGS TO *EVERYONE...* AND NO ONE PERSON OR THING SHOULD BE ALLOWED TO CONTROL IT! THAT'S WHY I'M HERE, AND THAT'S WHY I BROUGHT YOU HERE TO HELP ME!
EVERYBODY'S DREAM, huh?
WHAT TH--?!!
COOL!
RRIIIIPP!
DON'T
DO THAT!
AGAIN!
PINCH
YES MA'AM!
NO, NO! YOU'VE GOT IT ALL *WRONG!*
YUMPIN' YIMINY! I'M SO CONFUSED! THIS WOULD BE A LOT EASIER IF I JUST HAD SOME BAD GUYS TO HIT!
IF YOU WANT SOMETHING TO HIT, TRY LOOKING THROUGH THOSE BUSHES OVER THERE...
WHAT'S THAT SOUND? LIKE KIDS PLAYING...
...BUT...

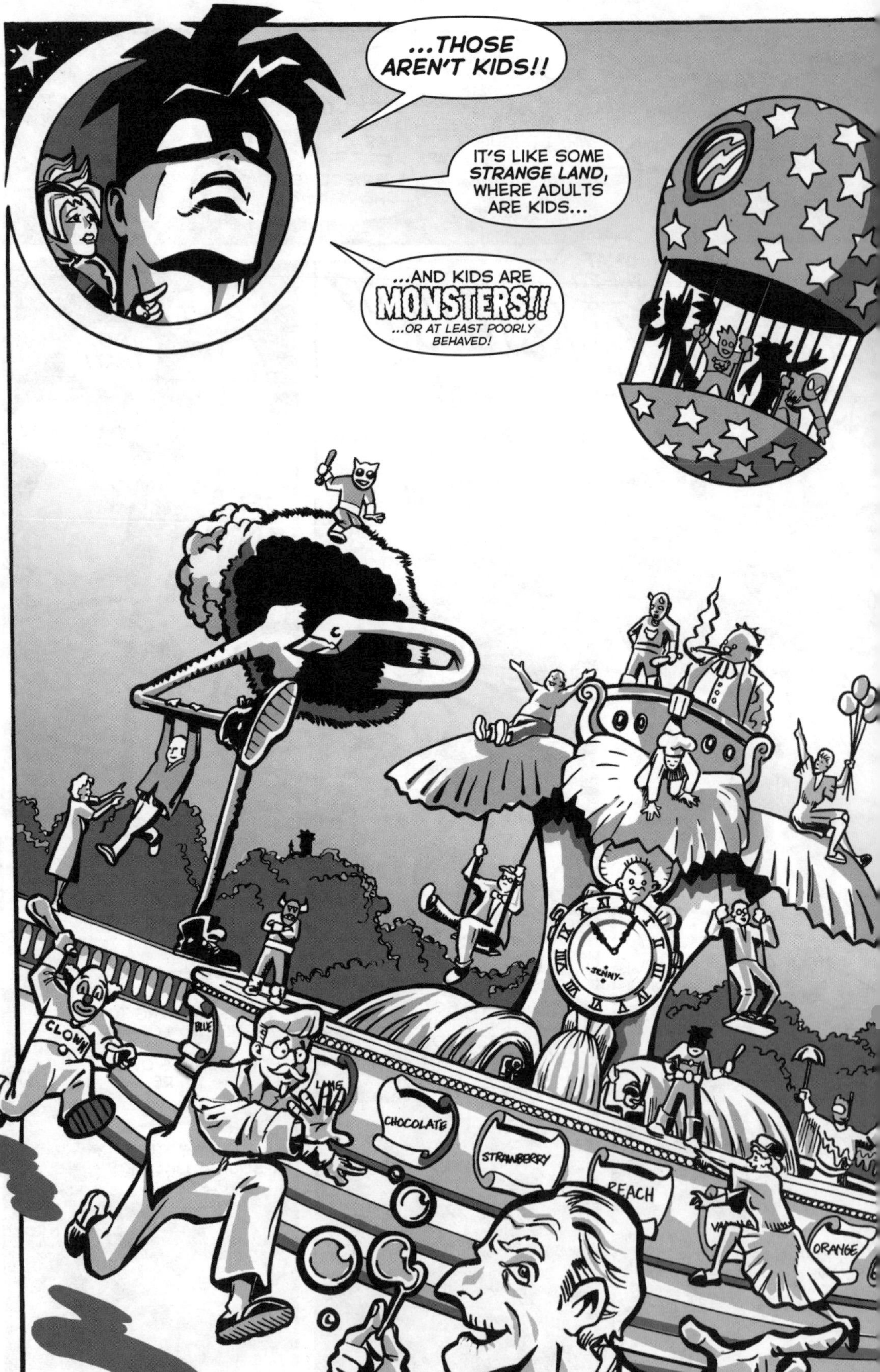
...THOSE AREN'T KIDS!!
IT'S LIKE SOME STRANGE LAND, WHERE ADULTS ARE KIDS...
...AND KIDS ARE MONSTERS!! ...OR AT LEAST POORLY BEHAVED!
CLOWN
BLUE
LIME
CHOCOLATE
STRAWBERRY
PEACH
ORANGE
JENNY
—AFTER McCAY!

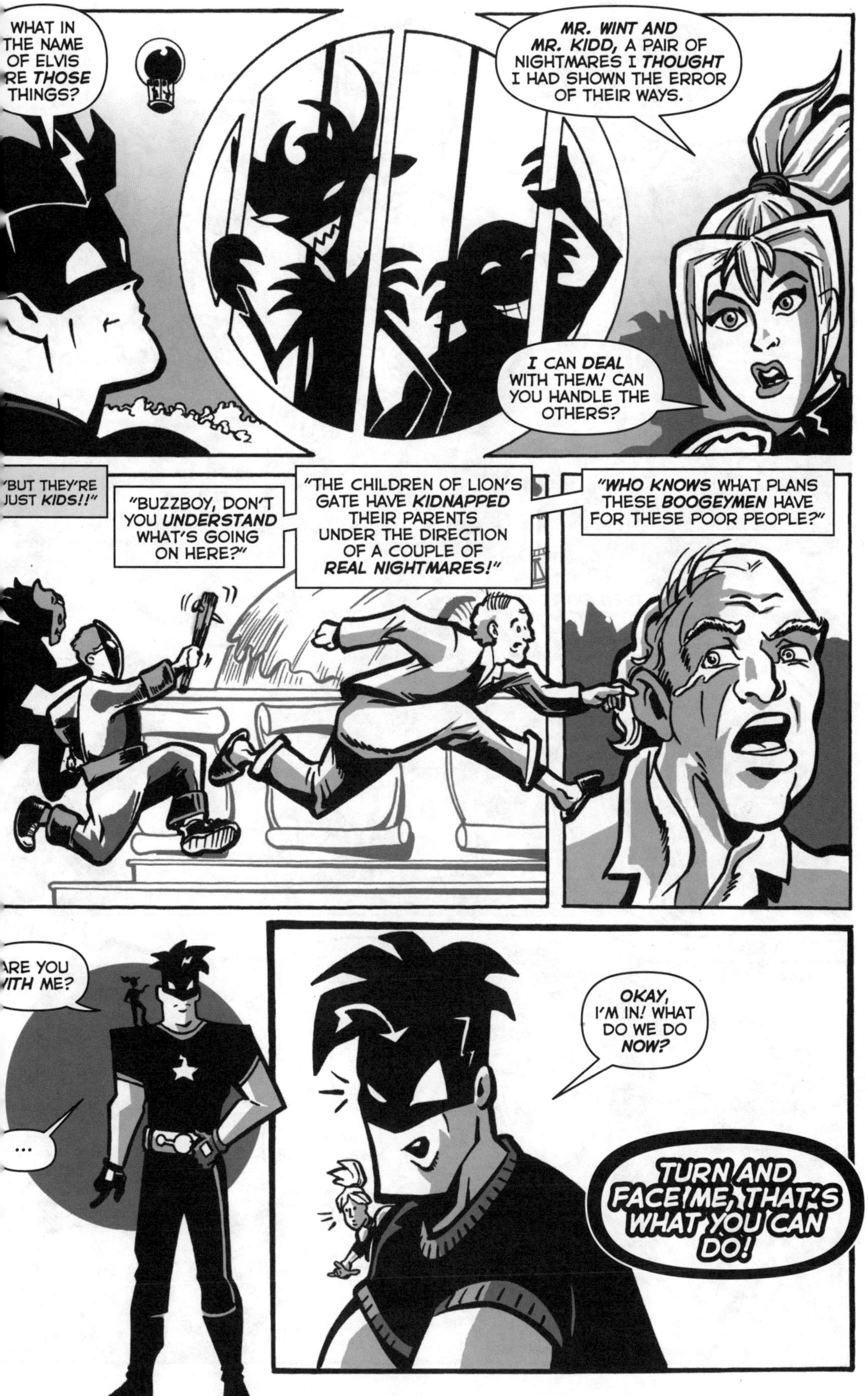
WHAT IN THE NAME OF ELVIS RE THOSE THINGS?
MR. WINT AND MR. KIDD, A PAIR OF NIGHTMARES I THOUGHT I HAD SHOWN THE ERROR OF THEIR WAYS.
I CAN DEAL WITH THEM! CAN YOU HANDLE THE OTHERS?
"BUT THEY'RE JUST KIDS!!"
"BUZZBOY, DON'T YOU UNDERSTAND WHAT'S GOING ON HERE?"
"THE CHILDREN OF LION'S GATE HAVE KIDNAPPED THEIR PARENTS UNDER THE DIRECTION OF A COUPLE OF REAL NIGHTMARES!"
"WHO KNOWS WHAT PLANS THESE BOOGEYMEN HAVE FOR THESE POOR PEOPLE?"
ARE YOU WITH ME?
...
OKAY, I'M IN! WHAT DO WE DO NOW?
TURN AND FACE ME, THAT'S WHAT YOU CAN DO!

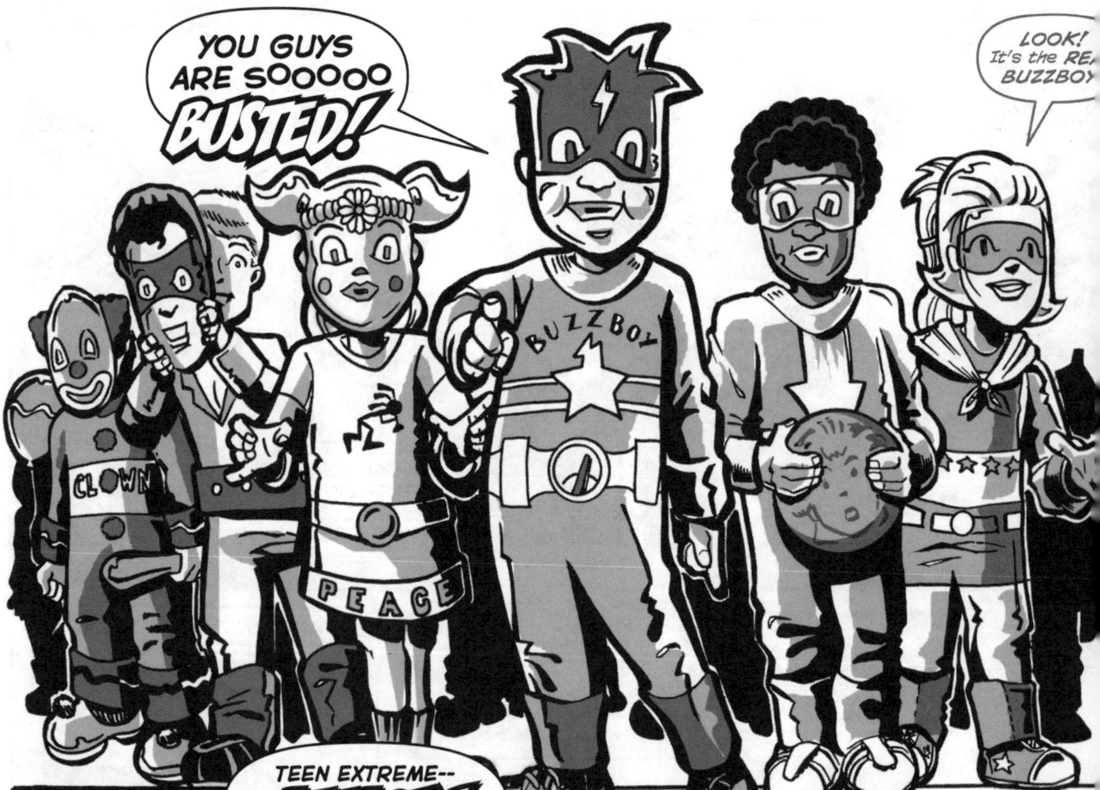
YOU GUYS ARE SOOOOO BUSTED!
LOOK! It's the
CLOWN
PEACE
BUZZBOY

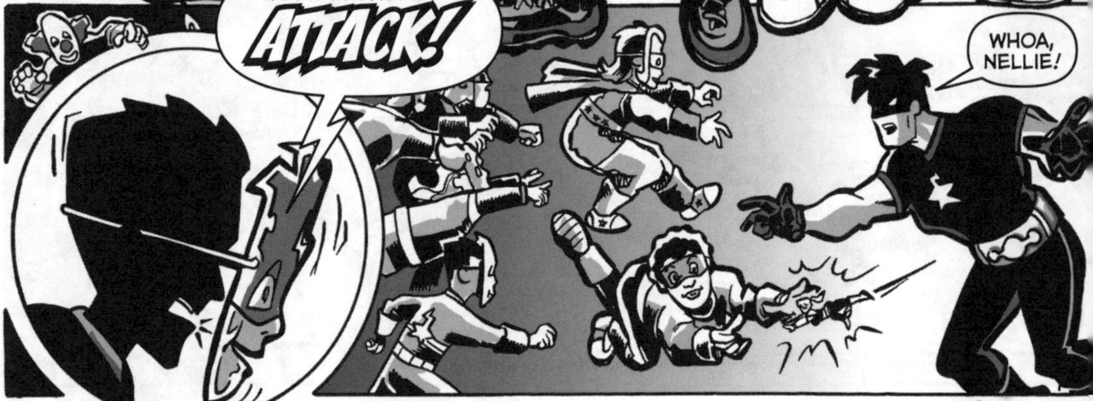
TEEN EXTREME-- ATTACK!
WHOA, NELLIE!

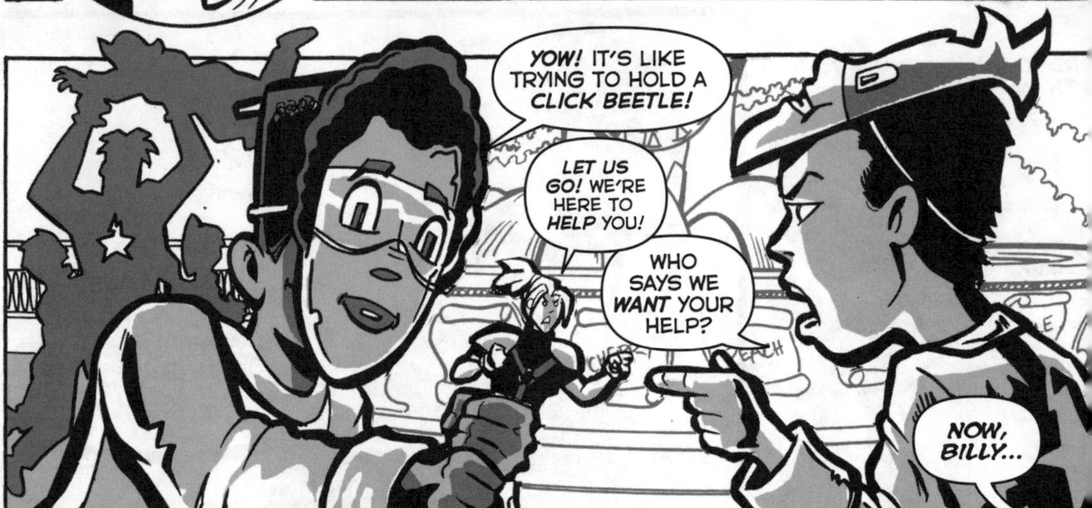
YOW! IT'S LIKE TRYING TO HOLD A CLICK BEETLE!
LET US GO! WE'RE HERE TO HELP YOU!
WHO SAYS WE WANT YOUR HELP?
NOW, BILLY...

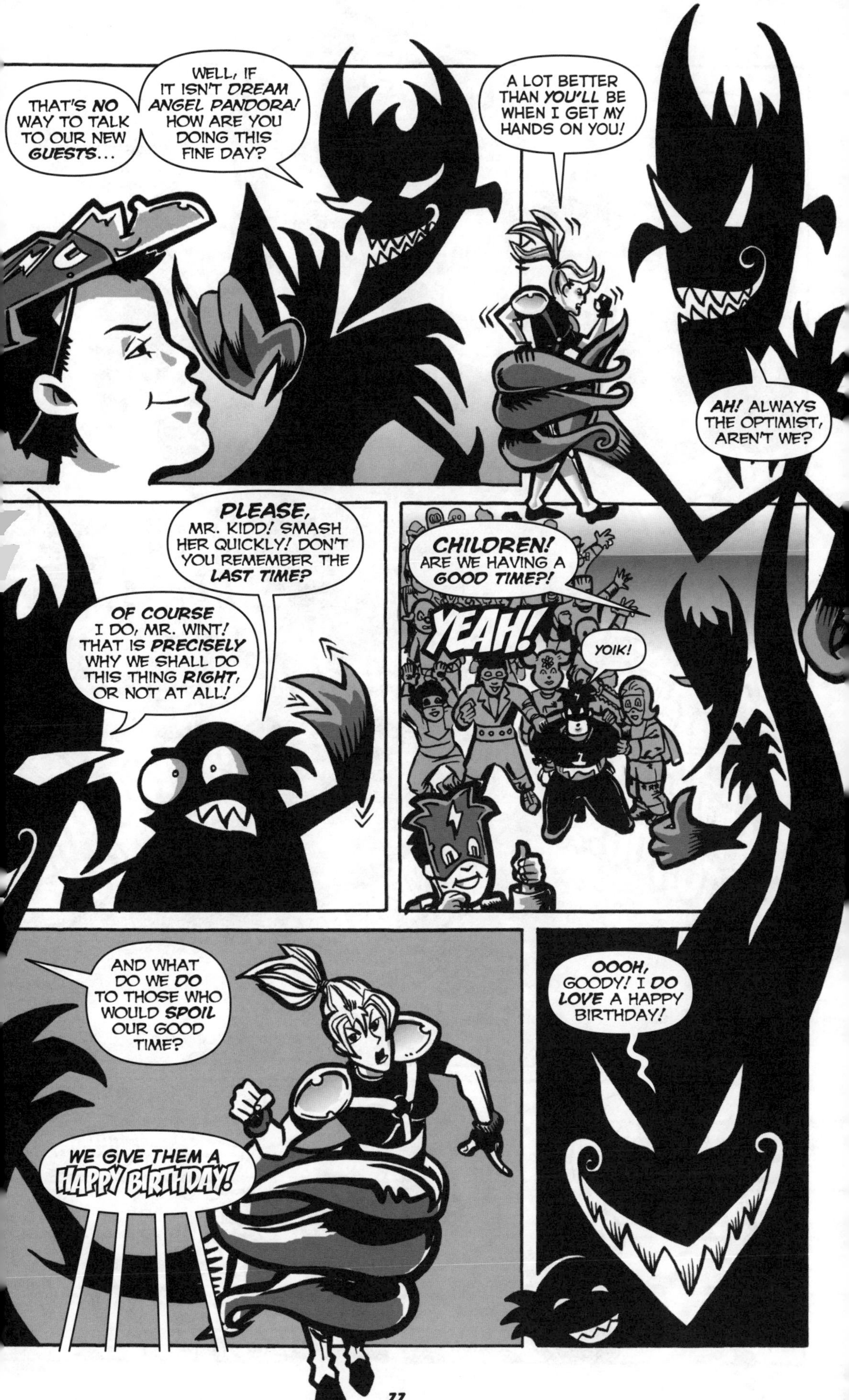
THAT'S NO WAY TO TALK TO OUR NEW GUESTS...
WELL, IF IT ISN'T DREAM ANGEL PANDORA! HOW ARE YOU DOING THIS FINE DAY?
A LOT BETTER THAN YOU'LL BE WHEN I GET MY HANDS ON YOU!
AH! ALWAYS THE OPTIMIST, AREN'T WE?
PLEASE, MR. KIDD! SMASH HER QUICKLY! DON'T YOU REMEMBER THE LAST TIME?
OF COURSE I DO, MR. WINT! THAT IS PRECISELY WHY WE SHALL DO THIS THING RIGHT, OR NOT AT ALL!
CHILDREN! ARE WE HAVING A GOOD TIME?!
YEAH!
YOIK!
AND WHAT DO WE DO TO THOSE WHO WOULD SPOIL OUR GOOD TIME?
WE GIVE THEM A HAPPY BIRTHDAY!
OOOH, GOODY! I DO LOVE A HAPPY BIRTHDAY!

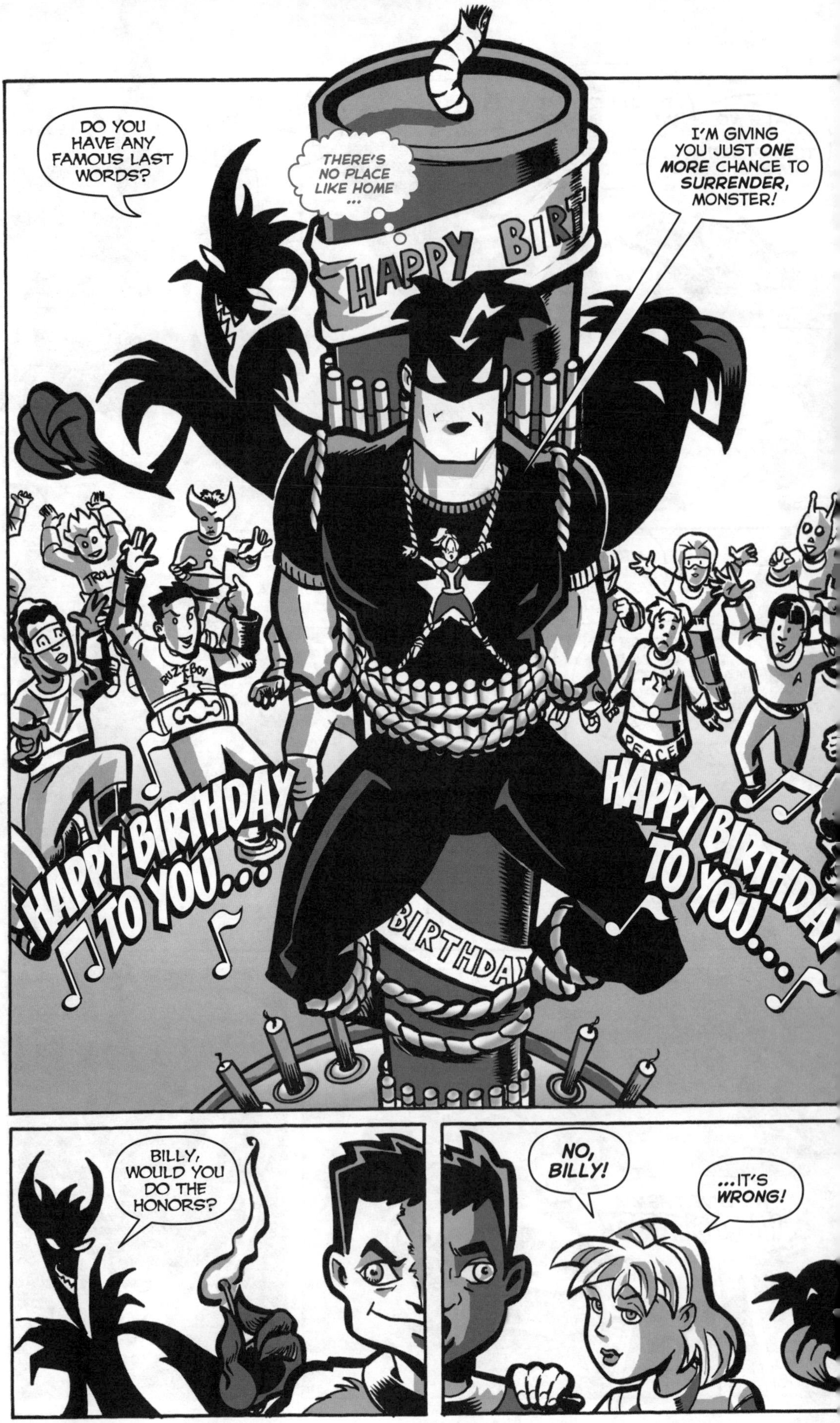
DO YOU HAVE ANY FAMOUS LAST WORDS?
THERE'S NO PLACE LIKE HOME ...
I'M GIVING YOU JUST ONE MORE CHANCE TO SURRENDER, MONSTER!
HAPPY BIRT
TROLL
BUZZ-BOY
PEACE
HAPPY BIRTHDAY TO YOU...
HAPPY BIRTHDAY TO YOU...
BIRTHDAY
BILLY, WOULD YOU DO THE HONORS?
NO, BILLY!
...IT'S WRONG!

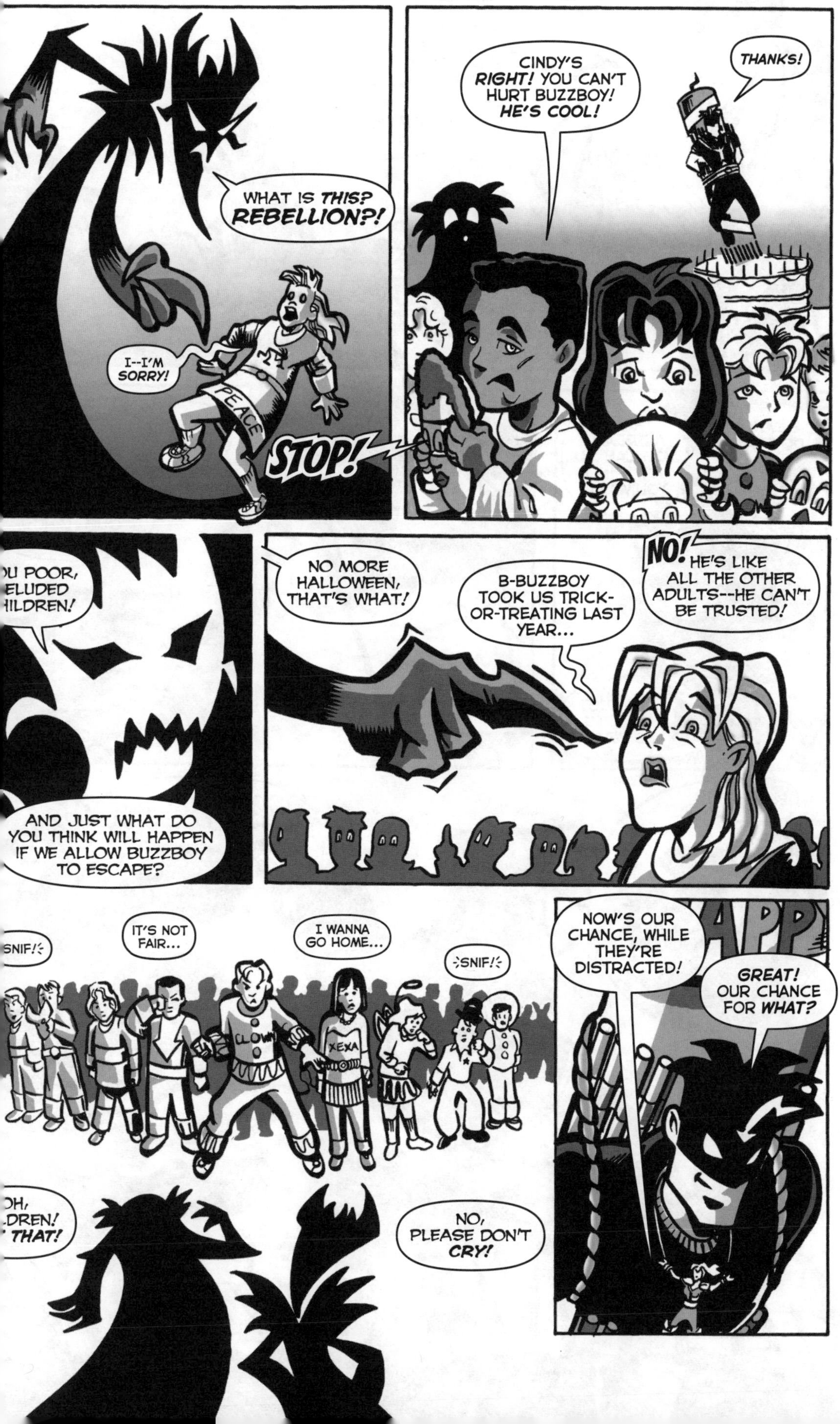
WHAT IS THIS? REBELLION?!
I--I'M SORRY!
STOP!
CINDY'S RIGHT! YOU CAN'T HURT BUZZBOY! HE'S COOL!
THANKS!
U POOR, ELUDED HILDREN!
AND JUST WHAT DO YOU THINK WILL HAPPEN IF WE ALLOW BUZZBOY TO ESCAPE?
NO MORE HALLOWEEN, THAT'S WHAT!
B-BUZZBOY TOOK US TRICK-OR-TREATING LAST YEAR...
NO! HE'S LIKE ALL THE OTHER ADULTS--HE CAN'T BE TRUSTED!
SNIF!
IT'S NOT FAIR...
I WANNA GO HOME...
SNIF!
OH, DREN! THAT!
NO, PLEASE DON'T CRY!
NOW'S OUR CHANCE, WHILE THEY'RE DISTRACTED!
GREAT! OUR CHANCE FOR WHAT?

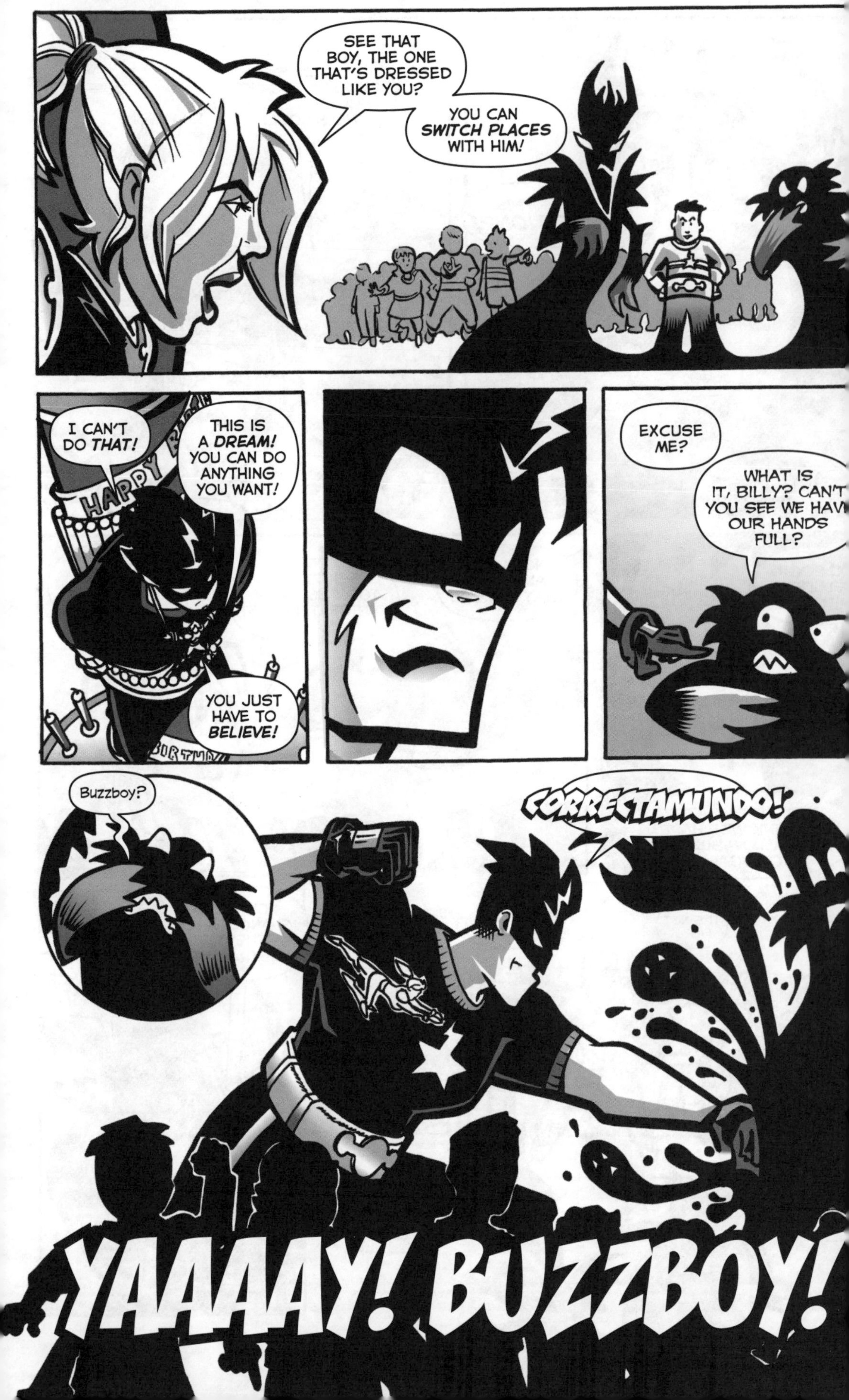
SEE THAT BOY, THE ONE THAT'S DRESSED LIKE YOU?
YOU CAN SWITCH PLACES WITH HIM!
I CAN'T DO THAT!
THIS IS A DREAM! YOU CAN DO ANYTHING YOU WANT!
YOU JUST HAVE TO BELIEVE!
EXCUSE ME?
WHAT IS IT, BILLY? CAN'T YOU SEE WE HAV OUR HANDS FULL?
Buzzboy?
CORRECTAMUNDO!
YAAAAY! BUZZBOY!

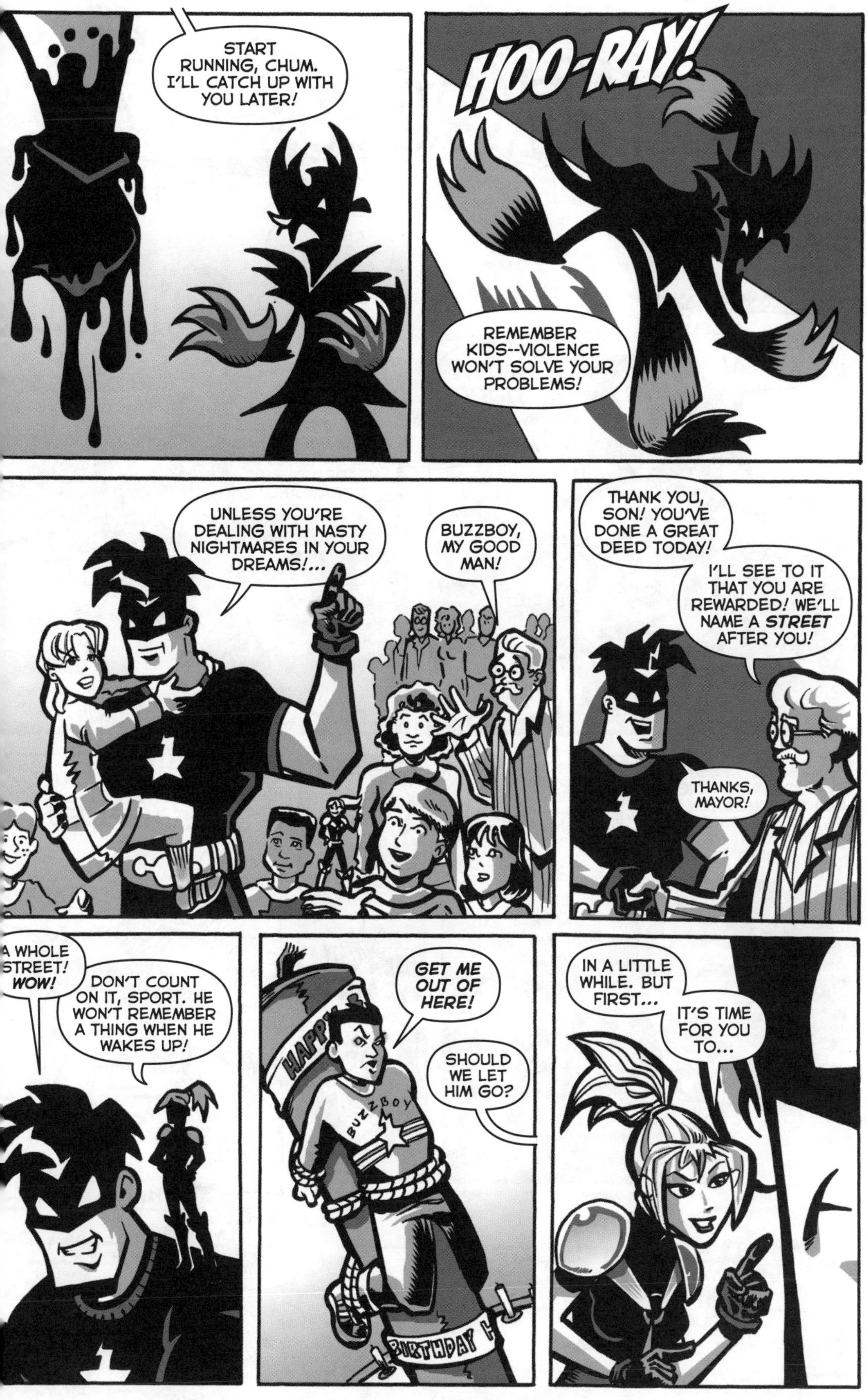
START RUNNING, CHUM. I'LL CATCH UP WITH YOU LATER!
HOO-RAY!
REMEMBER KIDS--VIOLENCE WON'T SOLVE YOUR PROBLEMS!
UNLESS YOU'RE DEALING WITH NASTY NIGHTMARES IN YOUR DREAMS!...
BUZZBOY, MY GOOD MAN!
THANK YOU, SON! YOU'VE DONE A GREAT DEED TODAY!
I'LL SEE TO IT THAT YOU ARE REWARDED! WE'LL NAME A STREET AFTER YOU!
THANKS, MAYOR!
A WHOLE STREET! WOW!
DON'T COUNT ON IT, SPORT. HE WON'T REMEMBER A THING WHEN HE WAKES UP!
GET ME OUT OF HERE!
SHOULD WE LET HIM GO?
IN A LITTLE WHILE. BUT FIRST...
IT'S TIME FOR YOU TO...

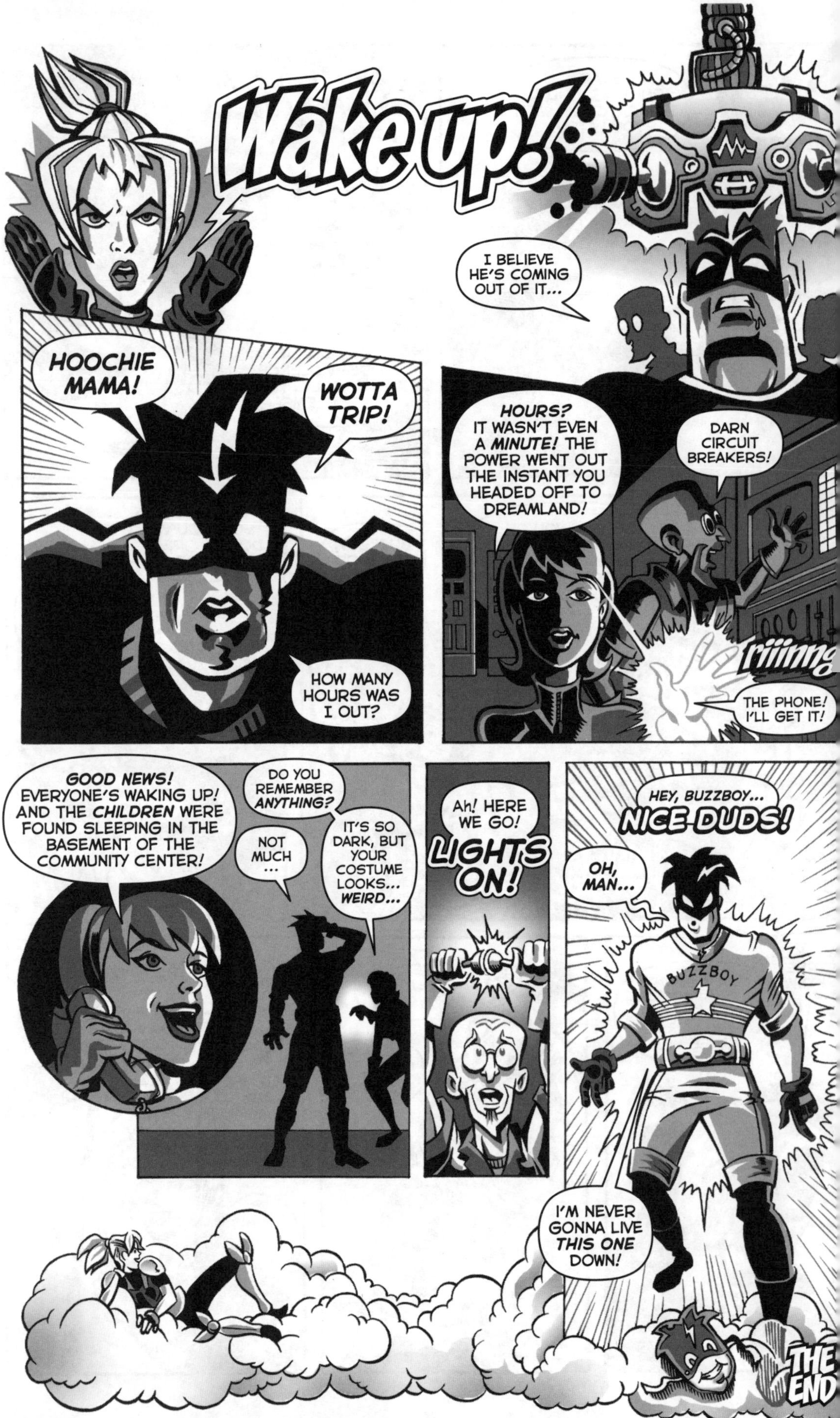
Wake up!
I BELIEVE HE'S COMING OUT OF IT...
HOOCHIE MAMA!
WOTTA TRIP!
HOW MANY HOURS WAS I OUT?
HOURS? IT WASN'T EVEN A MINUTE! THE POWER WENT OUT THE INSTANT YOU HEADED OFF TO DREAMLAND!
DARN CIRCUIT BREAKERS!
riiinng
THE PHONE! I'LL GET IT!
GOOD NEWS! EVERYONE'S WAKING UP! AND THE CHILDREN WERE FOUND SLEEPING IN THE BASEMENT OF THE COMMUNITY CENTER!
DO YOU REMEMBER ANYTHING?
NOT MUCH ...
IT'S SO DARK, BUT YOUR COSTUME LOOKS... WEIRD...
Ah! HERE WE GO!
LIGHTS ON!
HEY, BUZZBOY...
NICE DUDS!
OH, MAN...
BUZZBOY
I'M NEVER GONNA LIVE THIS ONE DOWN!
THE END

Third Course

"Cheeseboogie! Cheeseboogie! Cheeseboogie!"
- John Belushi
as the Greek Restauranter
Saturday Night Live

Milkshakes

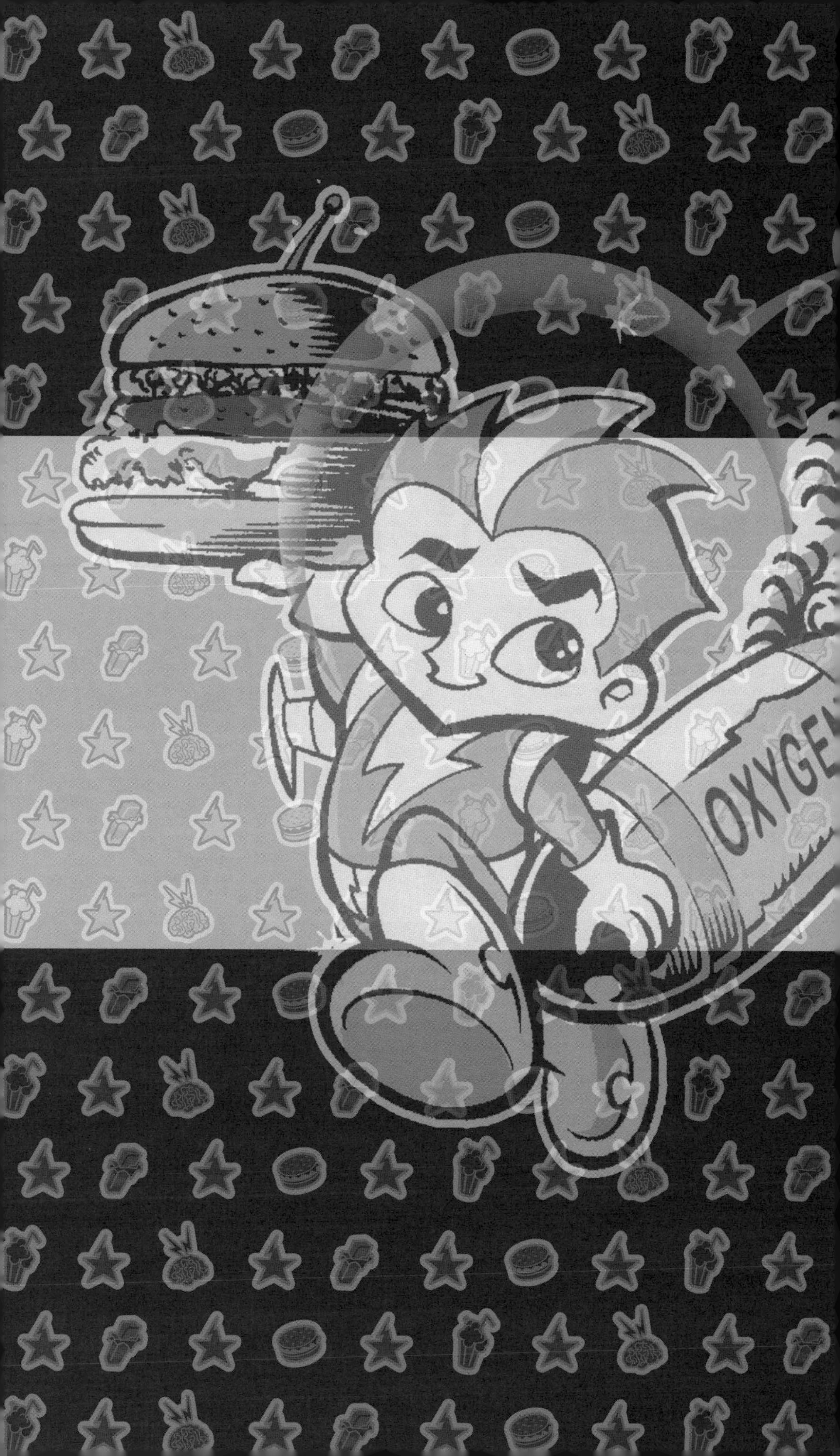
OXYGE

buzzography

POLICE OFFICER SAM BLUESTONE

STATS: ROOKIE COP SAM BLUESTONE IS NEW TO NEW PARADISE AND ALL ITS HEROES... AND VILLAINS. HE'S A GOOFY, YET DEDICATED PROTECTOR OF THE CITY'S CITIZENS, AND HAS CREATED A CLOSE BOND WITH BUZZBOY. HE HAS A WICKED CRUSH ON MARZ GRRL, AND IS GENERALLY FASCINATED WITH SUPER HEROES.

1ST APPEARANCE:
BUZZBOY: SHORT CUTS #1 COMIC BOOK
SAM BLUESTONE CREATED BY JOHN HEFFNER
™ AND ©2000 JOHN HEFFNER

LADY ARAKNID
REAL NAME: UNKNOWN

STATS: A MYSTERIOUS CAT BURGLAR WITH AN INTEREST IN ANYTHING RELATED TO SPIDERS. HER MECHANICAL APPENDAGES MAKE HER A FORMIDABLE FOE FOR ANY CRIME FIGHTER. RECENT RUMORS SUGGEST A ROMANTIC LINK BETWEEN LADY ARAKNID AND BUZZBOY, WHICH BOTH DENY VEHEMENTLY.

1ST APPEARANCE:
LOVE IN TIGHTS #3

BUNGEE

MAGGIE Z

TUATARA

NZ3 *(EN·ZED·THREE)*
REAL NAMES: UNKNOWN

STATS: NEW ZEALAND'S OFFICIAL SUPER TEAM, NZ3, IS COMPRISED OF A TRIO OF YOUNG HEROES W/ POWERS REPRESENTATIVE OF ASPECTS OF NEW ZEALAND. THEY HAVE MUCH TO LEARN ABOUT BEING HEROES, BUT THEIR LOYALTY TO THEIR COUNTRY MAKES THEM A FORCE TO BE RECKONED WITH.

1ST APPEARANCE:
BUZZBOY DAILY COMIC STRIP,
EPISODE 96

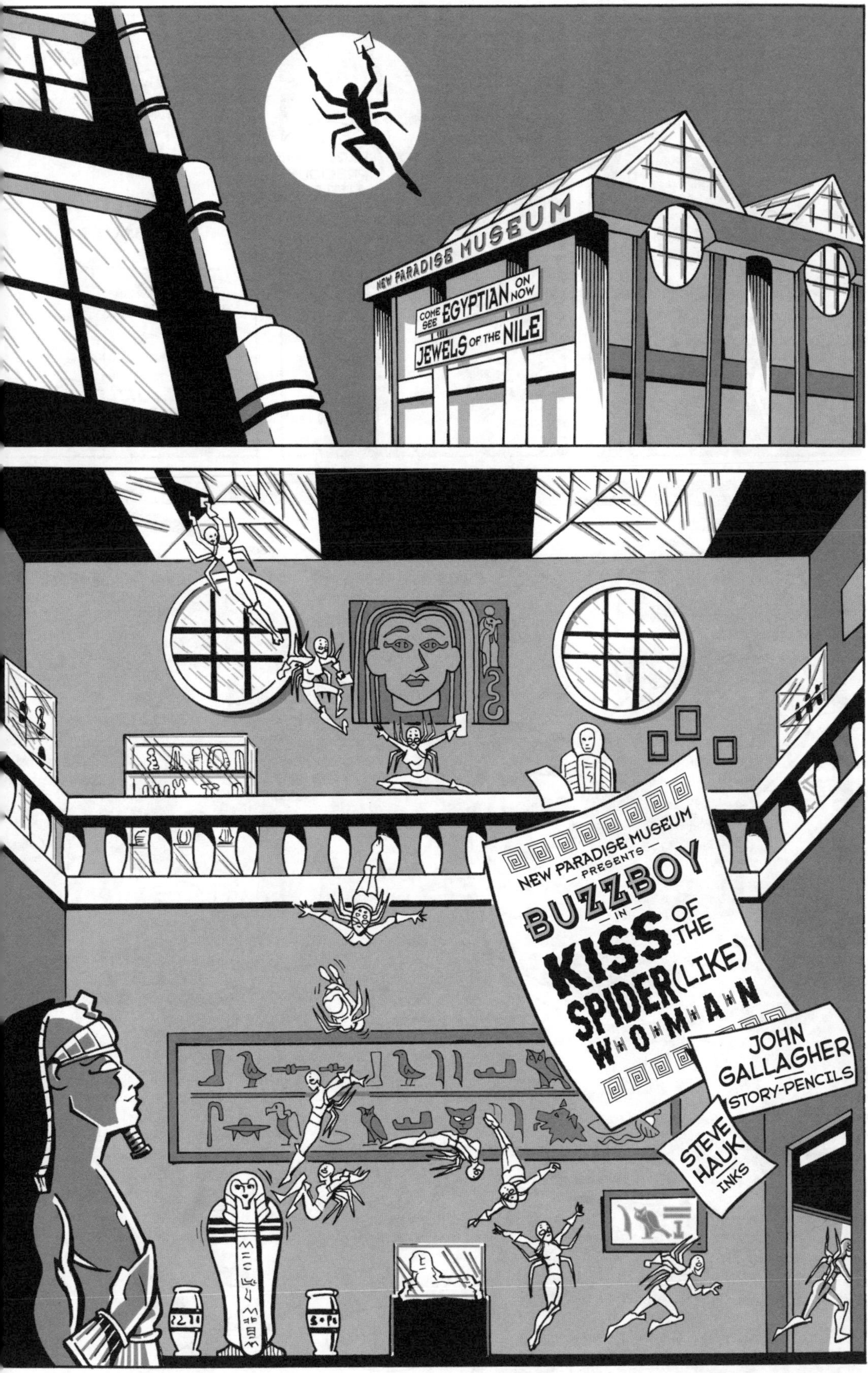

NEW PARADISE MUSEUM
COME SEE EGYPTIAN ON NOW
JEWELS OF THE NILE
NEW PARADISE MUSEUM
PRESENTS
BUZZBOY
IN
KISS OF THE SPIDER(LIKE) WOMAN
JOHN GALLAGHER
STORY-PENCILS
STEVE HAUK
INKS

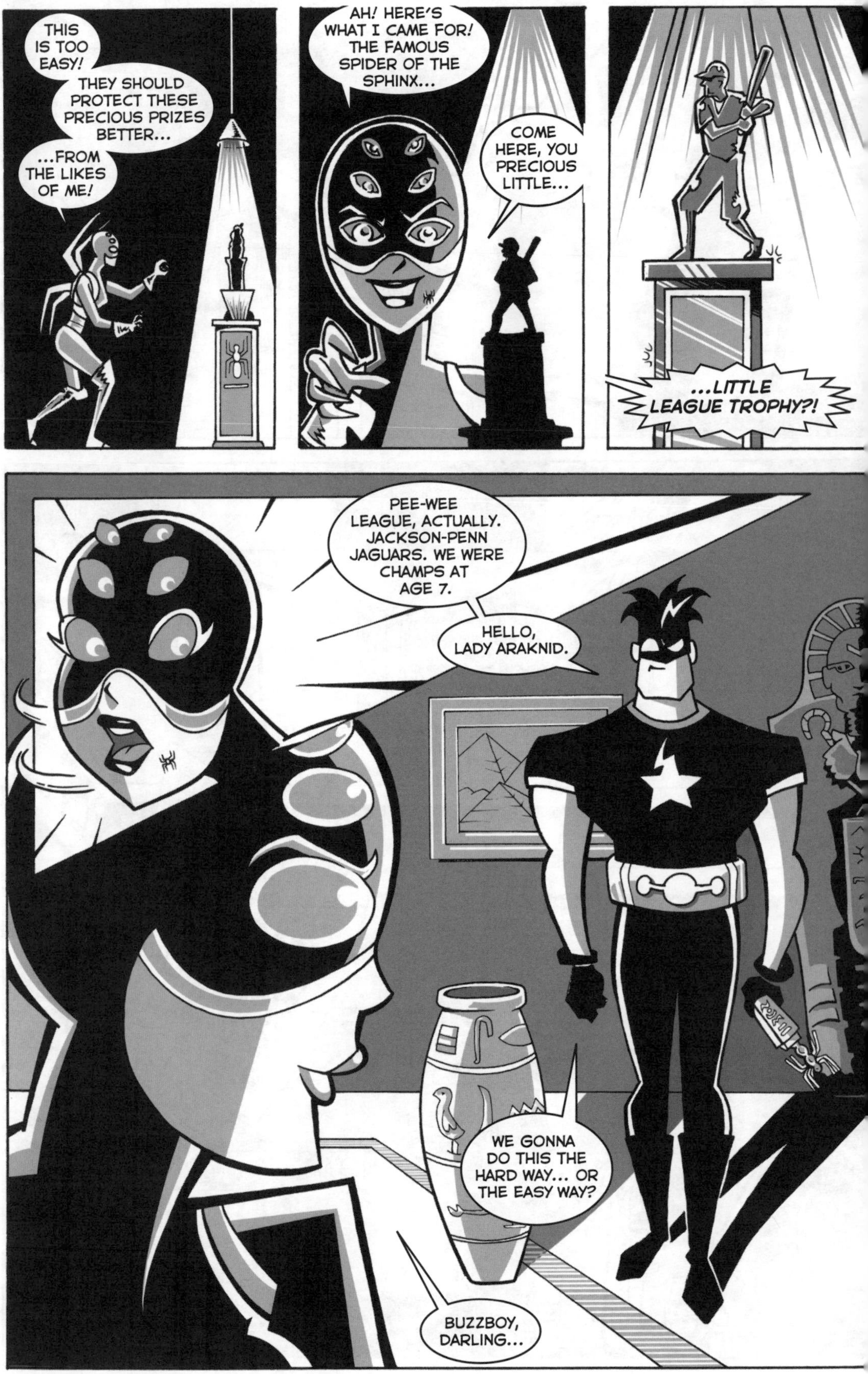
THIS IS TOO EASY!
THEY SHOULD PROTECT THESE PRECIOUS PRIZES BETTER...
...FROM THE LIKES OF ME!
AH! HERE'S WHAT I CAME FOR! THE FAMOUS SPIDER OF THE SPHINX...
COME HERE, YOU PRECIOUS LITTLE...
...LITTLE LEAGUE TROPHY?!
PEE-WEE LEAGUE, ACTUALLY. JACKSON-PENN JAGUARS. WE WERE CHAMPS AT AGE 7.
HELLO, LADY ARAKNID.
WE GONNA DO THIS THE HARD WAY... OR THE EASY WAY?
BUZZBOY, DARLING...

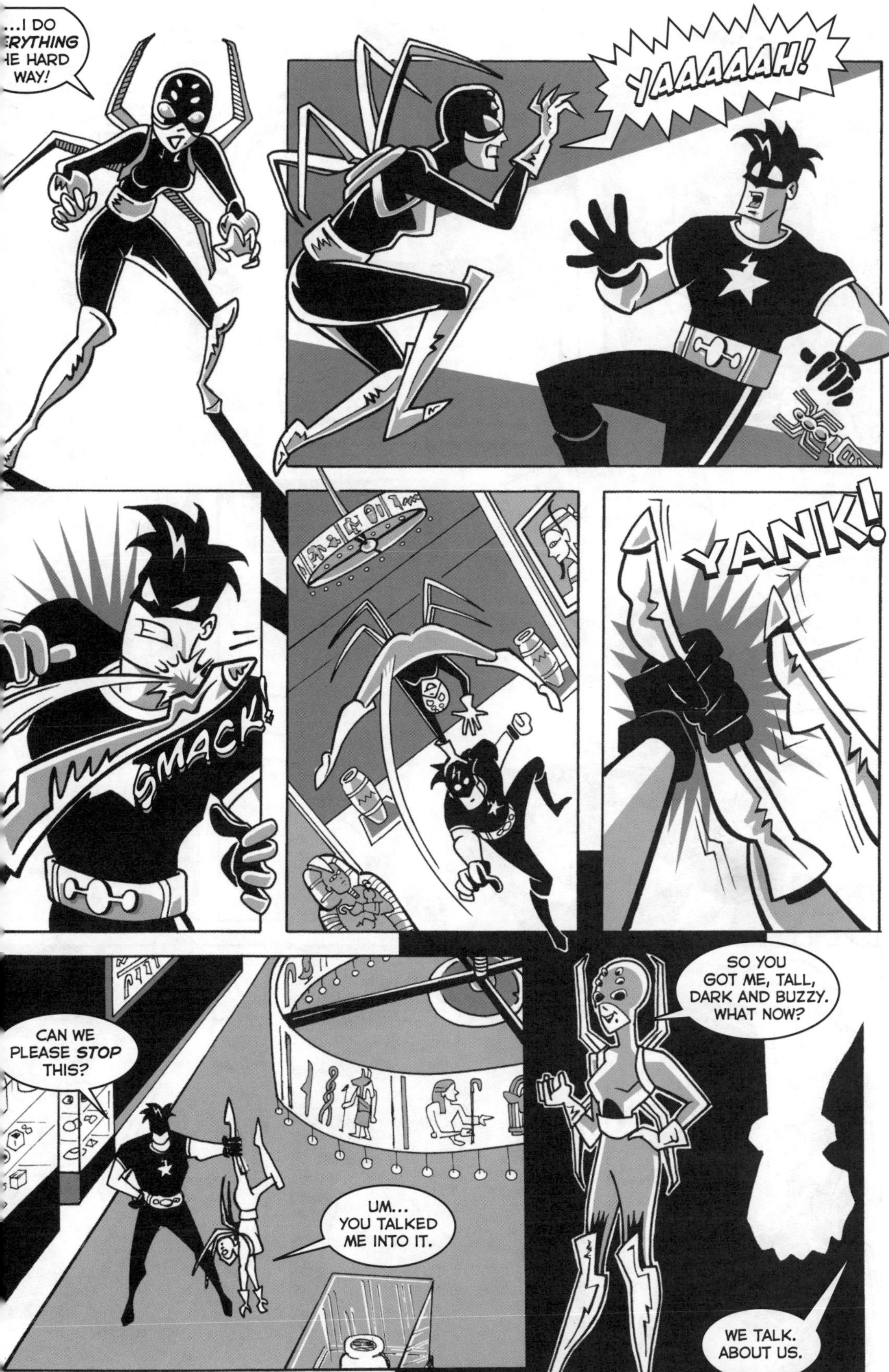
...I DO
ERYTHING
HE HARD
WAY!
YAAAAAH!
SMACK!
YANK!
CAN WE PLEASE STOP THIS?
UM... YOU TALKED ME INTO IT.
SO YOU GOT ME, TALL, DARK AND BUZZY. WHAT NOW?
WE TALK. ABOUT US.

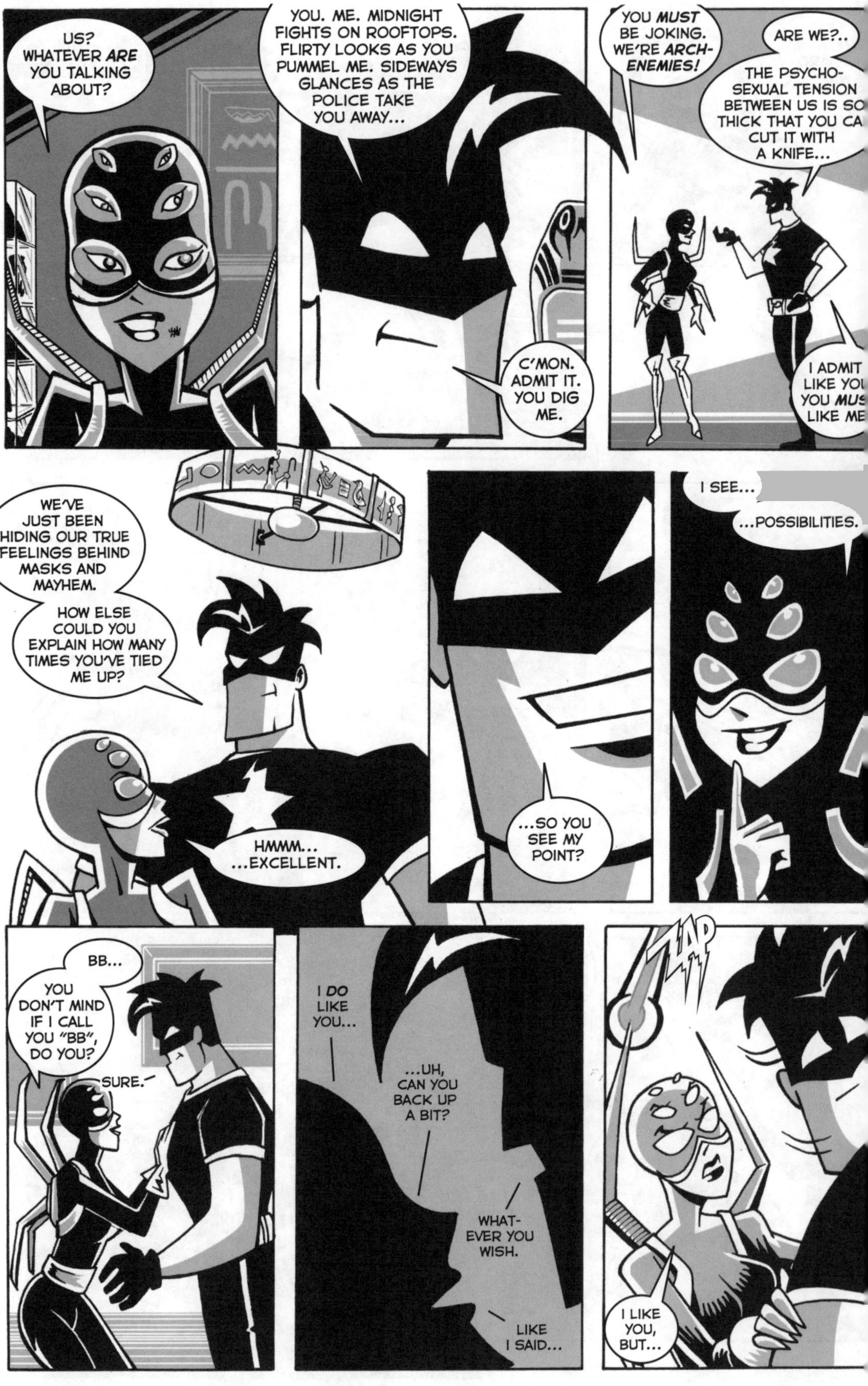
US? WHATEVER ARE YOU TALKING ABOUT?
YOU. ME. MIDNIGHT FIGHTS ON ROOFTOPS. FLIRTY LOOKS AS YOU PUMMEL ME. SIDEWAYS GLANCES AS THE POLICE TAKE YOU AWAY...
C'MON. ADMIT IT. YOU DIG ME.
YOU MUST BE JOKING. WE'RE ARCH-ENEMIES!
ARE WE?..
THE PSYCHO-SEXUAL TENSION BETWEEN US IS SO THICK THAT YOU CA CUT IT WITH A KNIFE...
I ADMIT LIKE YOU YOU MUS LIKE ME
WE'VE JUST BEEN HIDING OUR TRUE FEELINGS BEHIND MASKS AND MAYHEM.
HOW ELSE COULD YOU EXPLAIN HOW MANY TIMES YOU'VE TIED ME UP?
HMMM... ...EXCELLENT.
...SO YOU SEE MY POINT?
I SEE...
...POSSIBILITIES.
BB...
YOU DON'T MIND IF I CALL YOU "BB", DO YOU?
SURE.
I DO LIKE YOU...
...UH, CAN YOU BACK UP A BIT?
WHAT-EVER YOU WISH.
LIKE I SAID...
ZAP
I LIKE YOU, BUT...

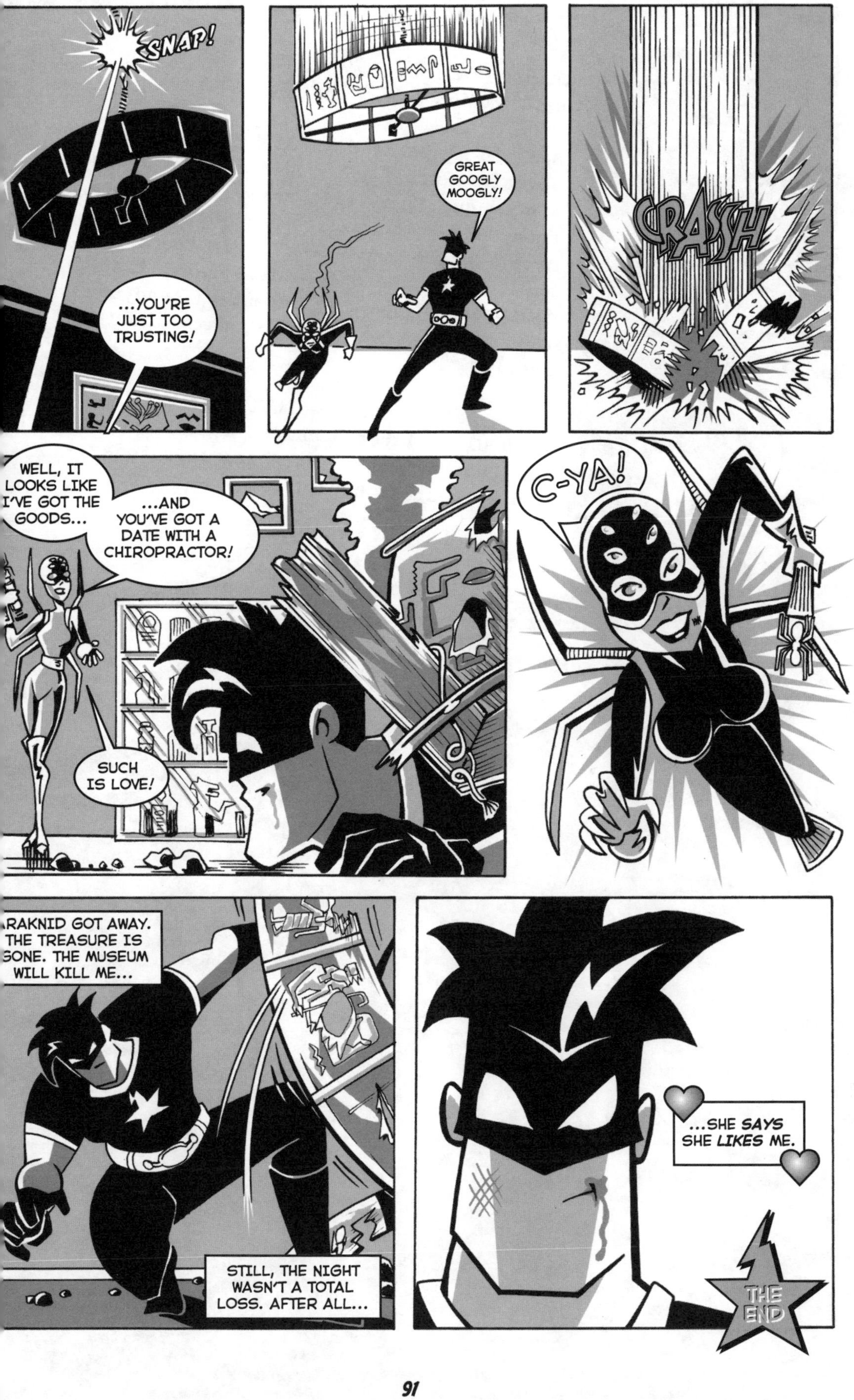
SNAP!
...YOU'RE JUST TOO TRUSTING!
GREAT GOOGLY MOOGLY!
CRASSH
WELL, IT LOOKS LIKE I'VE GOT THE GOODS...
...AND YOU'VE GOT A DATE WITH A CHIROPRACTOR!
SUCH IS LOVE!
C-YA!
RAKNID GOT AWAY. THE TREASURE IS GONE. THE MUSEUM WILL KILL ME...
STILL, THE NIGHT WASN'T A TOTAL LOSS. AFTER ALL...
...SHE *SAYS* SHE *LIKES* ME.
THE END

FROM THE FILES OF DOC CYBER...

HERO: BUZZBOY (50'S ERA)
REAL NAME: LARRY KANE

Back in my early days of being a super villain (luckilly I wised up, and became a good guy!), my arch enemy, Lord Ultra, took on a young ward-- Buzzboy, "The Mighty Mite!" While quite popular in the day, he stuck around only a few years, then disappeared. We only recently found out that he survived the 50's, with mixed results.*

Years later, the seemingly ageless Lord Ultra later acquired a new sidekick, the Buzzboy we all know and love today-- and my bestest buddy!

* To find out what happened to the original Buzzboy, and learn more about Lord Ultra, Becca, and Cyber, check out Buzzboy Volume 1: Trouble In Paradise, from Sky-Dog Press

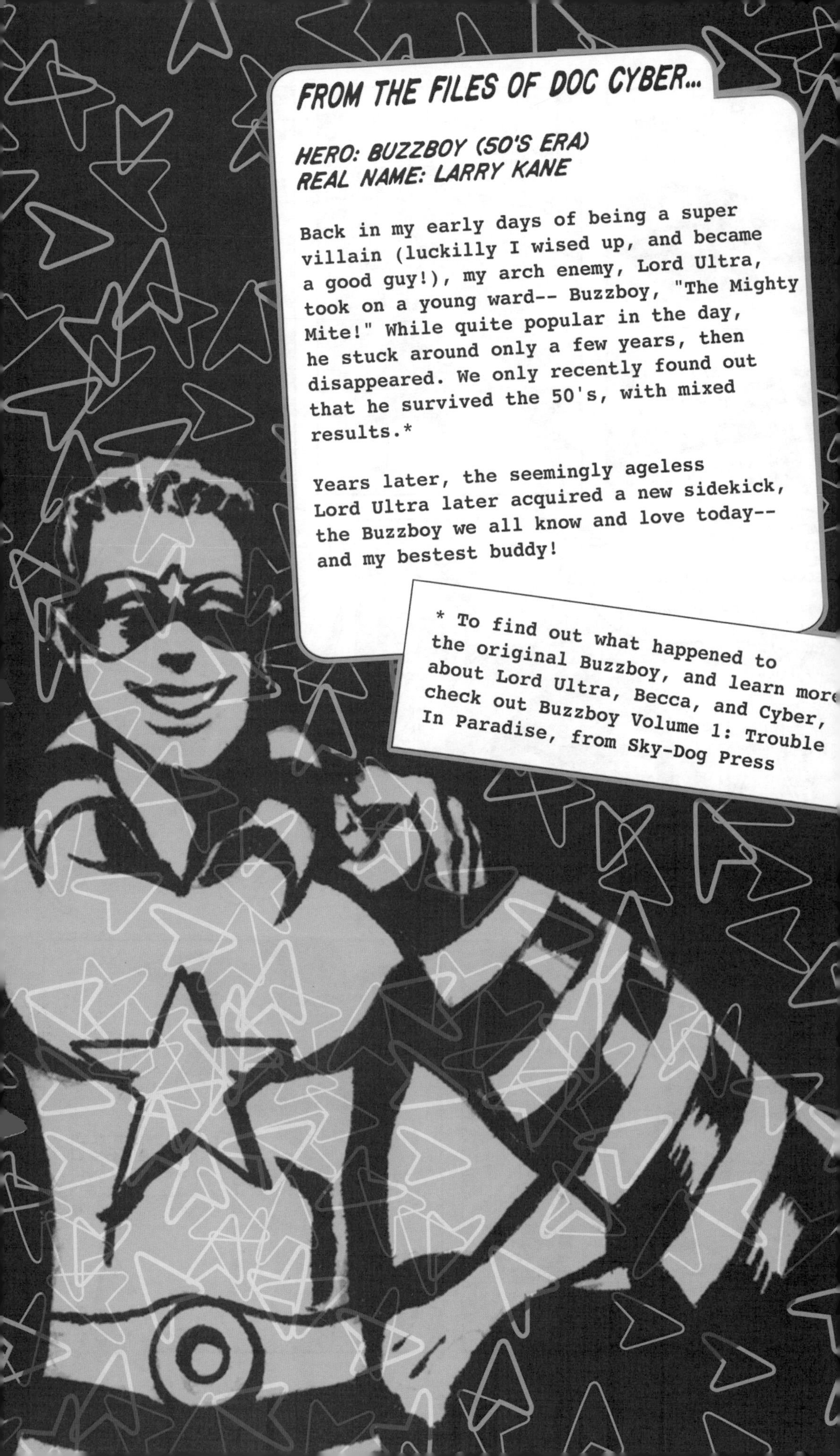

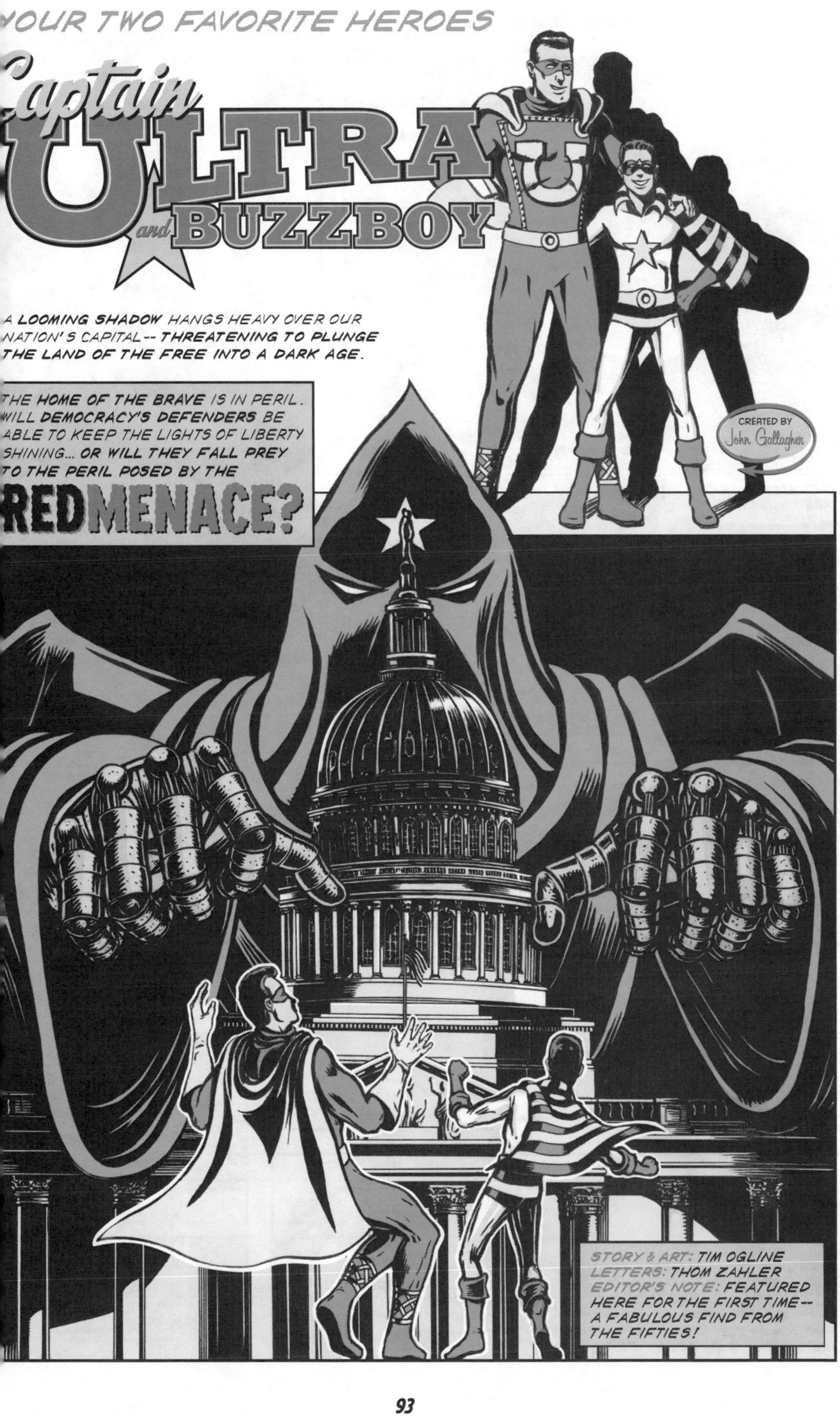
YOUR TWO FAVORITE HEROES
Captain ULTRA and BUZZBOY
CREATED BY John Gallagher
A LOOMING SHADOW HANGS HEAVY OVER OUR NATION'S CAPITAL -- THREATENING TO PLUNGE THE LAND OF THE FREE INTO A DARK AGE.
THE HOME OF THE BRAVE IS IN PERIL. WILL DEMOCRACY'S DEFENDERS BE ABLE TO KEEP THE LIGHTS OF LIBERTY SHINING... OR WILL THEY FALL PREY TO THE PERIL POSED BY THE
RED MENACE?
STORY & ART: TIM OGLINE
LETTERS: THOM ZAHLER
EDITOR'S NOTE: FEATURED HERE FOR THE FIRST TIME -- A FABULOUS FIND FROM THE FIFTIES!

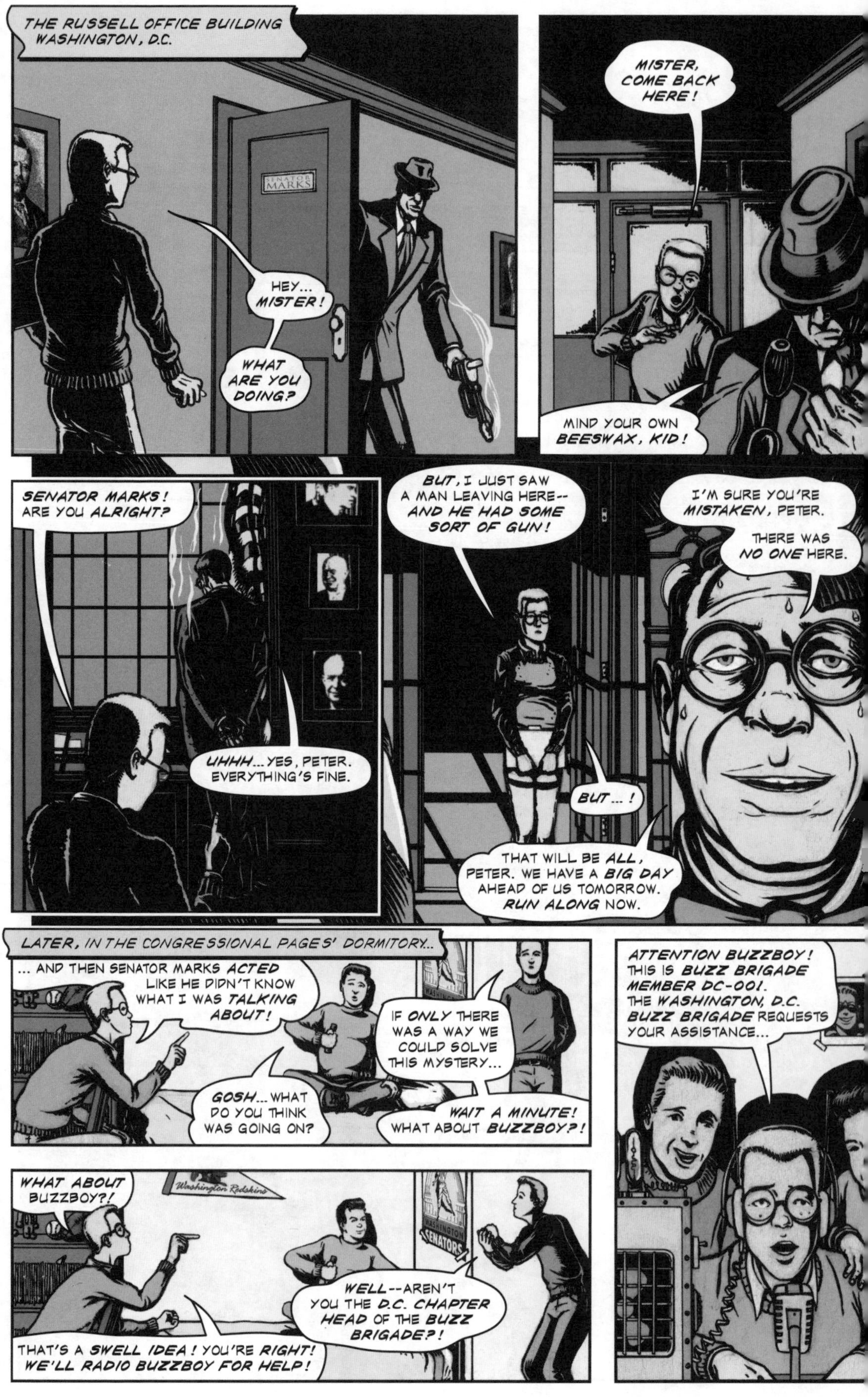
THE RUSSELL OFFICE BUILDING WASHINGTON, D.C.
SENATOR MARKS
HEY... MISTER!
WHAT ARE YOU DOING?
MISTER, COME BACK HERE!
MIND YOUR OWN BEESWAX, KID!
SENATOR MARKS! ARE YOU ALRIGHT?
UHHH... YES, PETER. EVERYTHING'S FINE.
BUT, I JUST SAW A MAN LEAVING HERE-- AND HE HAD SOME SORT OF GUN!
BUT... !
I'M SURE YOU'RE MISTAKEN, PETER.
THERE WAS NO ONE HERE.
THAT WILL BE ALL, PETER. WE HAVE A BIG DAY AHEAD OF US TOMORROW. RUN ALONG NOW.
LATER, IN THE CONGRESSIONAL PAGES' DORMITORY...
... AND THEN SENATOR MARKS ACTED LIKE HE DIDN'T KNOW WHAT I WAS TALKING ABOUT!
GOSH... WHAT DO YOU THINK WAS GOING ON?
IF ONLY THERE WAS A WAY WE COULD SOLVE THIS MYSTERY...
WAIT A MINUTE! WHAT ABOUT BUZZBOY?!
WHAT ABOUT BUZZBOY?!
Washington Redskins
WASHINGTON SENATORS
WELL--AREN'T YOU THE D.C. CHAPTER HEAD OF THE BUZZ BRIGADE?!
THAT'S A SWELL IDEA! YOU'RE RIGHT! WE'LL RADIO BUZZBOY FOR HELP!
ATTENTION BUZZBOY! THIS IS BUZZ BRIGADE MEMBER DC-001. THE WASHINGTON, D.C. BUZZ BRIGADE REQUESTS YOUR ASSISTANCE...

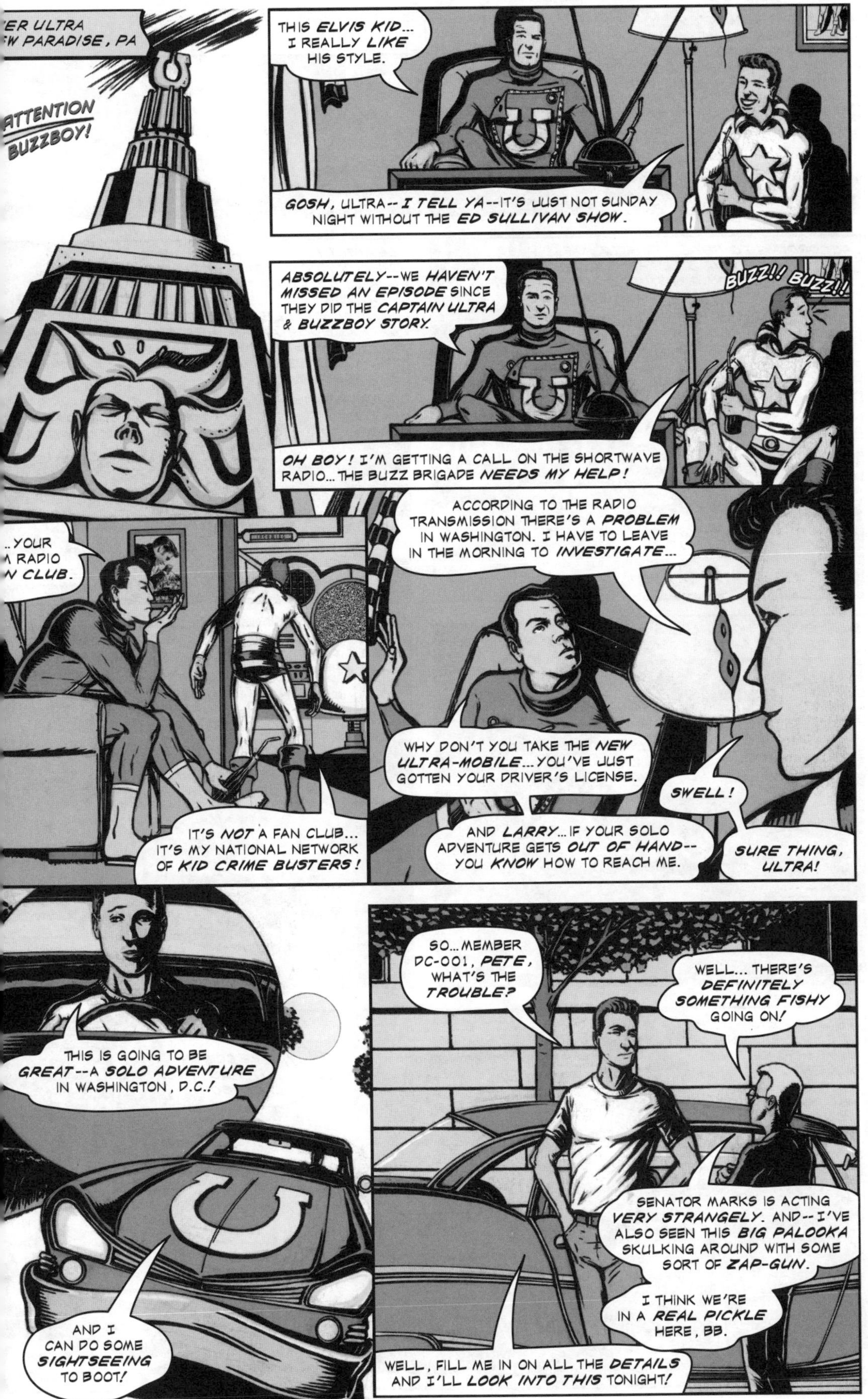
ER ULTRA
W PARADISE, PA
ATTENTION BUZZBOY!
THIS ELVIS KID... I REALLY LIKE HIS STYLE.
GOSH, ULTRA-- I TELL YA--IT'S JUST NOT SUNDAY NIGHT WITHOUT THE ED SULLIVAN SHOW.
ABSOLUTELY--WE HAVEN'T MISSED AN EPISODE SINCE THEY DID THE CAPTAIN ULTRA & BUZZBOY STORY.
BUZZ!! BUZZ!!
OH BOY! I'M GETTING A CALL ON THE SHORTWAVE RADIO... THE BUZZ BRIGADE NEEDS MY HELP!
..YOUR
A RADIO
N CLUB.
IT'S NOT A FAN CLUB... IT'S MY NATIONAL NETWORK OF KID CRIME BUSTERS!
ACCORDING TO THE RADIO TRANSMISSION THERE'S A PROBLEM IN WASHINGTON. I HAVE TO LEAVE IN THE MORNING TO INVESTIGATE...
WHY DON'T YOU TAKE THE NEW ULTRA-MOBILE... YOU'VE JUST GOTTEN YOUR DRIVER'S LICENSE.
SWELL!
AND LARRY... IF YOUR SOLO ADVENTURE GETS OUT OF HAND-- YOU KNOW HOW TO REACH ME.
SURE THING, ULTRA!
THIS IS GOING TO BE GREAT--A SOLO ADVENTURE IN WASHINGTON, D.C.!
AND I CAN DO SOME SIGHTSEEING TO BOOT!
SO... MEMBER DC-001, PETE, WHAT'S THE TROUBLE?
WELL... THERE'S DEFINITELY SOMETHING FISHY GOING ON!
SENATOR MARKS IS ACTING VERY STRANGELY. AND-- I'VE ALSO SEEN THIS BIG PALOOKA SKULKING AROUND WITH SOME SORT OF ZAP-GUN.
I THINK WE'RE IN A REAL PICKLE HERE, BB.
WELL, FILL ME IN ON ALL THE DETAILS AND I'LL LOOK INTO THIS TONIGHT!

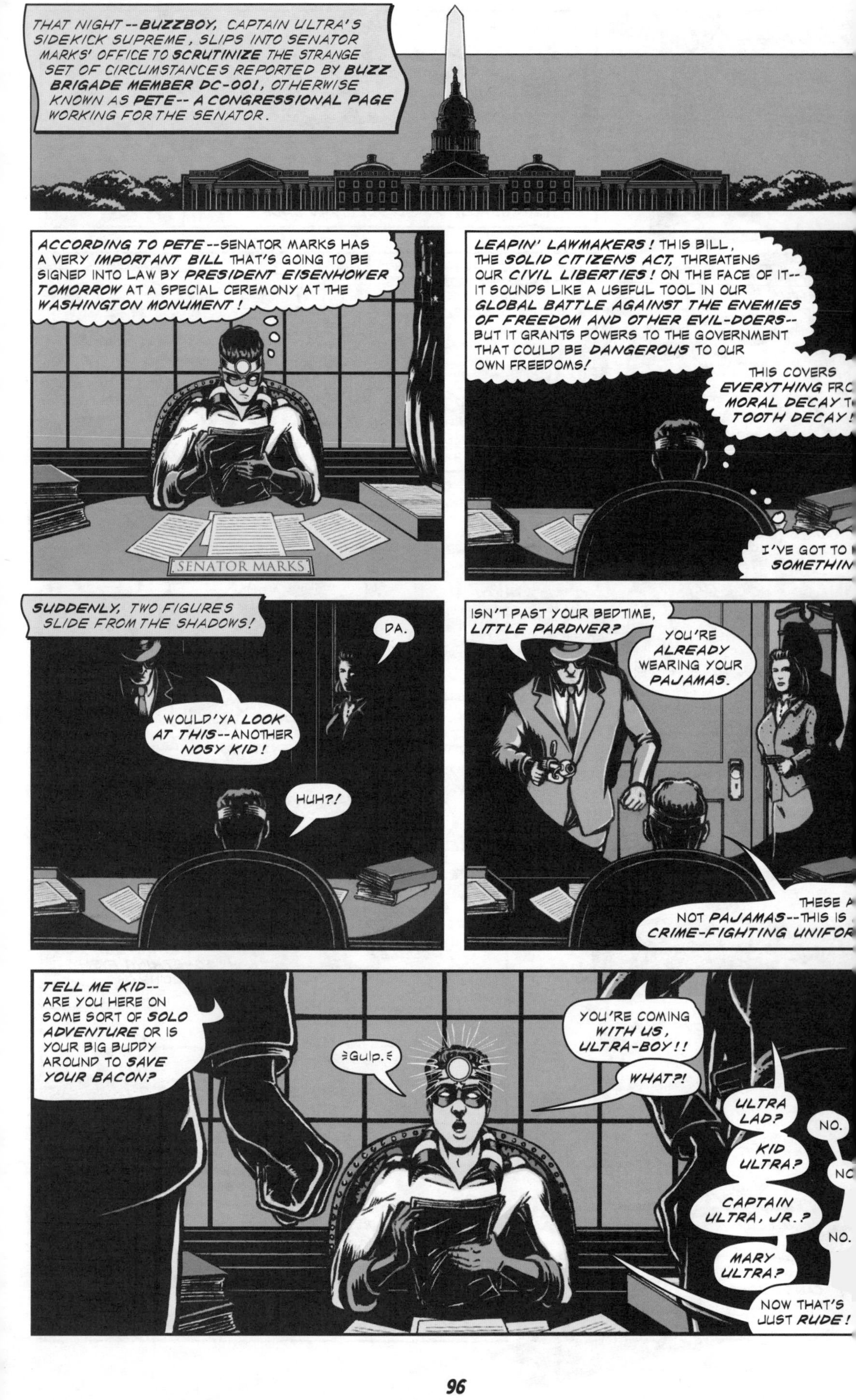
THAT NIGHT -- BUZZBOY, CAPTAIN ULTRA'S SIDEKICK SUPREME, SLIPS INTO SENATOR MARKS' OFFICE TO SCRUTINIZE THE STRANGE SET OF CIRCUMSTANCES REPORTED BY BUZZ BRIGADE MEMBER DC-001, OTHERWISE KNOWN AS PETE -- A CONGRESSIONAL PAGE WORKING FOR THE SENATOR.
ACCORDING TO PETE --SENATOR MARKS HAS A VERY IMPORTANT BILL THAT'S GOING TO BE SIGNED INTO LAW BY PRESIDENT EISENHOWER TOMORROW AT A SPECIAL CEREMONY AT THE WASHINGTON MONUMENT!
SENATOR MARKS
LEAPIN' LAWMAKERS! THIS BILL, THE SOLID CITIZENS ACT, THREATENS OUR CIVIL LIBERTIES! ON THE FACE OF IT-- IT SOUNDS LIKE A USEFUL TOOL IN OUR GLOBAL BATTLE AGAINST THE ENEMIES OF FREEDOM AND OTHER EVIL-DOERS-- BUT IT GRANTS POWERS TO THE GOVERNMENT THAT COULD BE DANGEROUS TO OUR OWN FREEDOMS!
THIS COVERS EVERYTHING FRC MORAL DECAY T TOOTH DECAY!
I'VE GOT TO SOMETHIN
SUDDENLY, TWO FIGURES SLIDE FROM THE SHADOWS!
DA.
WOULD'YA LOOK AT THIS--ANOTHER NOSY KID!
HUH?!
ISN'T PAST YOUR BEDTIME, LITTLE PARDNER?
YOU'RE ALREADY WEARING YOUR PAJAMAS.
THESE A NOT PAJAMAS--THIS IS CRIME-FIGHTING UNIFOR
TELL ME KID-- ARE YOU HERE ON SOME SORT OF SOLO ADVENTURE OR IS YOUR BIG BUDDY AROUND TO SAVE YOUR BACON?
Gulp.
YOU'RE COMING WITH US, ULTRA-BOY!!
WHAT?!
ULTRA LAD?
NO.
KID ULTRA?
NC
CAPTAIN ULTRA, JR.?
NO.
MARY ULTRA?
NOW THAT'S JUST RUDE!

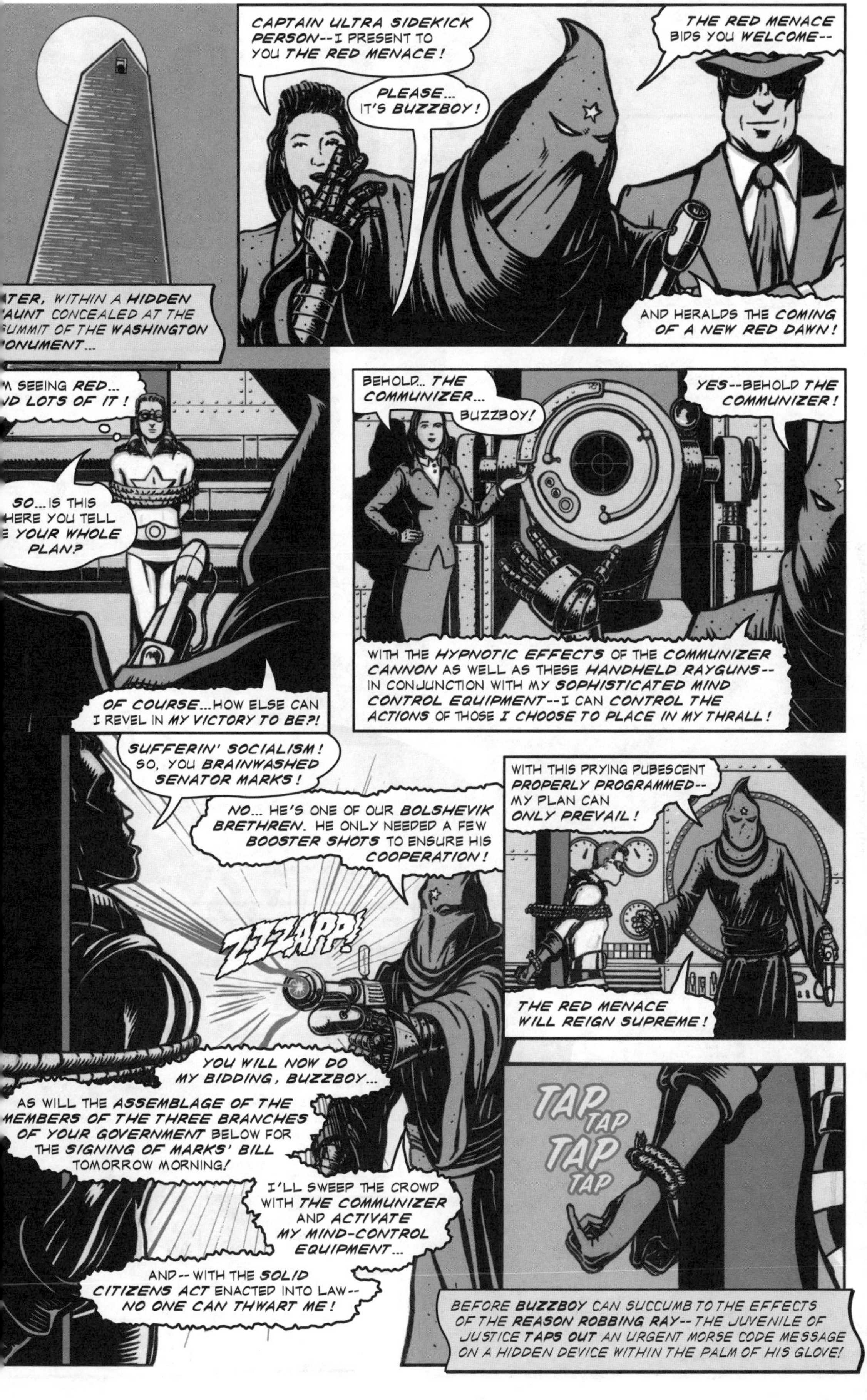

…TER, WITHIN A HIDDEN …AUNT CONCEALED AT THE …UMMIT OF THE WASHINGTON …ONUMENT...
CAPTAIN ULTRA SIDEKICK PERSON--I PRESENT TO YOU THE RED MENACE!
PLEASE... IT'S BUZZBOY!
THE RED MENACE BIDS YOU WELCOME--
AND HERALDS THE COMING OF A NEW RED DAWN!
…M SEEING RED... …D LOTS OF IT!
SO... IS THIS …HERE YOU TELL …E YOUR WHOLE PLAN?
OF COURSE... HOW ELSE CAN I REVEL IN MY VICTORY TO BE?!
BEHOLD... THE COMMUNIZER... BUZZBOY!
YES--BEHOLD THE COMMUNIZER!
WITH THE HYPNOTIC EFFECTS OF THE COMMUNIZER CANNON AS WELL AS THESE HANDHELD RAYGUNS-- IN CONJUNCTION WITH MY SOPHISTICATED MIND CONTROL EQUIPMENT--I CAN CONTROL THE ACTIONS OF THOSE I CHOOSE TO PLACE IN MY THRALL!
SUFFERIN' SOCIALISM! SO, YOU BRAINWASHED SENATOR MARKS!
NO... HE'S ONE OF OUR BOLSHEVIK BRETHREN. HE ONLY NEEDED A FEW BOOSTER SHOTS TO ENSURE HIS COOPERATION!
ZZZZAPP!
YOU WILL NOW DO MY BIDDING, BUZZBOY...
AS WILL THE ASSEMBLAGE OF THE MEMBERS OF THE THREE BRANCHES OF YOUR GOVERNMENT BELOW FOR THE SIGNING OF MARKS' BILL TOMORROW MORNING!
I'LL SWEEP THE CROWD WITH THE COMMUNIZER AND ACTIVATE MY MIND-CONTROL EQUIPMENT...
AND--WITH THE SOLID CITIZENS ACT ENACTED INTO LAW-- NO ONE CAN THWART ME!
WITH THIS PRYING PUBESCENT PROPERLY PROGRAMMED-- MY PLAN CAN ONLY PREVAIL!
THE RED MENACE WILL REIGN SUPREME!
TAP TAP TAP TAP
BEFORE BUZZBOY CAN SUCCUMB TO THE EFFECTS OF THE REASON ROBBING RAY--THE JUVENILE OF JUSTICE TAPS OUT AN URGENT MORSE CODE MESSAGE ON A HIDDEN DEVICE WITHIN THE PALM OF HIS GLOVE!

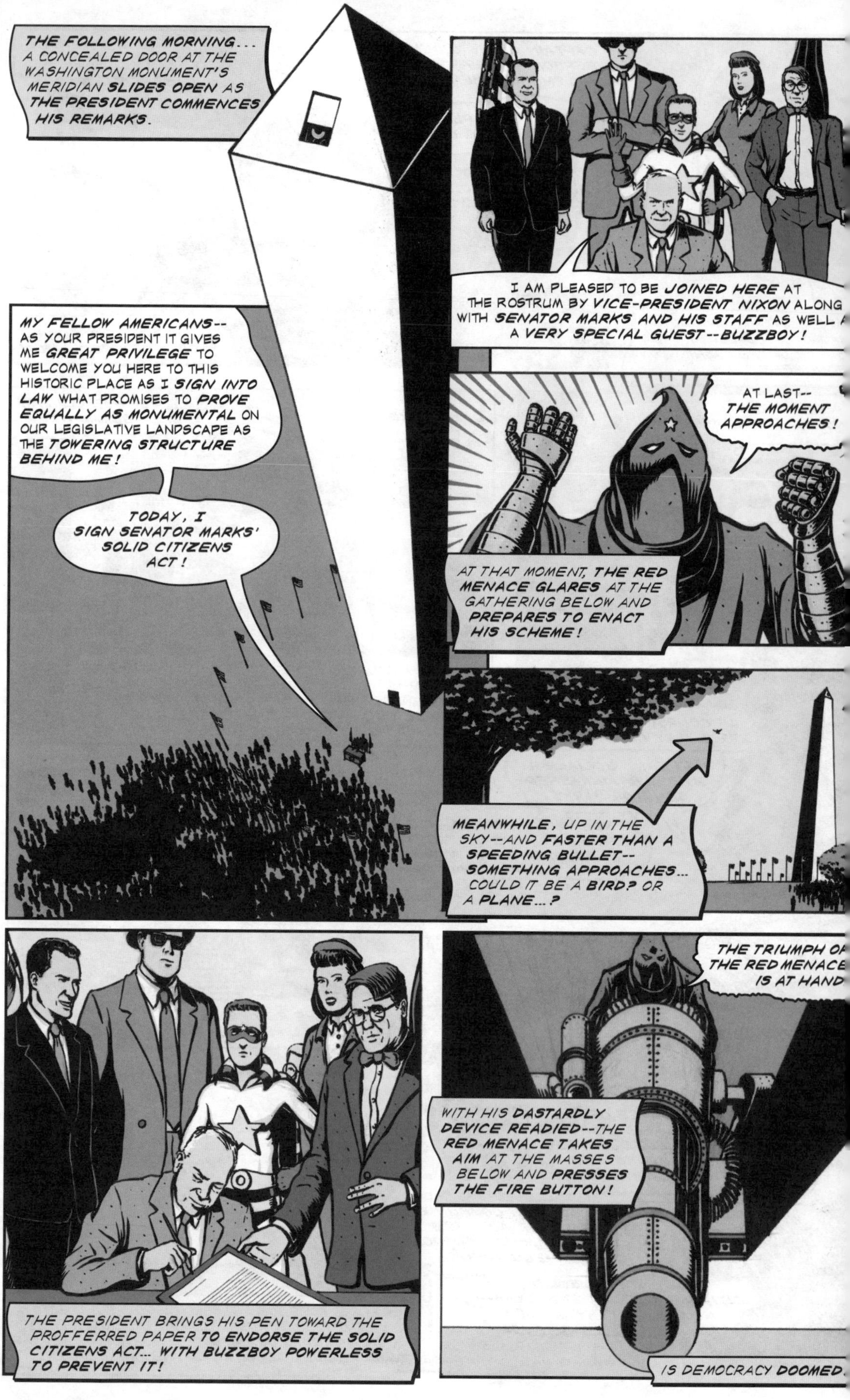
THE FOLLOWING MORNING... A CONCEALED DOOR AT THE WASHINGTON MONUMENT'S MERIDIAN SLIDES OPEN AS THE PRESIDENT COMMENCES HIS REMARKS.
I AM PLEASED TO BE JOINED HERE AT THE ROSTRUM BY VICE-PRESIDENT NIXON ALONG WITH SENATOR MARKS AND HIS STAFF AS WELL A A VERY SPECIAL GUEST--BUZZBOY!
MY FELLOW AMERICANS-- AS YOUR PRESIDENT IT GIVES ME GREAT PRIVILEGE TO WELCOME YOU HERE TO THIS HISTORIC PLACE AS I SIGN INTO LAW WHAT PROMISES TO PROVE EQUALLY AS MONUMENTAL ON OUR LEGISLATIVE LANDSCAPE AS THE TOWERING STRUCTURE BEHIND ME!
TODAY, I SIGN SENATOR MARKS' SOLID CITIZENS ACT!
AT LAST-- THE MOMENT APPROACHES!
AT THAT MOMENT, THE RED MENACE GLARES AT THE GATHERING BELOW AND PREPARES TO ENACT HIS SCHEME!
MEANWHILE, UP IN THE SKY--AND FASTER THAN A SPEEDING BULLET-- SOMETHING APPROACHES... COULD IT BE A BIRD? OR A PLANE...?
THE PRESIDENT BRINGS HIS PEN TOWARD THE PROFFERRED PAPER TO ENDORSE THE SOLID CITIZENS ACT... WITH BUZZBOY POWERLESS TO PREVENT IT!
THE TRIUMPH OF THE RED MENACE IS AT HAND
WITH HIS DASTARDLY DEVICE READIED--THE RED MENACE TAKES AIM AT THE MASSES BELOW AND PRESSES THE FIRE BUTTON!
IS DEMOCRACY DOOMED.

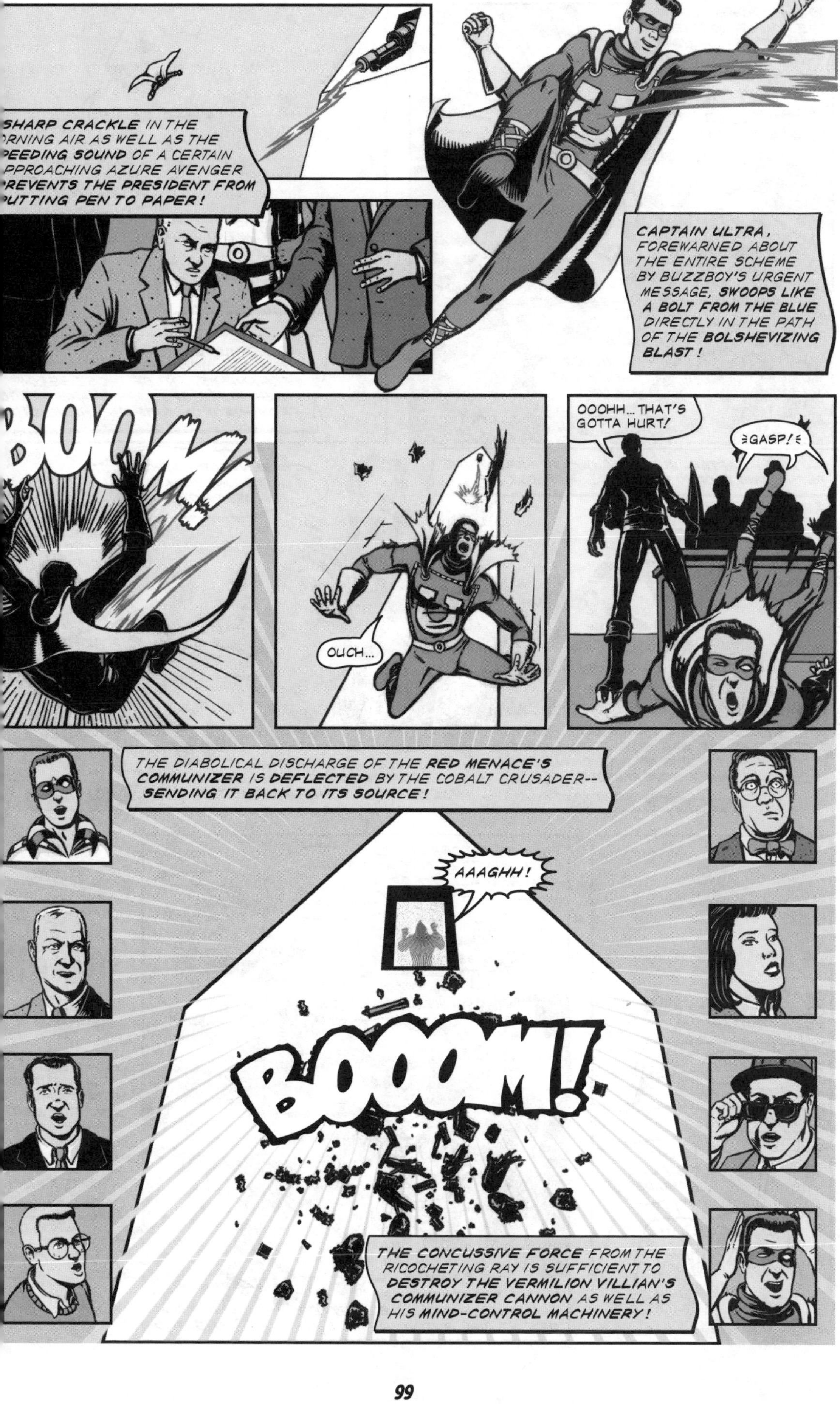
SHARP CRACKLE IN THE RNING AIR AS WELL AS THE PEEDING SOUND OF A CERTAIN PPROACHING AZURE AVENGER PREVENTS THE PRESIDENT FROM UTTING PEN TO PAPER!
CAPTAIN ULTRA, FOREWARNED ABOUT THE ENTIRE SCHEME BY BUZZBOY'S URGENT MESSAGE, SWOOPS LIKE A BOLT FROM THE BLUE DIRECTLY IN THE PATH OF THE BOLSHEVIZING BLAST!
BOOM
OUCH...
OOOHH... THAT'S GOTTA HURT!
GASP!
THE DIABOLICAL DISCHARGE OF THE RED MENACE'S COMMUNIZER IS DEFLECTED BY THE COBALT CRUSADER-- SENDING IT BACK TO ITS SOURCE!
AAAGHH!
BOOOM!
THE CONCUSSIVE FORCE FROM THE RICOCHETING RAY IS SUFFICIENT TO DESTROY THE VERMILION VILLIAN'S COMMUNIZER CANNON AS WELL AS HIS MIND-CONTROL MACHINERY!

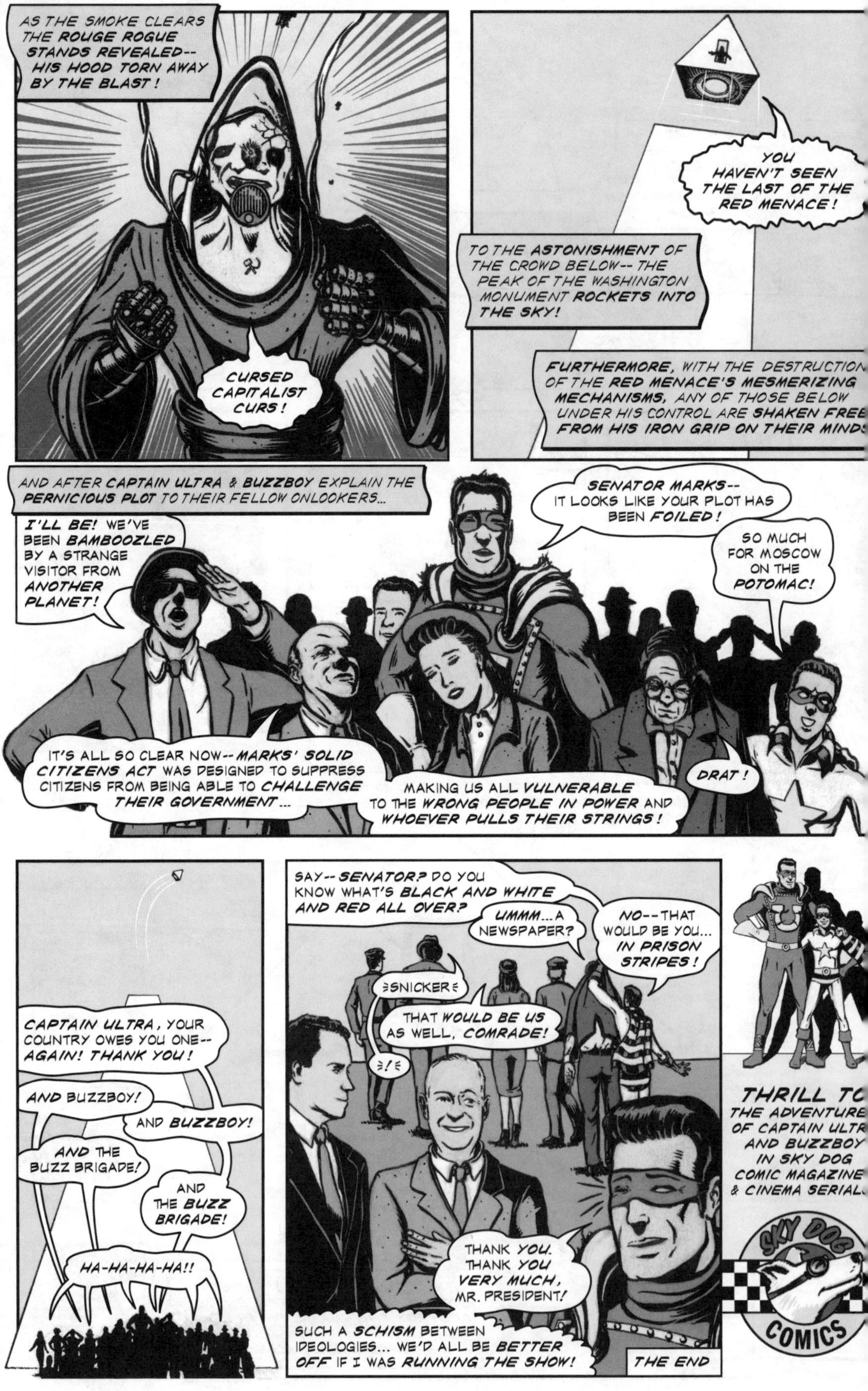
AS THE SMOKE CLEARS THE ROUGE ROGUE STANDS REVEALED-- HIS HOOD TORN AWAY BY THE BLAST!
CURSED CAPITALIST CURS!
YOU HAVEN'T SEEN THE LAST OF THE RED MENACE!
TO THE ASTONISHMENT OF THE CROWD BELOW-- THE PEAK OF THE WASHINGTON MONUMENT ROCKETS INTO THE SKY!
FURTHERMORE, WITH THE DESTRUCTION OF THE RED MENACE'S MESMERIZING MECHANISMS, ANY OF THOSE BELOW UNDER HIS CONTROL ARE SHAKEN FREE FROM HIS IRON GRIP ON THEIR MINDS
AND AFTER CAPTAIN ULTRA & BUZZBOY EXPLAIN THE PERNICIOUS PLOT TO THEIR FELLOW ONLOOKERS...
I'LL BE! WE'VE BEEN BAMBOOZLED BY A STRANGE VISITOR FROM ANOTHER PLANET!
SENATOR MARKS-- IT LOOKS LIKE YOUR PLOT HAS BEEN FOILED!
SO MUCH FOR MOSCOW ON THE POTOMAC!
IT'S ALL SO CLEAR NOW-- MARKS' SOLID CITIZENS ACT WAS DESIGNED TO SUPPRESS CITIZENS FROM BEING ABLE TO CHALLENGE THEIR GOVERNMENT...
MAKING US ALL VULNERABLE TO THE WRONG PEOPLE IN POWER AND WHOEVER PULLS THEIR STRINGS!
DRAT!
CAPTAIN ULTRA, YOUR COUNTRY OWES YOU ONE-- AGAIN! THANK YOU!
AND BUZZBOY!
AND BUZZBOY!
AND THE BUZZ BRIGADE!
AND THE BUZZ BRIGADE!
HA-HA-HA-HA!!
SAY-- SENATOR? DO YOU KNOW WHAT'S BLACK AND WHITE AND RED ALL OVER?
UMMM... A NEWSPAPER?
NO-- THAT WOULD BE YOU... IN PRISON STRIPES!
SNICKER
THAT WOULD BE US AS WELL, COMRADE!
!
THANK YOU. THANK YOU VERY MUCH, MR. PRESIDENT!
SUCH A SCHISM BETWEEN IDEOLOGIES... WE'D ALL BE BETTER OFF IF I WAS RUNNING THE SHOW!
THE END
THRILL TO THE ADVENTURES OF CAPTAIN ULTRA AND BUZZBOY IN SKY DOG COMIC MAGAZINES & CINEMA SERIALS
SKY DOG COMICS

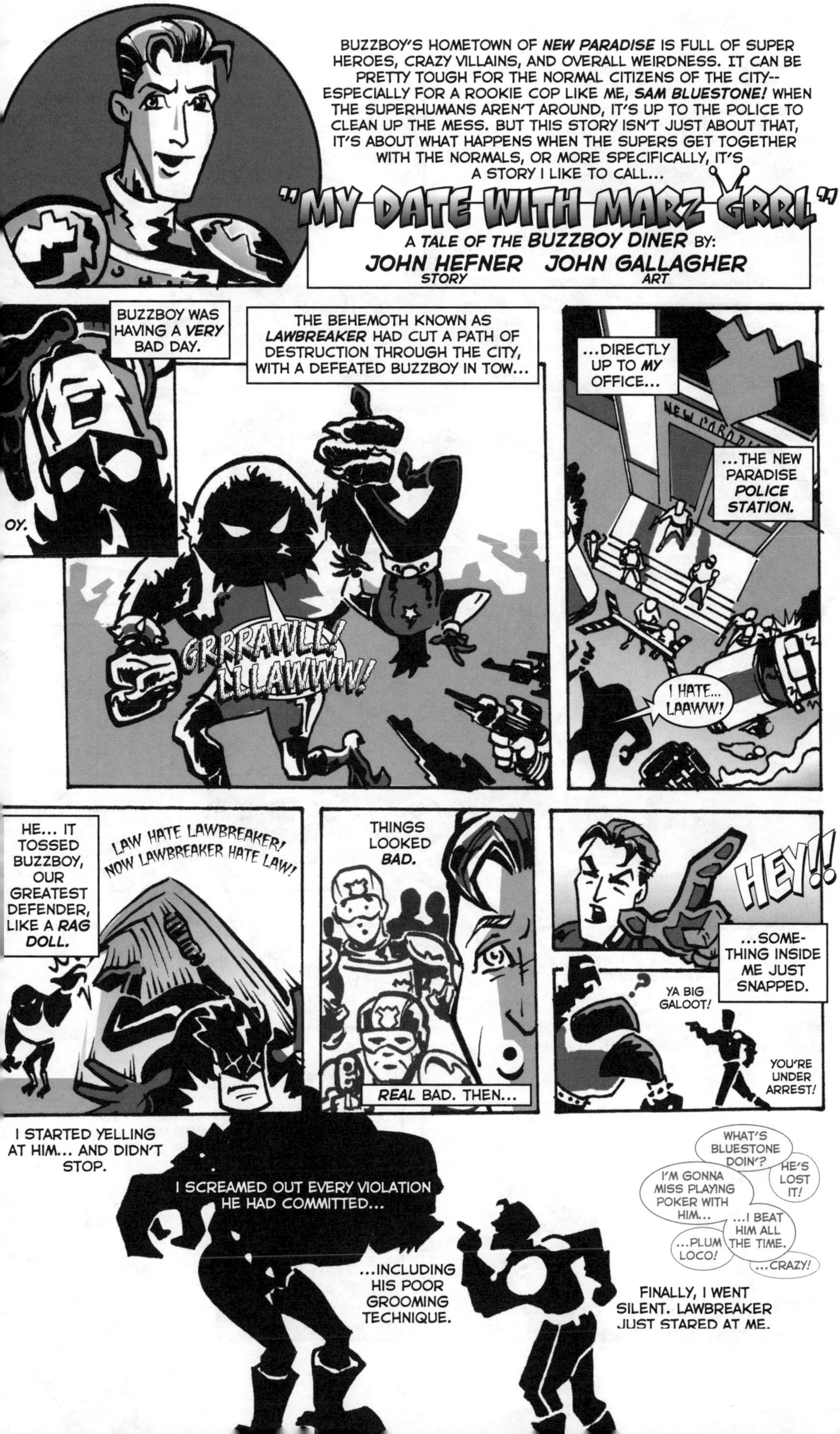
BUZZBOY'S HOMETOWN OF NEW PARADISE IS FULL OF SUPER HEROES, CRAZY VILLAINS, AND OVERALL WEIRDNESS. IT CAN BE PRETTY TOUGH FOR THE NORMAL CITIZENS OF THE CITY-- ESPECIALLY FOR A ROOKIE COP LIKE ME, SAM BLUESTONE! WHEN THE SUPERHUMANS AREN'T AROUND, IT'S UP TO THE POLICE TO CLEAN UP THE MESS. BUT THIS STORY ISN'T JUST ABOUT THAT, IT'S ABOUT WHAT HAPPENS WHEN THE SUPERS GET TOGETHER WITH THE NORMALS, OR MORE SPECIFICALLY, IT'S A STORY I LIKE TO CALL...
"MY DATE WITH MARZ GRRL"
A TALE OF THE BUZZBOY DINER BY:
JOHN HEFNER STORY
JOHN GALLAGHER ART
BUZZBOY WAS HAVING A VERY BAD DAY.
OY.
THE BEHEMOTH KNOWN AS LAWBREAKER HAD CUT A PATH OF DESTRUCTION THROUGH THE CITY, WITH A DEFEATED BUZZBOY IN TOW...
GRRRAWLL! LLLAWWW!
...DIRECTLY UP TO MY OFFICE...
NEW PARADI
...THE NEW PARADISE POLICE STATION.
I HATE... LAAWW!
HE... IT TOSSED BUZZBOY, OUR GREATEST DEFENDER, LIKE A RAG DOLL.
LAW HATE LAWBREAKER! NOW LAWBREAKER HATE LAW!
THINGS LOOKED BAD.
REAL BAD. THEN...
HEY!!
...SOMETHING INSIDE ME JUST SNAPPED.
?
YA BIG GALOOT!
YOU'RE UNDER ARREST!
I STARTED YELLING AT HIM... AND DIDN'T STOP.
I SCREAMED OUT EVERY VIOLATION HE HAD COMMITTED...
...INCLUDING HIS POOR GROOMING TECHNIQUE.
WHAT'S BLUESTONE DOIN'?
HE'S LOST IT!
I'M GONNA MISS PLAYING POKER WITH HIM...
...I BEAT HIM ALL THE TIME.
...PLUM LOCO!
...CRAZY!
FINALLY, I WENT SILENT. LAWBREAKER JUST STARED AT ME.

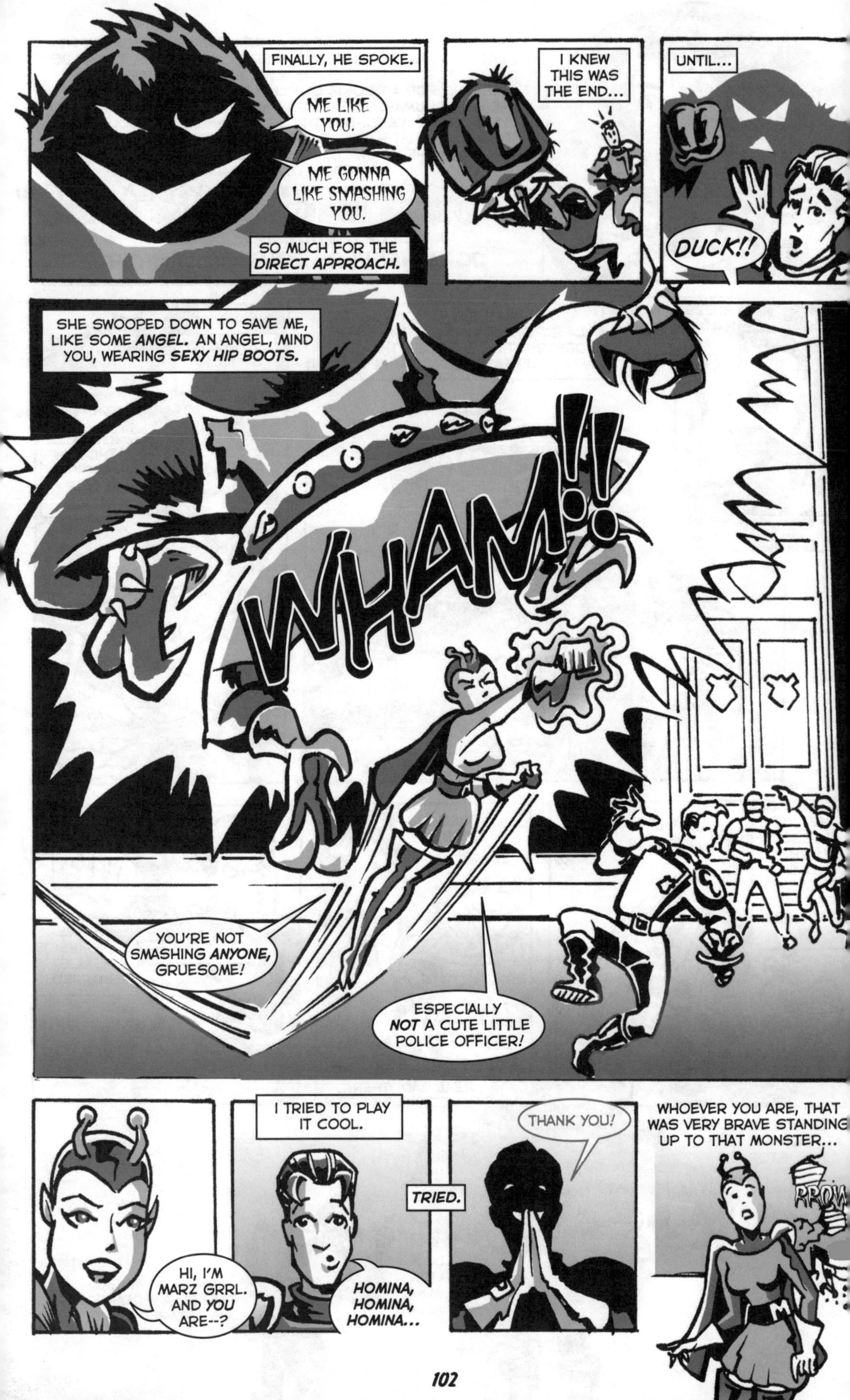
FINALLY, HE SPOKE.
ME LIKE YOU.
ME GONNA LIKE SMASHING YOU.
SO MUCH FOR THE *DIRECT APPROACH.*
I KNEW THIS WAS THE END...
UNTIL...
DUCK!!
SHE SWOOPED DOWN TO SAVE ME, LIKE SOME *ANGEL.* AN ANGEL, MIND YOU, WEARING *SEXY HIP BOOTS.*
WHAM!!
YOU'RE NOT SMASHING *ANYONE,* GRUESOME!
ESPECIALLY *NOT* A CUTE LITTLE POLICE OFFICER!
HI, I'M MARZ GRRL. AND *YOU* ARE--?
I TRIED TO PLAY IT COOL.
TRIED.
HOMINA, HOMINA, HOMINA...
THANK YOU!
WHOEVER YOU ARE, THAT WAS VERY BRAVE STANDING UP TO THAT MONSTER...

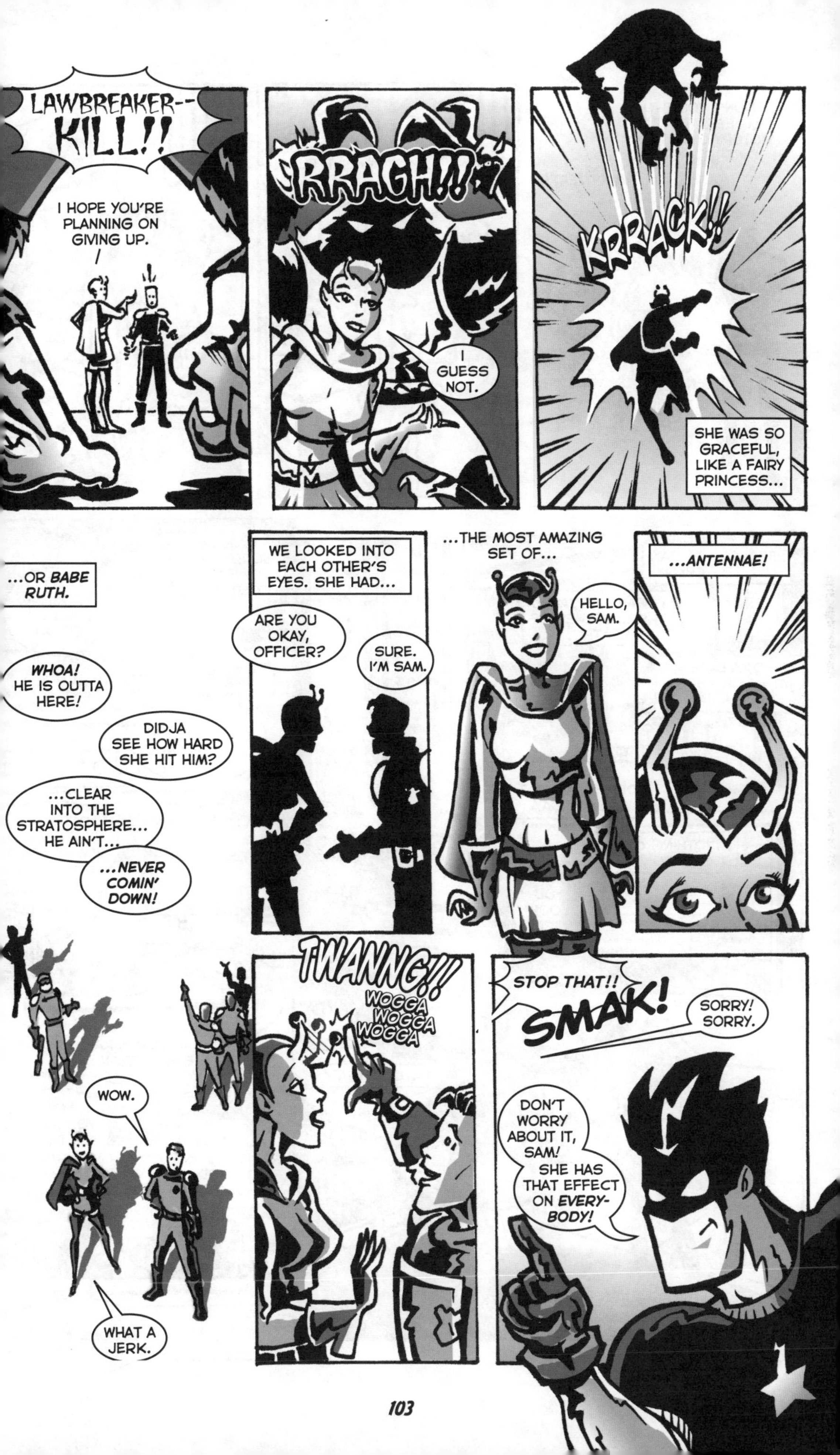
LAWBREAKER--KILL!!
I HOPE YOU'RE PLANNING ON GIVING UP.
RRAGH!!
I GUESS NOT.
KRRACK!!
SHE WAS SO GRACEFUL, LIKE A FAIRY PRINCESS...
...OR *BABE RUTH.*
WHOA! HE IS OUTTA HERE!
DIDJA SEE HOW HARD SHE HIT HIM?
...CLEAR INTO THE STRATOSPHERE... HE AIN'T...
...NEVER COMIN' DOWN!
WE LOOKED INTO EACH OTHER'S EYES. SHE HAD...
ARE YOU OKAY, OFFICER?
SURE. I'M SAM.
...THE MOST AMAZING SET OF...
HELLO, SAM.
...ANTENNAE!
WOW.
WHAT A JERK.
TWANNG!!
WOGGA WOGGA WOGGA
STOP THAT!!
SMAK!
SORRY! SORRY.
DON'T WORRY ABOUT IT, SAM!
SHE HAS THAT EFFECT ON *EVERY-BODY!*

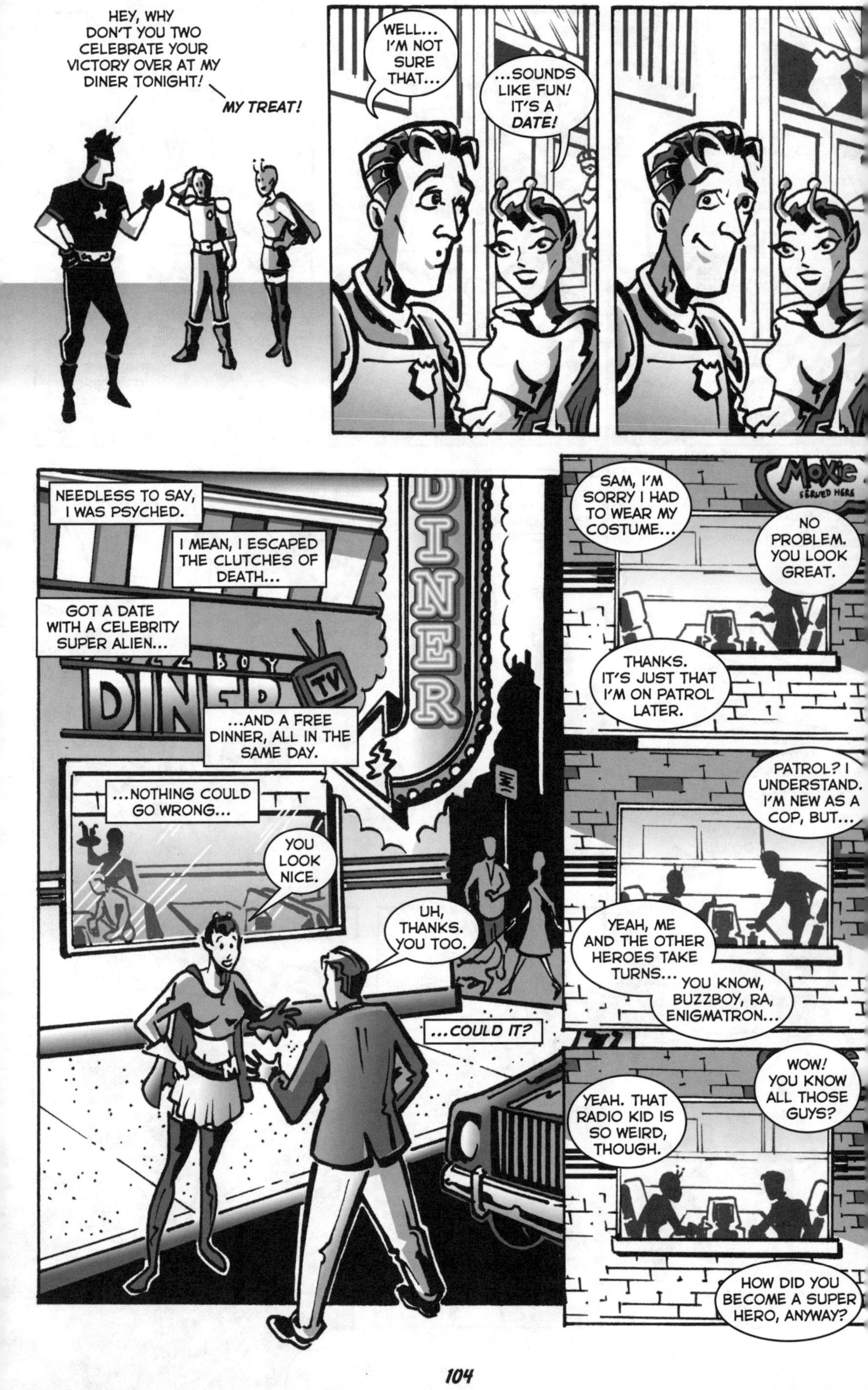
HEY, WHY DON'T YOU TWO CELEBRATE YOUR VICTORY OVER AT MY DINER TONIGHT!
MY TREAT!
WELL... I'M NOT SURE THAT...
...SOUNDS LIKE FUN! IT'S A DATE!
NEEDLESS TO SAY, I WAS PSYCHED.
I MEAN, I ESCAPED THE CLUTCHES OF DEATH...
GOT A DATE WITH A CELEBRITY SUPER ALIEN...
TV
DINER
...AND A FREE DINNER, ALL IN THE SAME DAY.
...NOTHING COULD GO WRONG...
YOU LOOK NICE.
UH, THANKS. YOU TOO.
...COULD IT?
Moxie SERVED HERE
SAM, I'M SORRY I HAD TO WEAR MY COSTUME...
NO PROBLEM. YOU LOOK GREAT.
THANKS. IT'S JUST THAT I'M ON PATROL LATER.
PATROL? I UNDERSTAND. I'M NEW AS A COP, BUT...
YEAH, ME AND THE OTHER HEROES TAKE TURNS...
YOU KNOW, BUZZBOY, RA, ENIGMATRON...
WOW! YOU KNOW ALL THOSE GUYS?
YEAH. THAT RADIO KID IS SO WEIRD, THOUGH.
HOW DID YOU BECOME A SUPER HERO, ANYWAY?

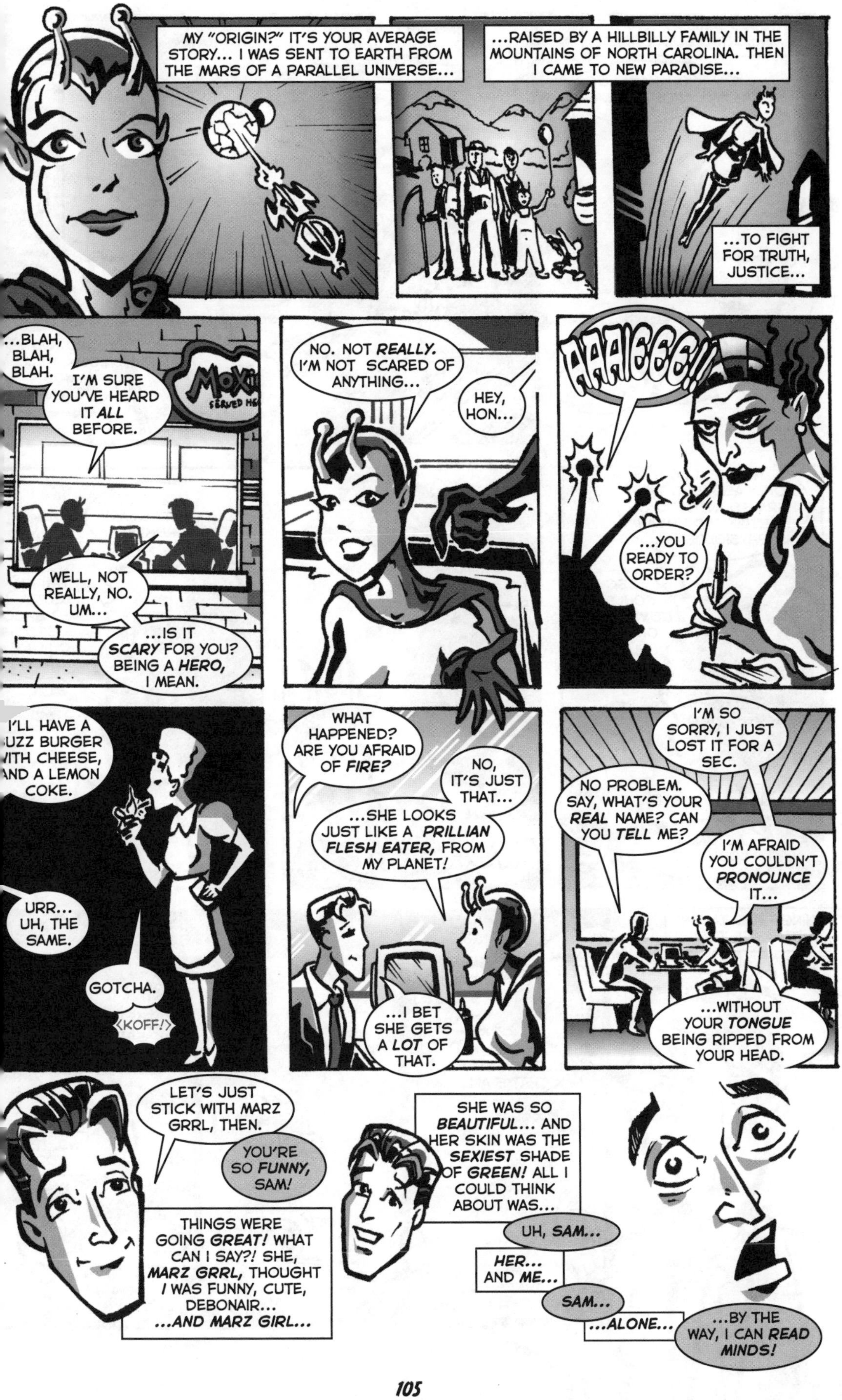
MY "ORIGIN?" IT'S YOUR AVERAGE STORY... I WAS SENT TO EARTH FROM THE MARS OF A PARALLEL UNIVERSE...
...RAISED BY A HILLBILLY FAMILY IN THE MOUNTAINS OF NORTH CAROLINA. THEN I CAME TO NEW PARADISE...
...TO FIGHT FOR TRUTH, JUSTICE...
...BLAH, BLAH, BLAH.
I'M SURE YOU'VE HEARD IT ALL BEFORE.
WELL, NOT REALLY, NO. UM...
...IS IT SCARY FOR YOU? BEING A HERO, I MEAN.
NO. NOT REALLY. I'M NOT SCARED OF ANYTHING...
HEY, HON...
AAAIEEE!!
...YOU READY TO ORDER?
I'LL HAVE A UZZ BURGER ITH CHEESE, ND A LEMON COKE.
URR... UH, THE SAME.
GOTCHA.
<KOFF!>
WHAT HAPPENED? ARE YOU AFRAID OF FIRE?
NO, IT'S JUST THAT...
...SHE LOOKS JUST LIKE A PRILLIAN FLESH EATER, FROM MY PLANET!
...I BET SHE GETS A LOT OF THAT.
I'M SO SORRY, I JUST LOST IT FOR A SEC.
NO PROBLEM. SAY, WHAT'S YOUR REAL NAME? CAN YOU TELL ME?
I'M AFRAID YOU COULDN'T PRONOUNCE IT...
...WITHOUT YOUR TONGUE BEING RIPPED FROM YOUR HEAD.
LET'S JUST STICK WITH MARZ GRRL, THEN.
YOU'RE SO FUNNY, SAM!
THINGS WERE GOING GREAT! WHAT CAN I SAY?! SHE, MARZ GRRL, THOUGHT I WAS FUNNY, CUTE, DEBONAIR... ...AND MARZ GIRL...
SHE WAS SO BEAUTIFUL... AND HER SKIN WAS THE SEXIEST SHADE OF GREEN! ALL I COULD THINK ABOUT WAS...
UH, SAM...
HER... AND ME...
SAM...
...ALONE...
...BY THE WAY, I CAN READ MINDS!

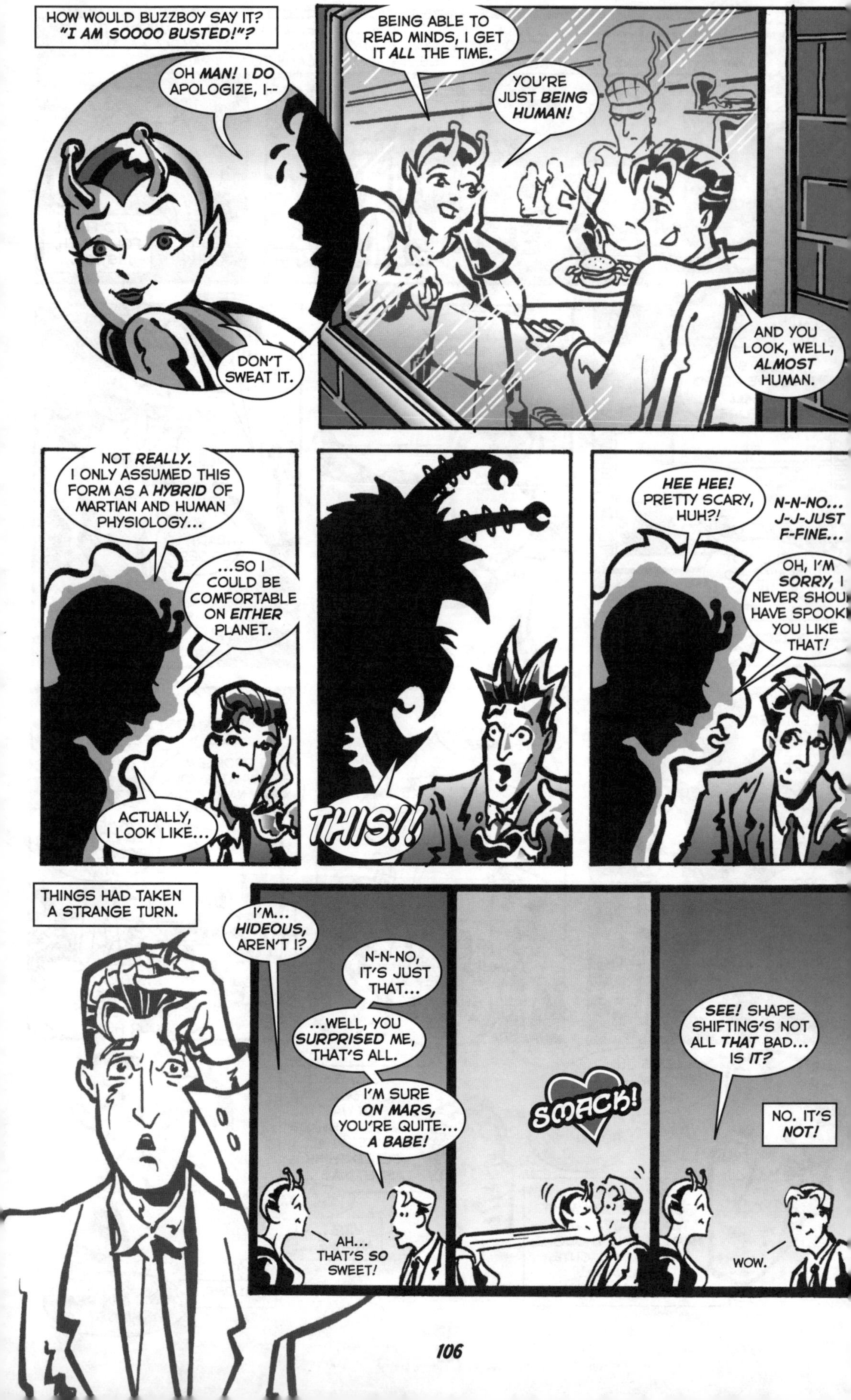
HOW WOULD BUZZBOY SAY IT? "I AM SOOOO BUSTED!"?
OH MAN! I DO APOLOGIZE, I--
DON'T SWEAT IT.
BEING ABLE TO READ MINDS, I GET IT ALL THE TIME.
YOU'RE JUST BEING HUMAN!
AND YOU LOOK, WELL, ALMOST HUMAN.
NOT REALLY. I ONLY ASSUMED THIS FORM AS A HYBRID OF MARTIAN AND HUMAN PHYSIOLOGY...
...SO I COULD BE COMFORTABLE ON EITHER PLANET.
ACTUALLY, I LOOK LIKE...
THIS!!
HEE HEE! PRETTY SCARY, HUH?!
N-N-NO... J-J-JUST F-FINE...
OH, I'M SORRY, I NEVER SHOU HAVE SPOOK YOU LIKE THAT!
THINGS HAD TAKEN A STRANGE TURN.
I'M... HIDEOUS, AREN'T I?
N-N-NO, IT'S JUST THAT...
...WELL, YOU SURPRISED ME, THAT'S ALL.
I'M SURE ON MARS, YOU'RE QUITE... A BABE!
AH... THAT'S SO SWEET!
SMACK!
SEE! SHAPE SHIFTING'S NOT ALL THAT BAD... IS IT?
NO. IT'S NOT!
WOW.

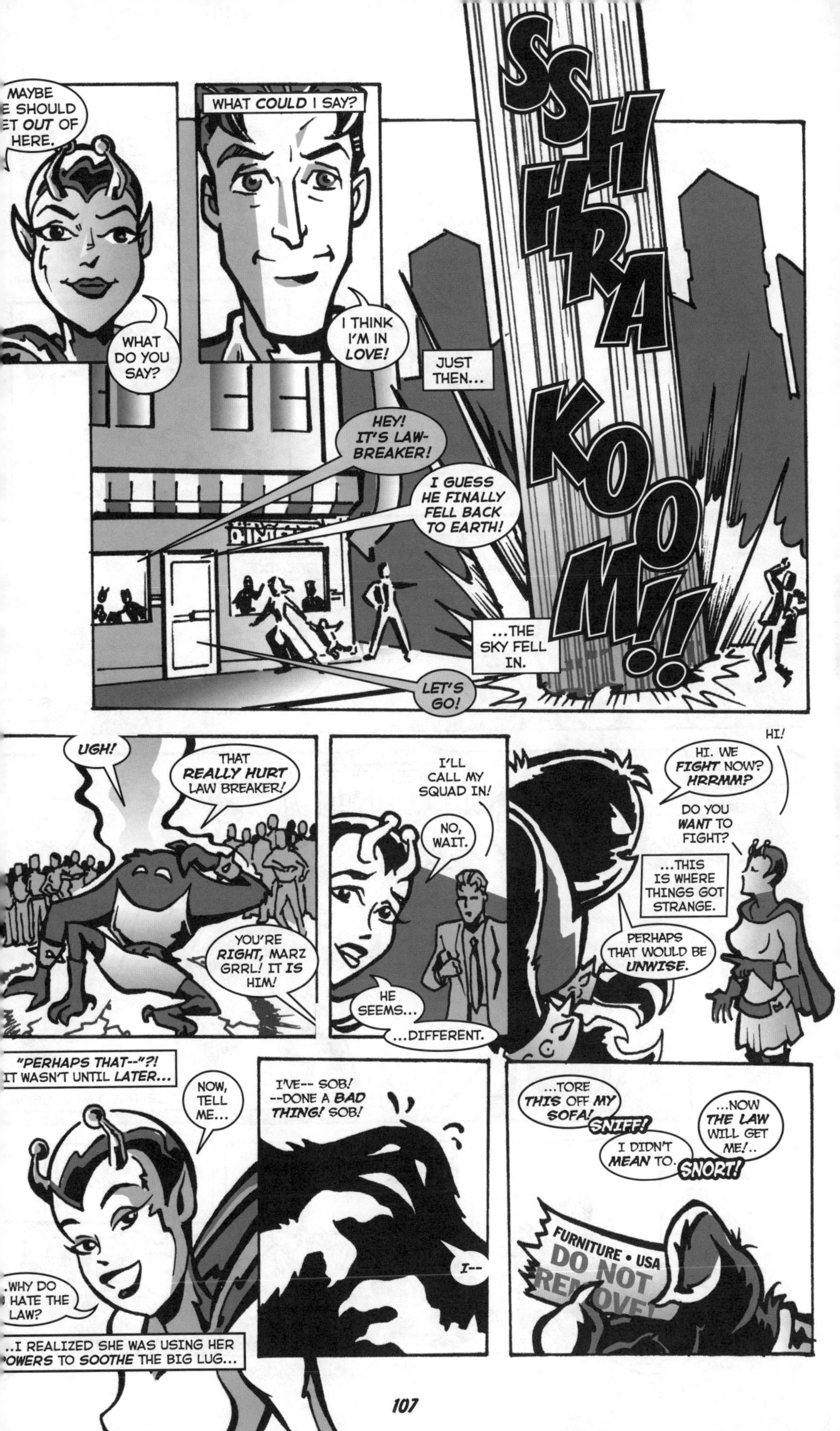
MAYBE
E SHOULD
ET OUT OF
HERE.
WHAT DO YOU SAY?
WHAT COULD I SAY?
I THINK I'M IN LOVE!
JUST THEN...
SSHHRAKOOOM!!
HEY! IT'S LAW-BREAKER!
I GUESS HE FINALLY FELL BACK TO EARTH!
...THE SKY FELL IN.
LET'S GO!
UGH!
THAT REALLY HURT LAW BREAKER!
YOU'RE RIGHT, MARZ GRRL! IT IS HIM!
I'LL CALL MY SQUAD IN!
NO, WAIT.
HE SEEMS...
...DIFFERENT.
HI. WE FIGHT NOW? HRRMM?
HI!
DO YOU WANT TO FIGHT?
...THIS IS WHERE THINGS GOT STRANGE.
PERHAPS THAT WOULD BE UNWISE.
"PERHAPS THAT--"?!
IT WASN'T UNTIL LATER...
NOW, TELL ME...
.WHY DO
HATE THE
LAW?
..I REALIZED SHE WAS USING HER
OWERS TO SOOTHE THE BIG LUG...
I'VE-- SOB! --DONE A BAD THING! SOB!
I--
...TORE THIS OFF MY SOFA!
SNIFF!
I DIDN'T MEAN TO.
SNORT!
...NOW THE LAW WILL GET ME!..
FURNITURE • USA
DO NOT
REMOVE!

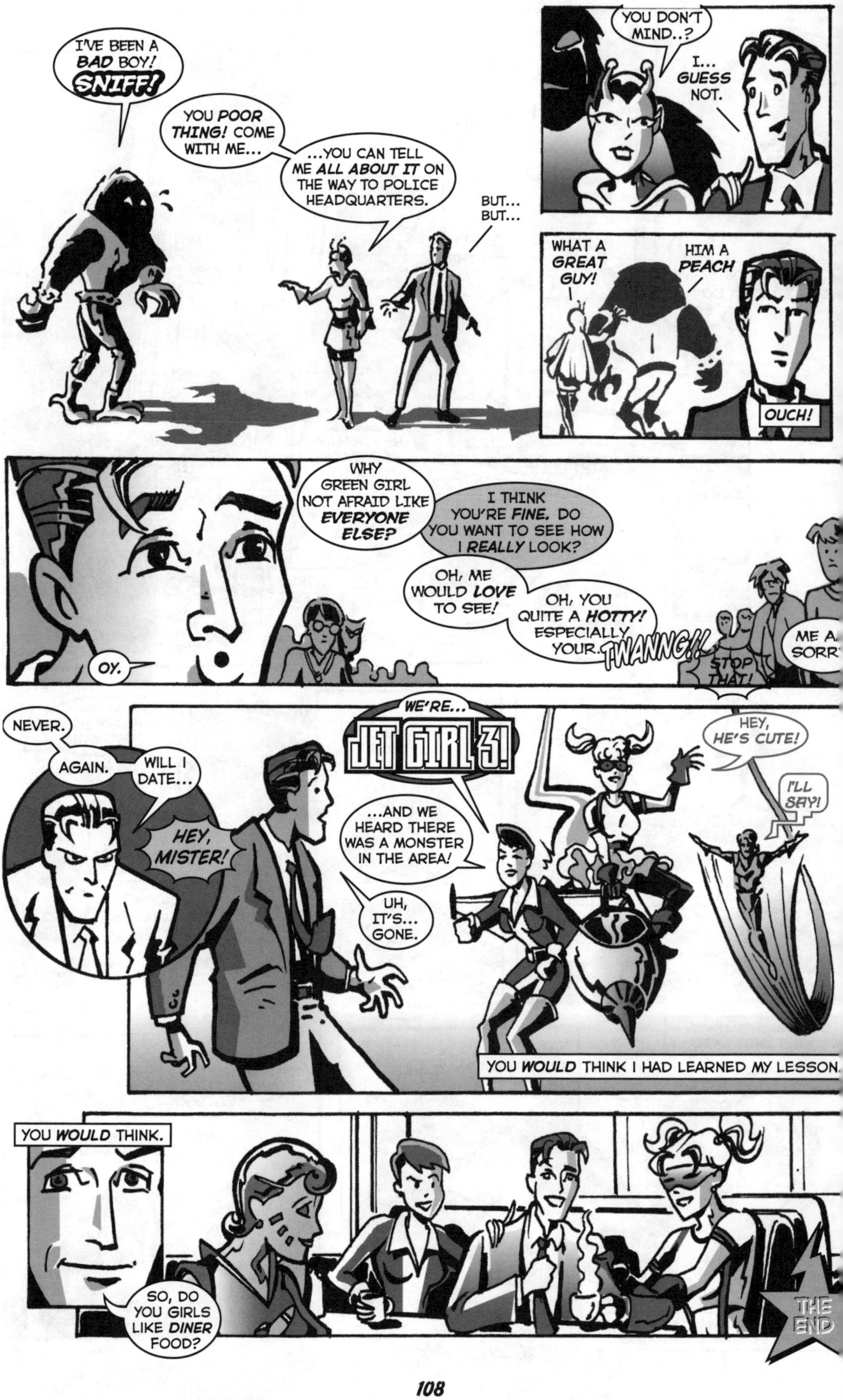
I'VE BEEN A BAD BOY! SNIFF!
YOU POOR THING! COME WITH ME...
...YOU CAN TELL ME ALL ABOUT IT ON THE WAY TO POLICE HEADQUARTERS.
BUT... BUT...
YOU DON'T MIND..?
I... GUESS NOT.
WHAT A GREAT GUY!
HIM A PEACH
OUCH!
WHY GREEN GIRL NOT AFRAID LIKE EVERYONE ELSE?
I THINK YOU'RE FINE. DO YOU WANT TO SEE HOW I REALLY LOOK?
OH, ME WOULD LOVE TO SEE!
OH, YOU QUITE A HOTTY! ESPECIALLY YOUR...
TWANNG!!
STOP THAT!
ME A SORR
OY.
NEVER.
AGAIN.
WILL I DATE...
HEY, MISTER!
WE'RE... JET GIRL 3!
...AND WE HEARD THERE WAS A MONSTER IN THE AREA!
UH, IT'S... GONE.
HEY, HE'S CUTE!
I'LL SAY!
YOU WOULD THINK I HAD LEARNED MY LESSON.
YOU WOULD THINK.
SO, DO YOU GIRLS LIKE DINER FOOD?
THE END

THE WORLD'S GREATEST
HEROES BAND TOGETHER
TO SAVE THE UNIVERSE!

CROSSOVER CLASSICS

STORY BY
AL NICKERSON
GREG HYLAND
MICHAEL KORNSTEIN
JOHN GALLAGHER
STEVE REMEN

ART BY
MICHAEL KORNSTEIN
AL NICKERSON
GREG HYLAND

AFTER KEVIN MAGUIRE

In 2001, Crossover Classics ran on the internet at the Argghh!! Chroncles and Lethargic Lad websites. Featuring a variety of online heroes, including Buzzboy, in a galaxy-spanning, hilarious adventure. Enjoy this star-spangled tale, here in print for the first time, then head over to the internet to see more of these characters in action...

Crossover Classics Character Profiles

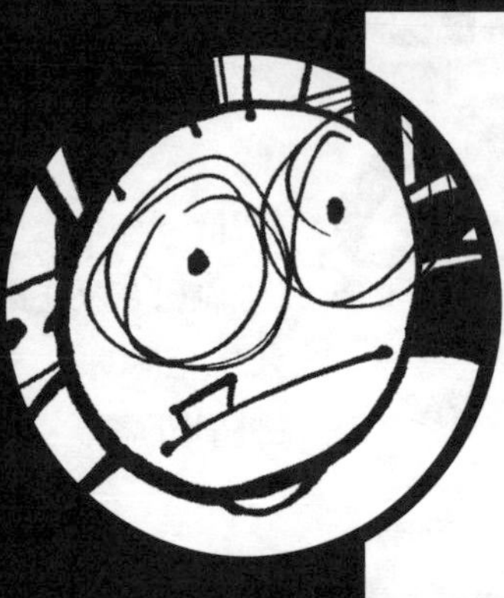

LETHARGIC LAD:

Lethargic Lad was born an extremely lethargic baby, who was immediately put in an orphanage. The young lethargic baby was adopted by Herman and Lilly Ladhands. As Larry Ladhands grew olde[r] he was bombarded by cosmic rays, caught in a gamma bomb explosion, bitten by a radioactive spider, forced to flee Boneville, and found a magical uru hammer. Later he drank orange juice, watched 'Blue Velvet' repeatedly, and listened to Patsy Cline records. Soon he became the crime fighting sidekick of Mr. West. After Mr. West's tragic death at the hands of the Evil Similey Face Guy, Larry Ladhands decided to follow in his mentor's footsteps, to become Lethargic Lad, the world's greatest superhero.

www.lethargiclad.com

NIHILIST-MAN:

While pursuing a villain from his home universe, DIMENSION X, Nihilist-Man became trapped on our world. Knowing he will never be able to return to DIMENSION X, Nihilist-Man has become a champion for our universe and Earth's supreme super-hero. Nihilist-Man's favorite pass time is to kick bad-guy butt and have a few brews afterward.

albert.nickerson.tripod.com/home.html

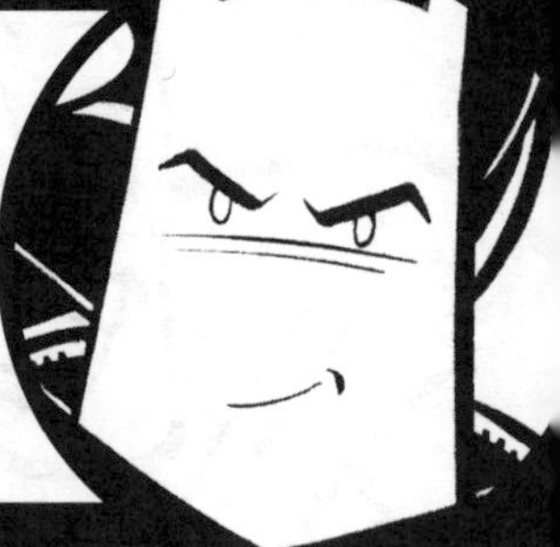

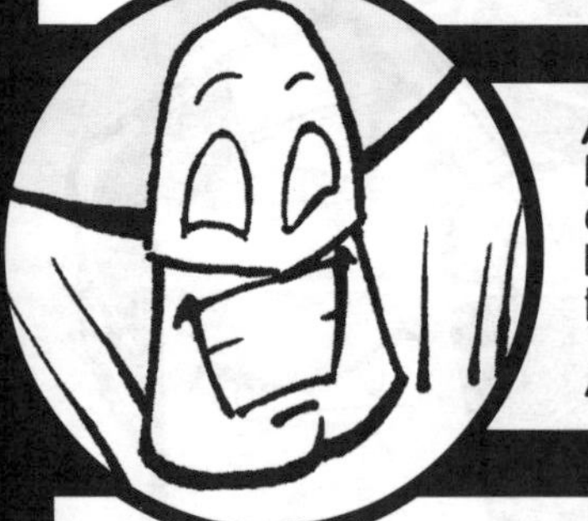

HIM:

HIM is one of Infantino city's greatest heroes. Since the dark days of World War Two; fighting crime and corn dogs have been his passion. It has been said that HIM can pose down with the best... and win!

Him can be seen at: www.lethargiclad.com

HUNTER:

From the year 2117, comes the vigilante known as Hunter. Hunter is a man with extra-ordinary senses and abilities. How he acquired them is a mystery. All Hunter knows is that it all started with a phone call setting him on an unstoppable course of destruction and causing the Ecoast crime faction's eventual fall. Problem is, Hunter doesn't know why he does what he does, only that it feels right. But to what end? Hunter doesn't know. One thing is for certain, Hunter sure as heck doesn't think of himself as a hero, and he'll be darned if he wears a cape.

Hunter can be seen at: albert.nickerson.tripod.com/home.html

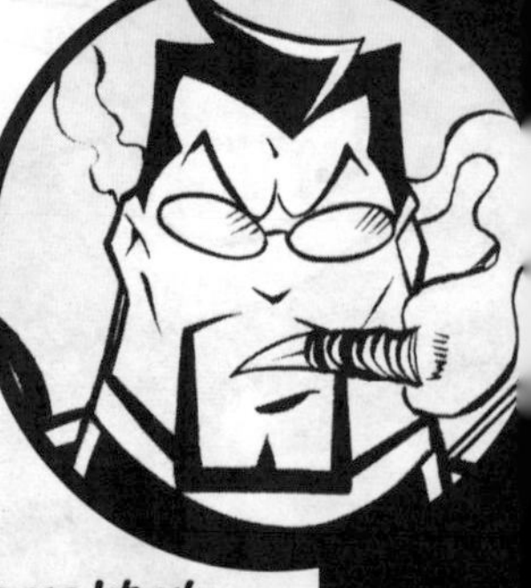

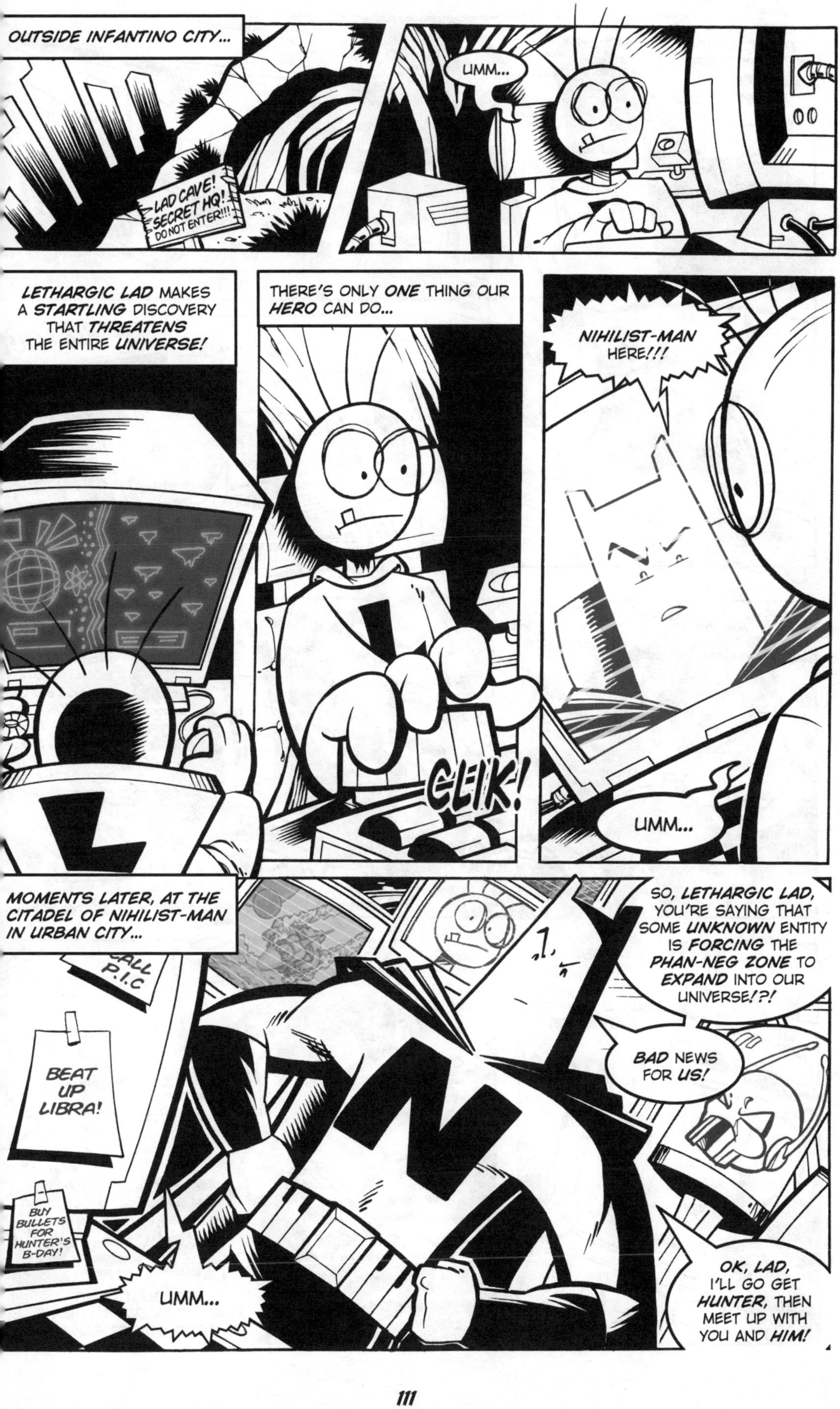
OUTSIDE INFANTINO CITY...
LAD CAVE! SECRET HQ! DO NOT ENTER!!!
UMM...
LETHARGIC LAD MAKES A STARTLING DISCOVERY THAT THREATENS THE ENTIRE UNIVERSE!
THERE'S ONLY ONE THING OUR HERO CAN DO...
CLIK!
NIHILIST-MAN HERE!!!
UMM...
MOMENTS LATER, AT THE CITADEL OF NIHILIST-MAN IN URBAN CITY...
CALL P.I.C
BEAT UP LIBRA!
BUY BULLETS FOR HUNTER'S B-DAY!
UMM...
SO, LETHARGIC LAD, YOU'RE SAYING THAT SOME UNKNOWN ENTITY IS FORCING THE PHAN-NEG ZONE TO EXPAND INTO OUR UNIVERSE!?!
BAD NEWS FOR US!
OK, LAD, I'LL GO GET HUNTER, THEN MEET UP WITH YOU AND HIM!

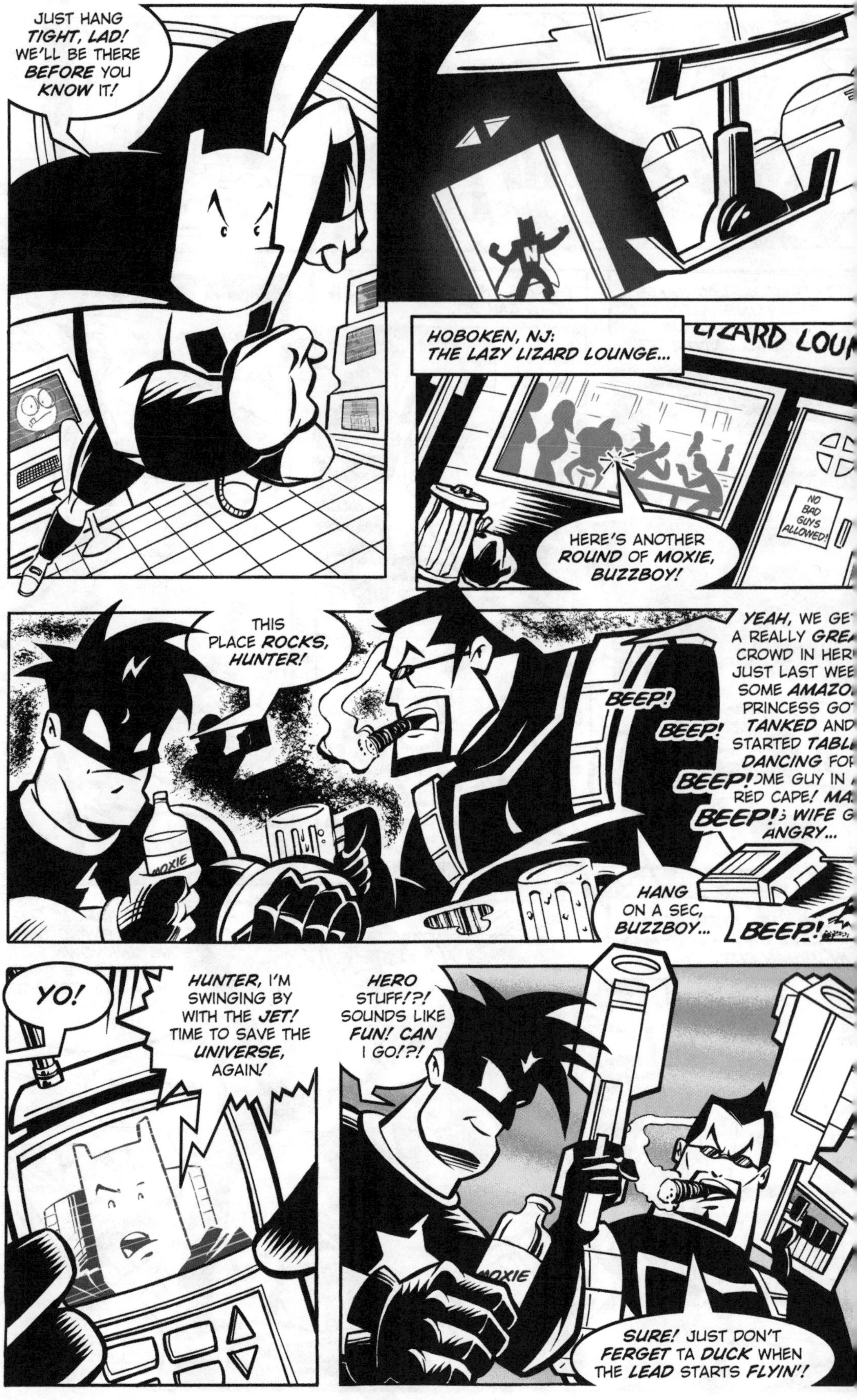
JUST HANG TIGHT, LAD! WE'LL BE THERE BEFORE YOU KNOW IT!
HOBOKEN, NJ: THE LAZY LIZARD LOUNGE...
IZARD LOUN
NO BAD GUYS ALLOWED!
HERE'S ANOTHER ROUND OF MOXIE, BUZZBOY!
THIS PLACE ROCKS, HUNTER!
MOXIE
YEAH, WE GE
BEEP!
BEEP!
BEEP!
BEEP!
BEEP!
HANG ON A SEC, BUZZBOY...
YO!
HUNTER, I'M SWINGING BY WITH THE JET! TIME TO SAVE THE UNIVERSE, AGAIN!
HERO STUFF!?! SOUNDS LIKE FUN! CAN I GO!?!
MOXIE
SURE! JUST DON'T FERGET TA DUCK WHEN THE LEAD STARTS FLYIN'!

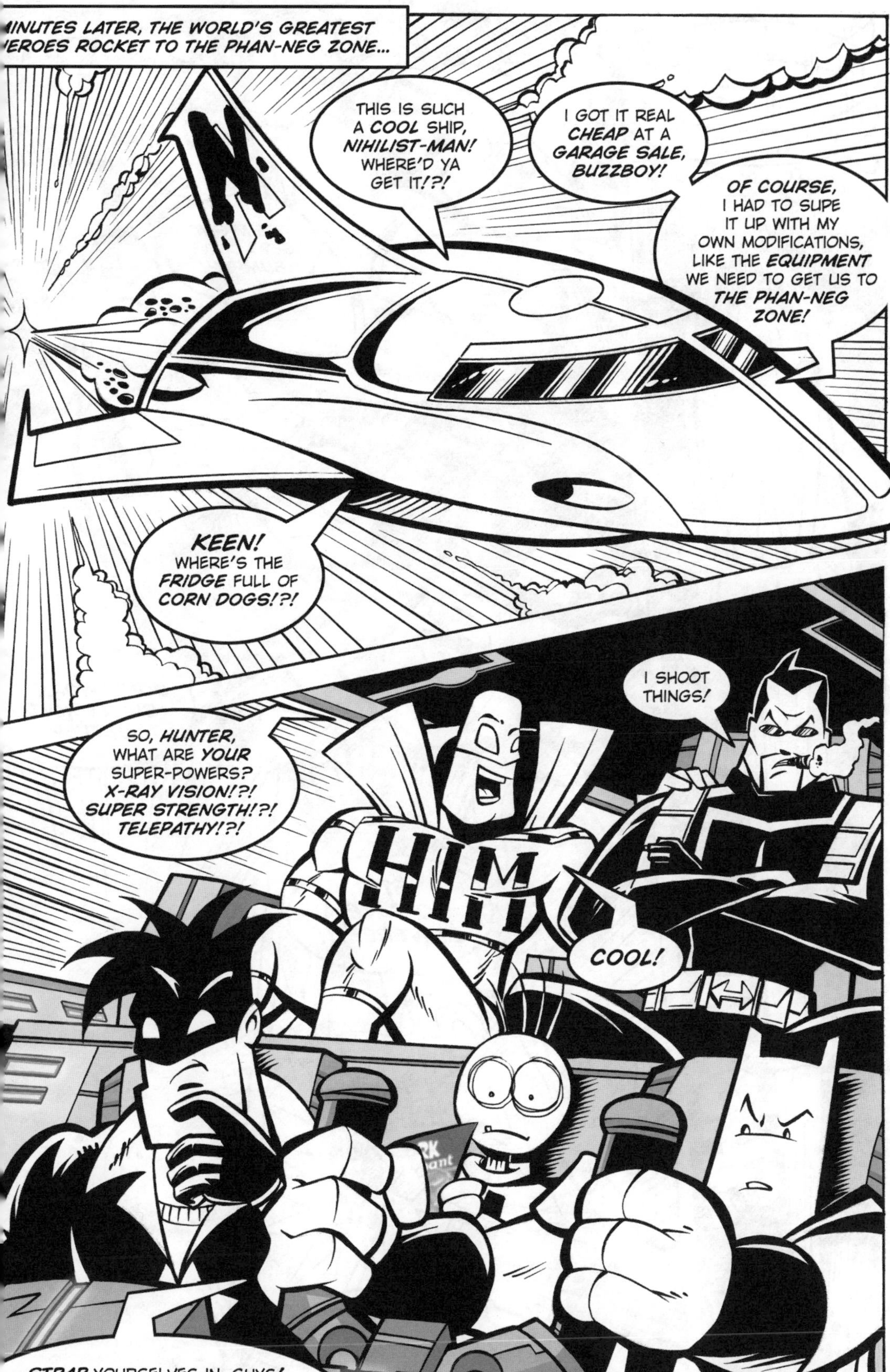

INUTES LATER, THE WORLD'S GREATEST
EROES ROCKET TO THE PHAN-NEG ZONE...
THIS IS SUCH A COOL SHIP, NIHILIST-MAN! WHERE'D YA GET IT!?!
I GOT IT REAL CHEAP AT A GARAGE SALE, BUZZBOY!
OF COURSE, I HAD TO SUPE IT UP WITH MY OWN MODIFICATIONS, LIKE THE EQUIPMENT WE NEED TO GET US TO THE PHAN-NEG ZONE!
KEEN! WHERE'S THE FRIDGE FULL OF CORN DOGS!?!
SO, HUNTER, WHAT ARE YOUR SUPER-POWERS? X-RAY VISION!?! SUPER STRENGTH!?! TELEPATHY!?!
I SHOOT THINGS!
HIM
COOL!
STRAP YOURSELVES IN, GUYS! I'M ABOUT TO BRING THE EMPORAL FUSION ENGINES ONLINE!

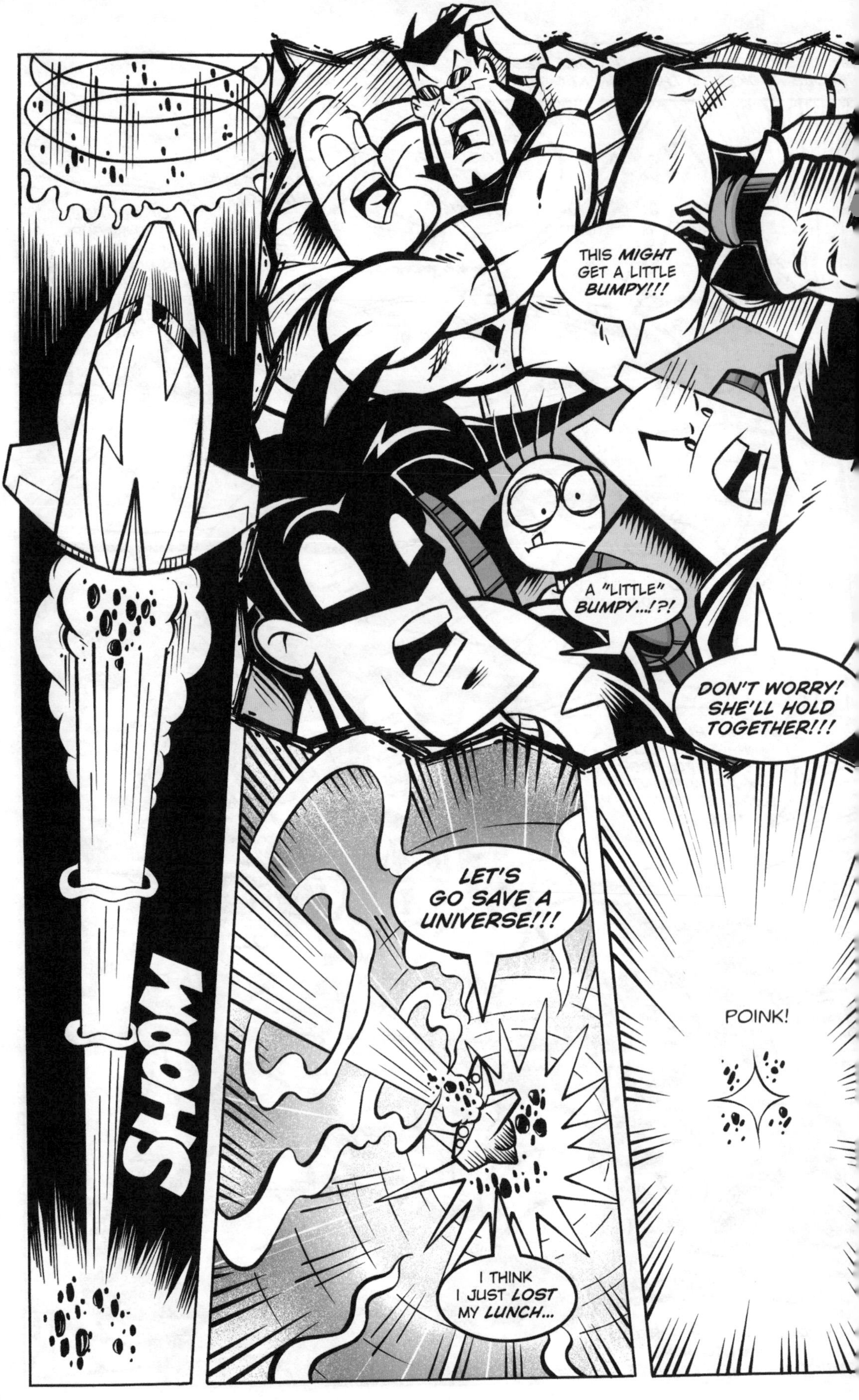
SHOOM
THIS MIGHT GET A LITTLE BUMPY!!!
A "LITTLE" BUMPY...!?!
DON'T WORRY! SHE'LL HOLD TOGETHER!!!
LET'S GO SAVE A UNIVERSE!!!
I THINK I JUST LOST MY LUNCH...
POINK!

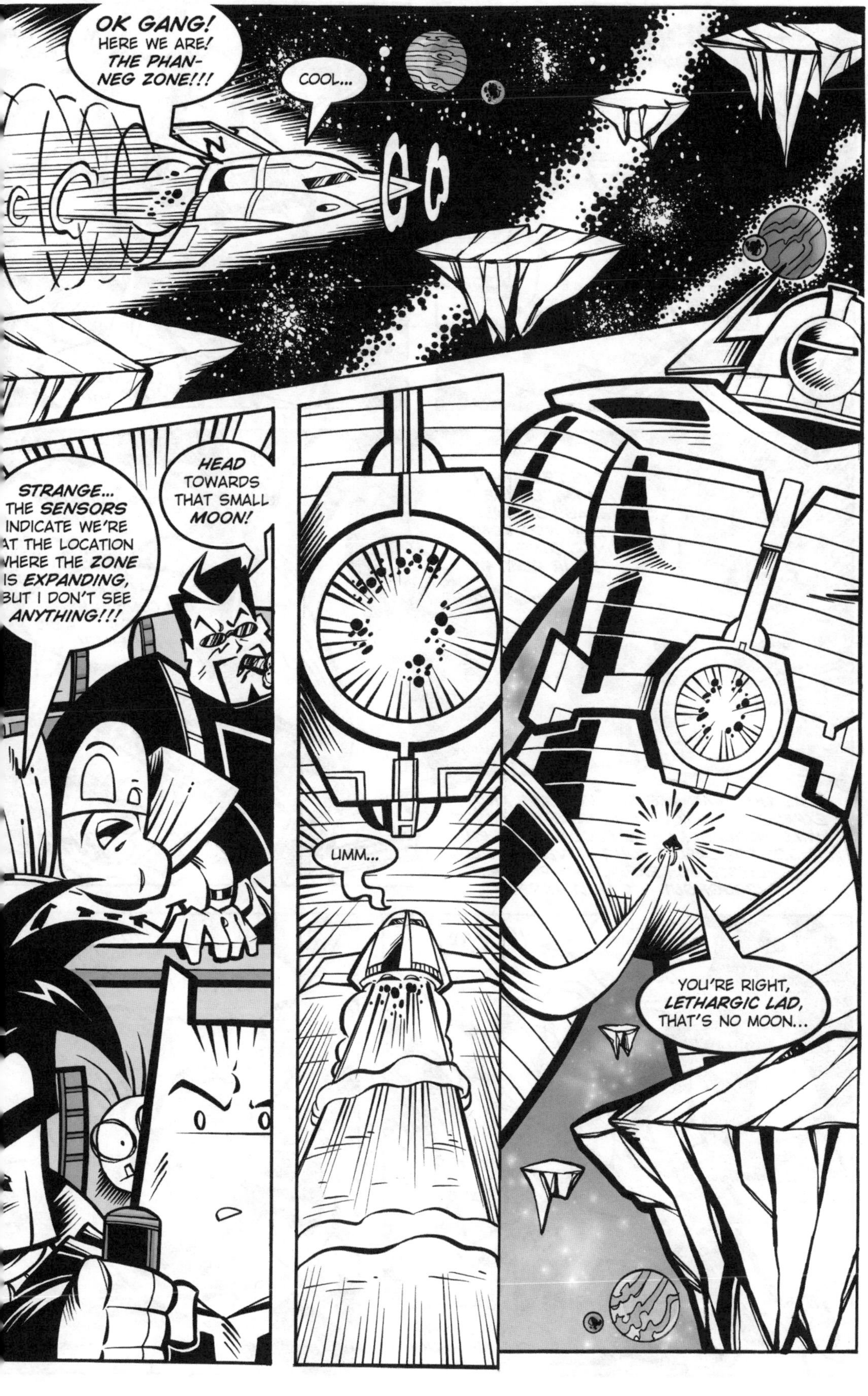
OK GANG! HERE WE ARE! THE PHAN-NEG ZONE!!!
COOL...
STRANGE... THE SENSORS INDICATE WE'RE AT THE LOCATION WHERE THE ZONE IS EXPANDING, BUT I DON'T SEE ANYTHING!!!
HEAD TOWARDS THAT SMALL MOON!
UMM...
YOU'RE RIGHT, LETHARGIC LAD, THAT'S NO MOON...

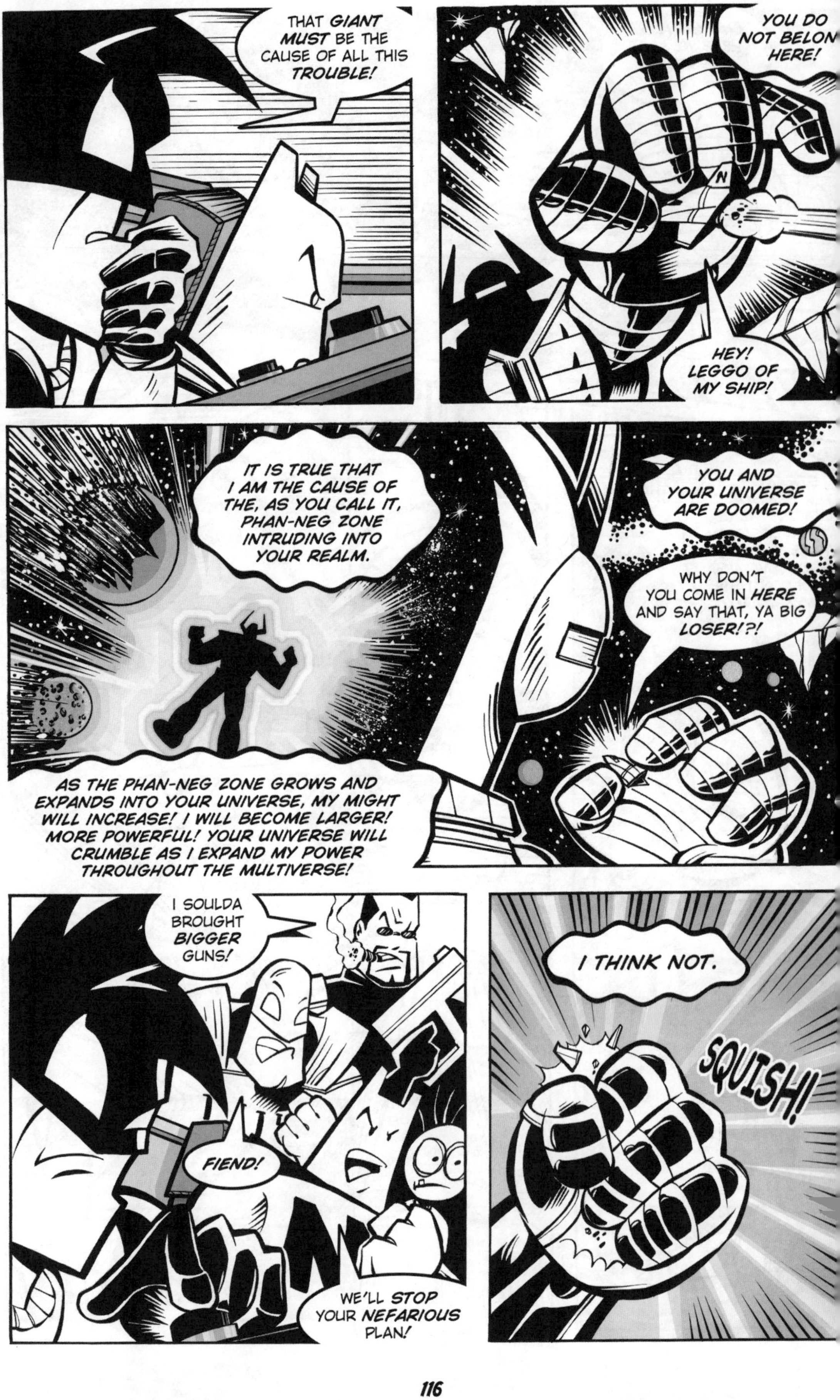
THAT GIANT MUST BE THE CAUSE OF ALL THIS TROUBLE!
YOU DO NOT BELON HERE!
HEY! LEGGO OF MY SHIP!
IT IS TRUE THAT I AM THE CAUSE OF THE, AS YOU CALL IT, PHAN-NEG ZONE INTRUDING INTO YOUR REALM.
AS THE PHAN-NEG ZONE GROWS AND EXPANDS INTO YOUR UNIVERSE, MY MIGHT WILL INCREASE! I WILL BECOME LARGER! MORE POWERFUL! YOUR UNIVERSE WILL CRUMBLE AS I EXPAND MY POWER THROUGHOUT THE MULTIVERSE!
YOU AND YOUR UNIVERSE ARE DOOMED!
WHY DON'T YOU COME IN HERE AND SAY THAT, YA BIG LOSER!?!
I SOULDA BROUGHT BIGGER GUNS!
FIEND!
WE'LL STOP YOUR NEFARIOUS PLAN!
I THINK NOT.
SQUISH!

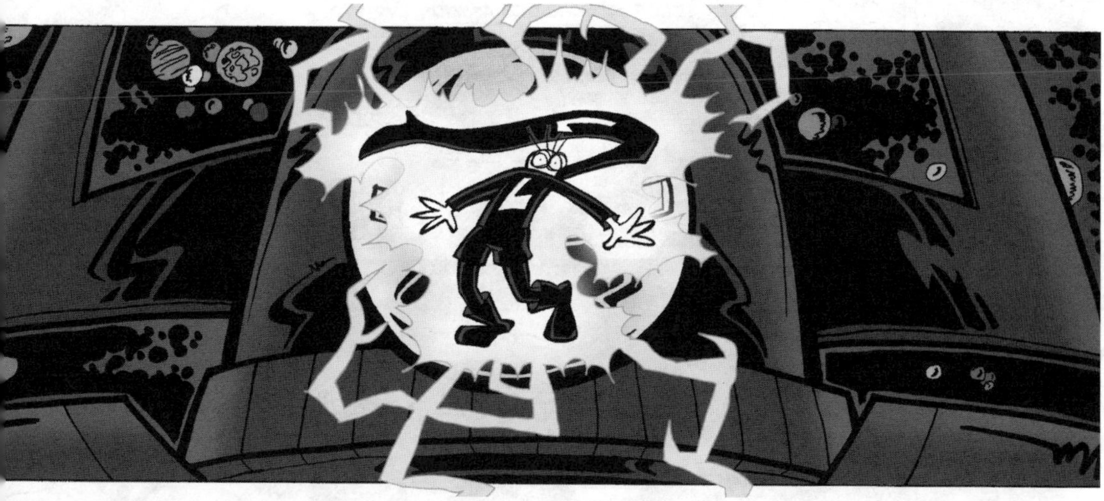

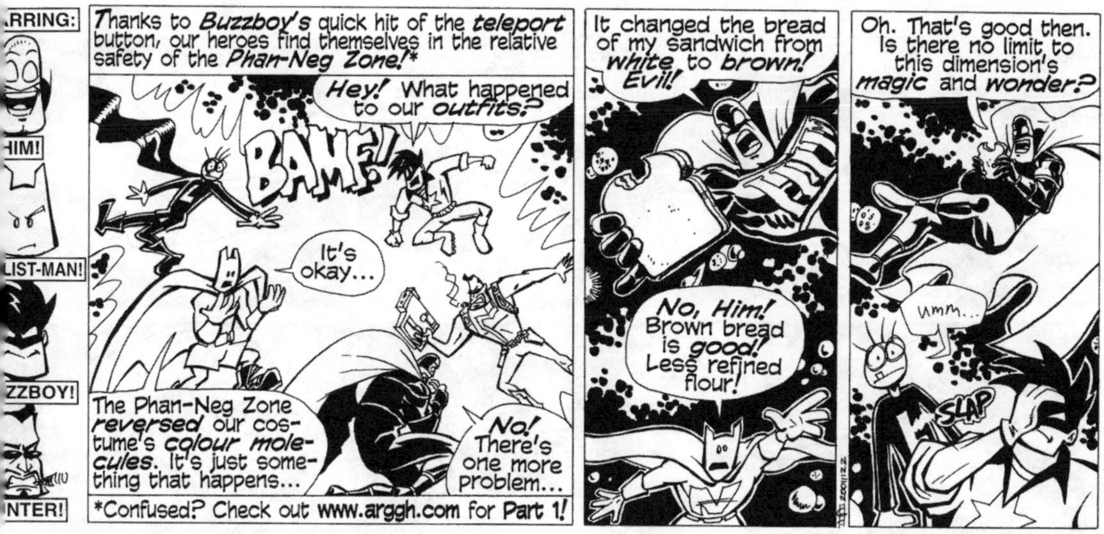
RRING:
HIM!
LIST-MAN!
ZZBOY!
NTER!
Thanks to Buzzboy's quick hit of the teleport button, our heroes find themselves in the relative safety of the Phan-Neg Zone!*
Hey! What happened to our outfits?
BAMF!!
It's okay...
The Phan-Neg Zone reversed our costume's colour molecules. It's just something that happens...
No! There's one more problem...
*Confused? Check out www.arggh.com for Part 1!
It changed the bread of my sandwich from white to brown! Evil!
No, Him! Brown bread is good! Less refined flour!
Oh. That's good then. Is there no limit to this dimension's magic and wonder?
umm...
SLAP

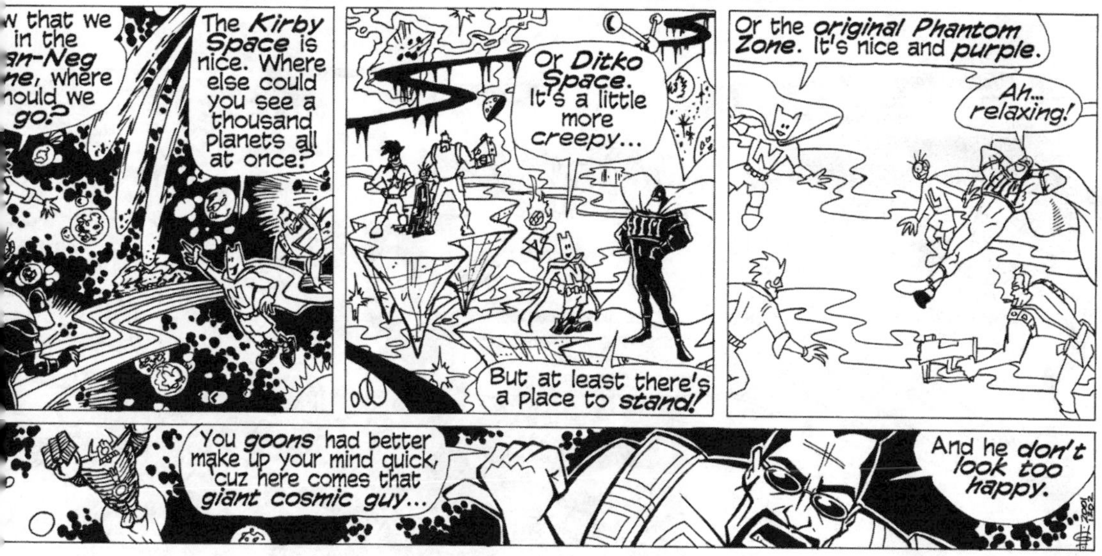
w that we in the an-Neg ne, where hould we go?
The Kirby Space is nice. Where else could you see a thousand planets all at once?
Or Ditko Space. It's a little more creepy...
But at least there's a place to stand!
Or the original Phantom Zone. It's nice and purple.
Ah... relaxing!
You goons had better make up your mind quick, cuz here comes that giant cosmic guy...
And he don't look too happy.

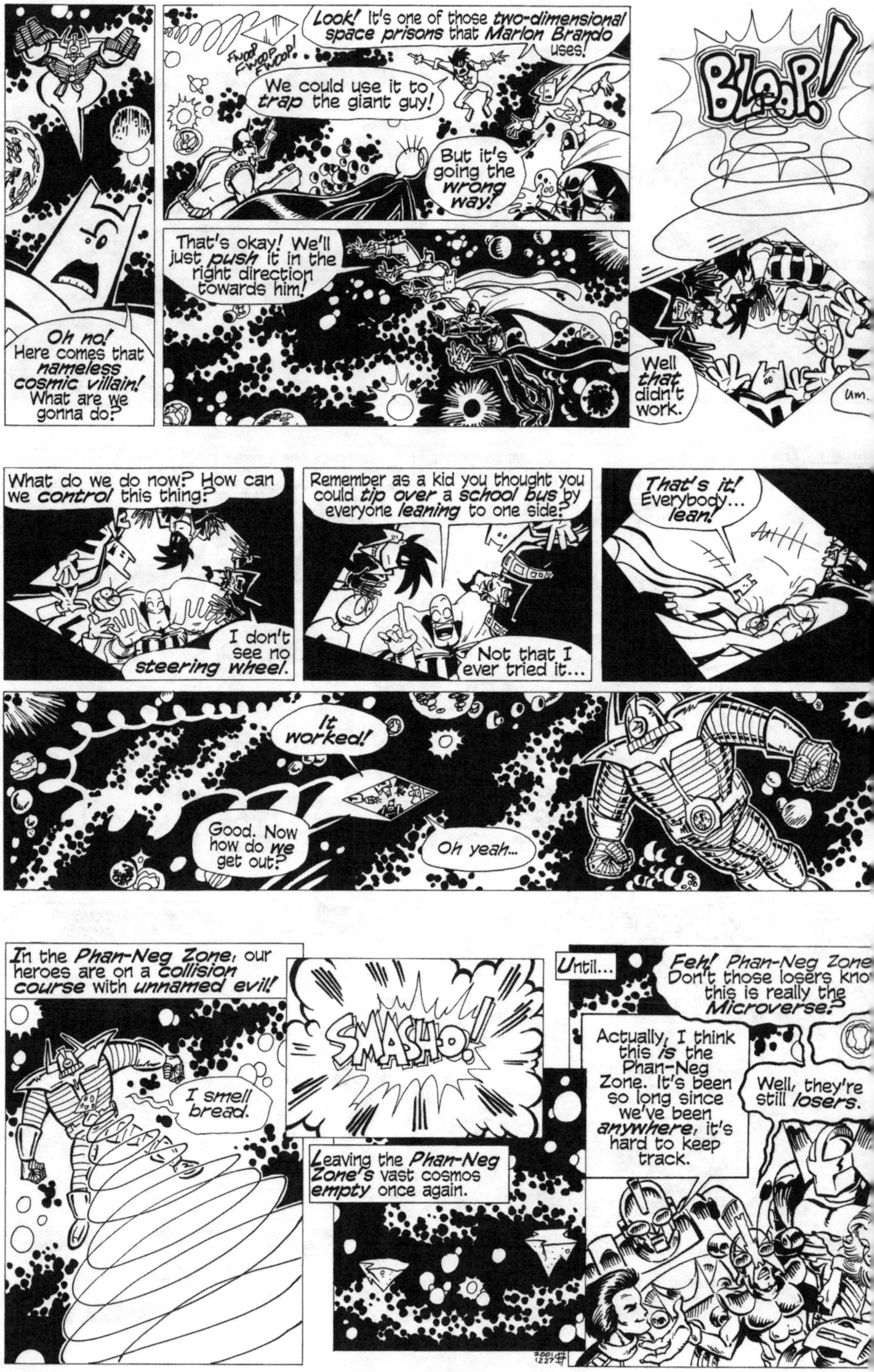
Oh no! Here comes that nameless cosmic villain! What are we gonna do?
FWOOP FWOOP FWOOP!
Look! It's one of those two-dimensional space prisons that Marlon Brando uses!
We could use it to trap the giant guy!
But it's going the wrong way!
That's okay! We'll just push it in the right direction towards him!
BLOOP!
Well that didn't work.
Um.
What do we do now? How can we control this thing?
I don't see no steering wheel.
Remember as a kid you thought you could tip over a school bus by everyone leaning to one side?
Not that I ever tried it...
That's it! Everybody... lean!
It worked!
Good. Now how do we get out?
Oh yeah...
In the Phan-Neg Zone, our heroes are on a collision course with unnamed evil!
I smell bread.
SMASHO!
Leaving the Phan-Neg Zone's vast cosmos empty once again.
Until...
Feh! Phan-Neg Zone
Don't those losers kno
this is really the Microverse?
Actually, I think this is the Phan-Neg Zone. It's been so long since we've been anywhere, it's hard to keep track.
Well, they're still losers.
2001 1227

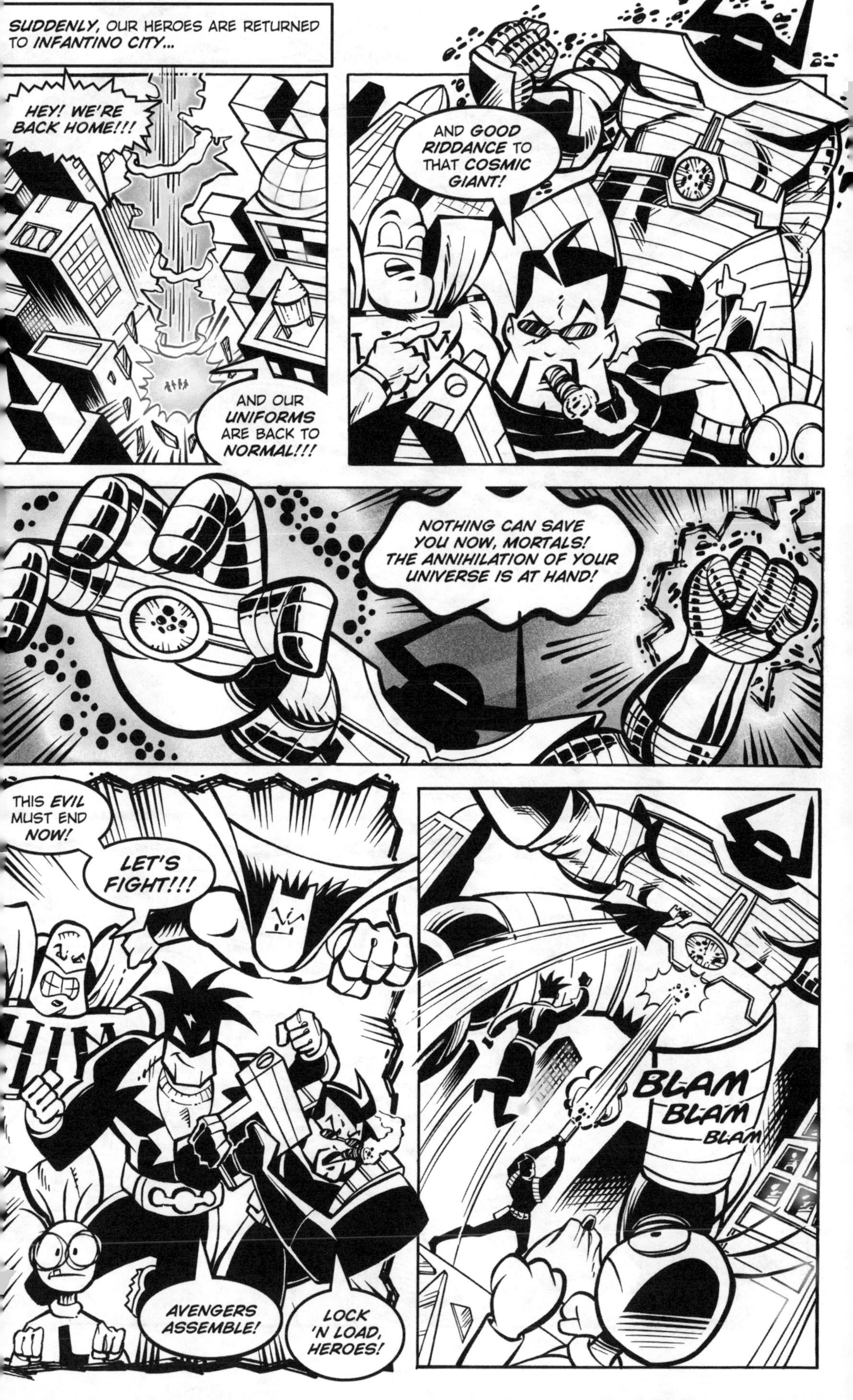
SUDDENLY, OUR HEROES ARE RETURNED TO INFANTINO CITY...
HEY! WE'RE BACK HOME!!!
AND OUR UNIFORMS ARE BACK TO NORMAL!!!
AND GOOD RIDDANCE TO THAT COSMIC GIANT!
NOTHING CAN SAVE YOU NOW, MORTALS! THE ANNIHILATION OF YOUR UNIVERSE IS AT HAND!
THIS EVIL MUST END NOW!
LET'S FIGHT!!!
AVENGERS ASSEMBLE!
LOCK 'N LOAD, HEROES!
BLAM
BLAM
BLAM

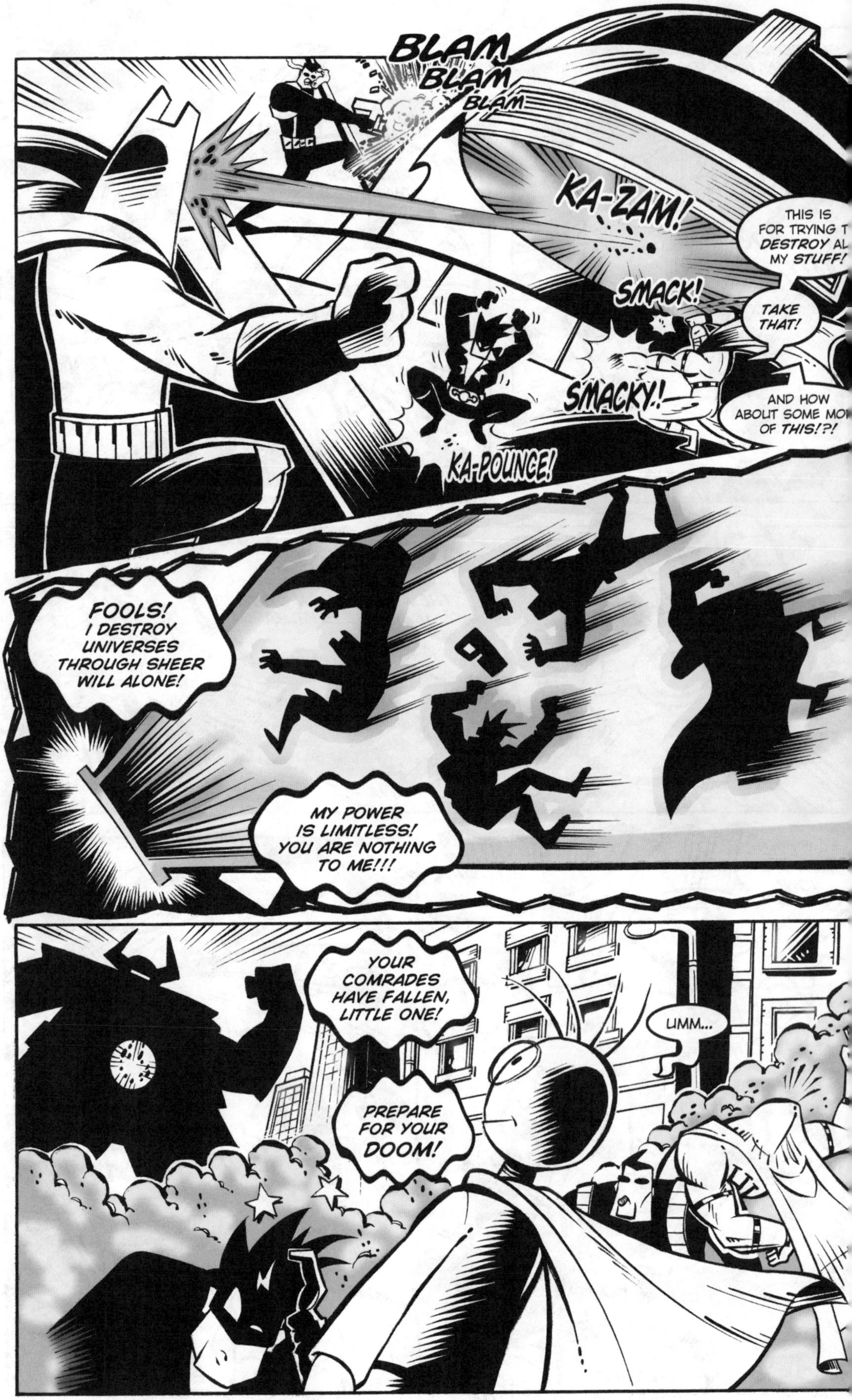
BLAM
BLAM
BLAM
KA-ZAM!
THIS IS FOR TRYING T DESTROY AL MY STUFF!
SMACK!
TAKE THAT!
SMACKY!
AND HOW ABOUT SOME MO OF THIS!?!
KA-POUNCE!
FOOLS! I DESTROY UNIVERSES THROUGH SHEER WILL ALONE!
MY POWER IS LIMITLESS! YOU ARE NOTHING TO ME!!!
YOUR COMRADES HAVE FALLEN, LITTLE ONE!
UMM...
PREPARE FOR YOUR DOOM!

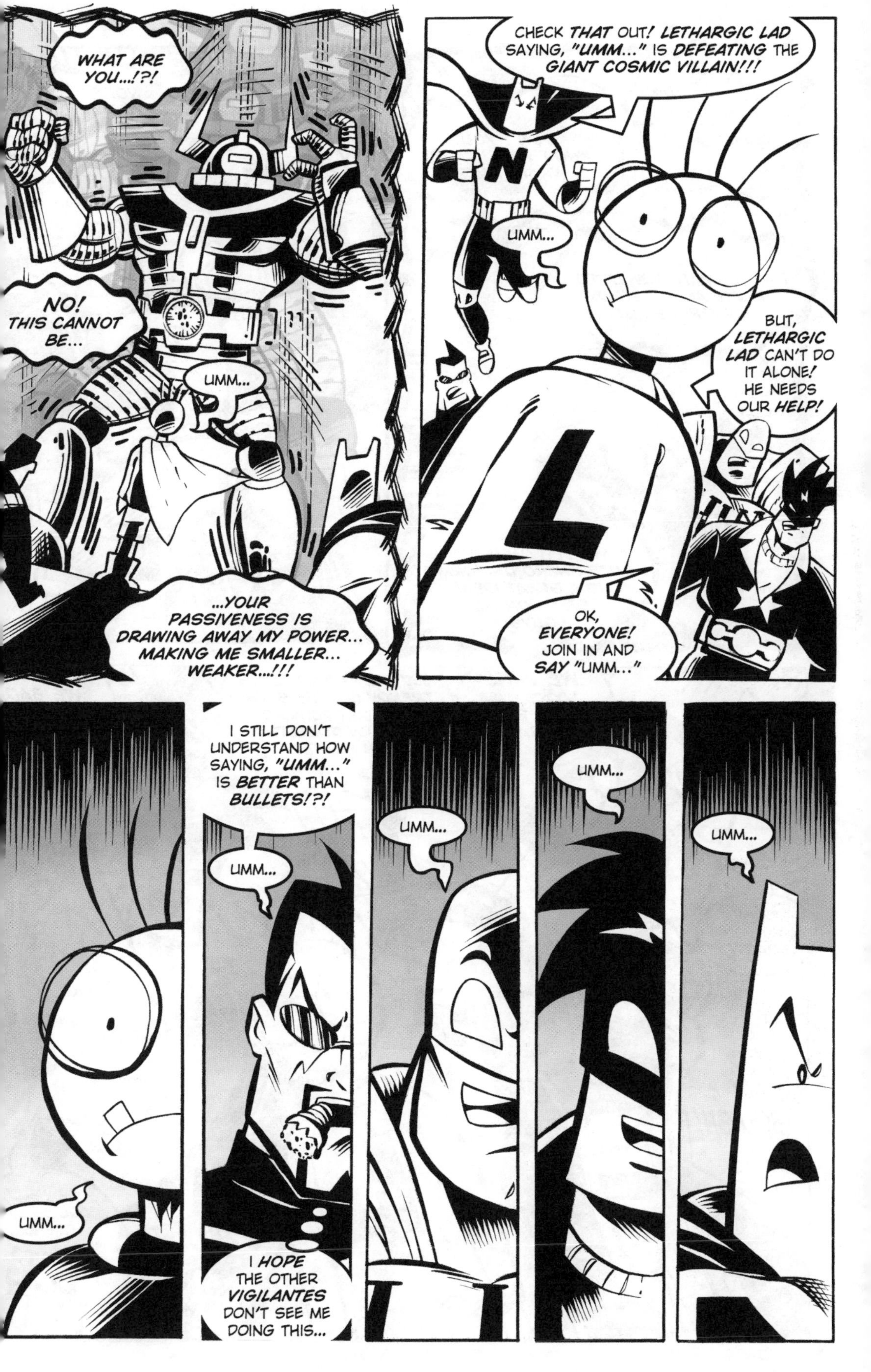
WHAT ARE YOU...!?!
NO! THIS CANNOT BE...
UMM...
...YOUR PASSIVENESS IS DRAWING AWAY MY POWER... MAKING ME SMALLER... WEAKER...!!!
CHECK THAT OUT! LETHARGIC LAD SAYING, "UMM..." IS DEFEATING THE GIANT COSMIC VILLAIN!!!
UMM...
BUT, LETHARGIC LAD CAN'T DO IT ALONE! HE NEEDS OUR HELP!
OK, EVERYONE! JOIN IN AND SAY "UMM..."
UMM...
I STILL DON'T UNDERSTAND HOW SAYING, "UMM..." IS BETTER THAN BULLETS!?!
UMM...
I HOPE THE OTHER VIGILANTES DON'T SEE ME DOING THIS...
UMM...
UMM...
UMM...

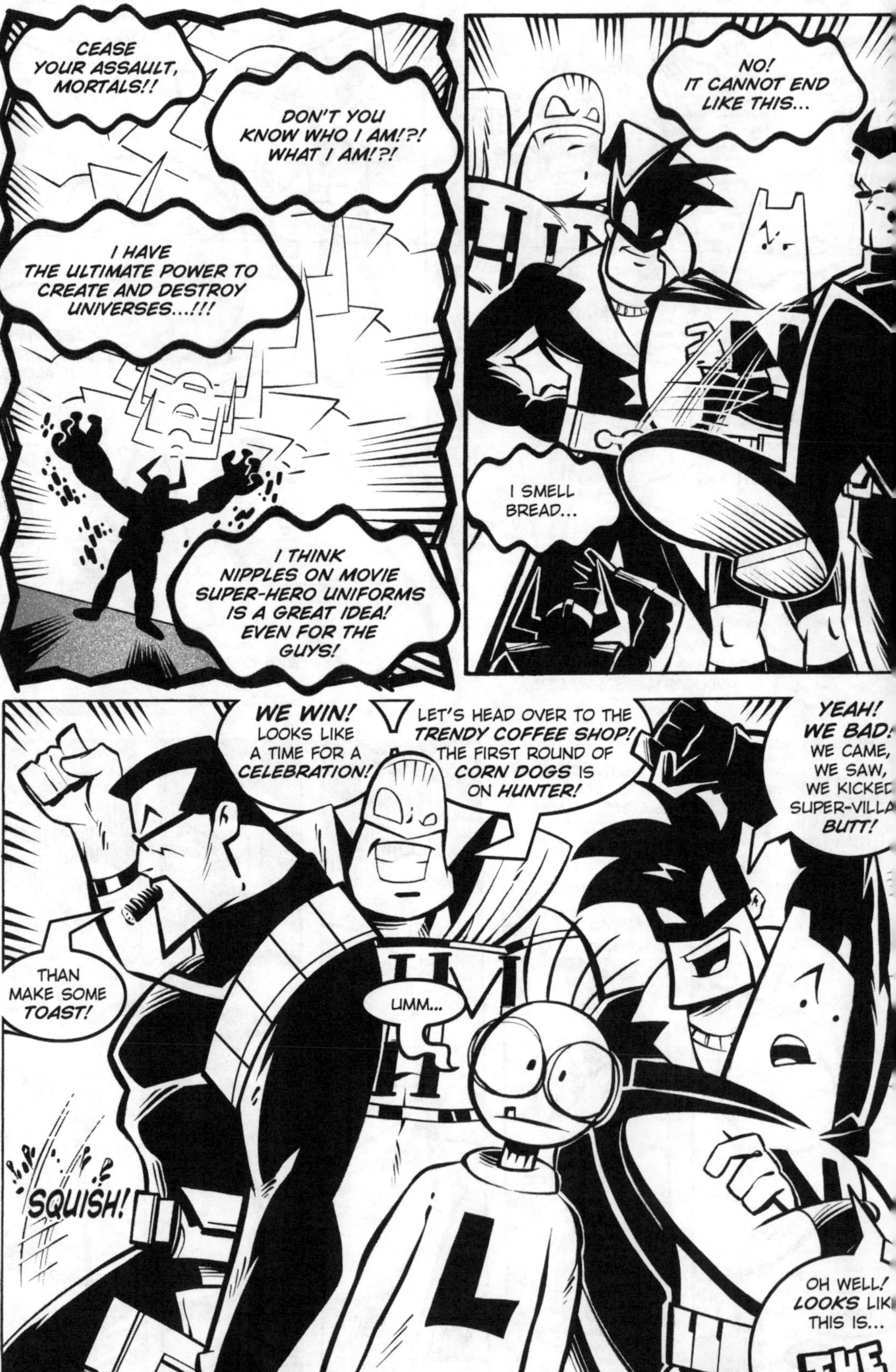
CEASE YOUR ASSAULT, MORTALS!!
DON'T YOU KNOW WHO I AM!?! WHAT I AM!?!
I HAVE THE ULTIMATE POWER TO CREATE AND DESTROY UNIVERSES...!!!
I THINK NIPPLES ON MOVIE SUPER-HERO UNIFORMS IS A GREAT IDEA! EVEN FOR THE GUYS!
NO! IT CANNOT END LIKE THIS...
I SMELL BREAD...
WE WIN! LOOKS LIKE A TIME FOR A CELEBRATION!
LET'S HEAD OVER TO THE TRENDY COFFEE SHOP! THE FIRST ROUND OF CORN DOGS IS ON HUNTER!
YEAH! WE BAD! WE CAME, WE SAW, WE KICKE SUPER-VILLA BUTT!
THAN MAKE SOME TOAST!
UMM...
SQUISH!
OH WELL! LOOKS LIK THIS IS...
THE END

The Buzzboy SECTION

NEW PARADISE
PICAYUNE

SPECIAL SAN DIEGO COMIC-CON EDITION - 2003

TRUTH Justice ★ ALL·U·CAN·EAT!

THE MOON! FOR CENTURIES UNTOLD, IT HAS BEEN A *MYSTERY!*

TO THE ANCIENT GREEKS, IT WAS CALLED *"SELENE."*

TO THE ITALIANS, IT WAS *"LUNA."* TO THE RUSSIANS, ALSO *"LUNA."*

TO THE SPANISH, IT WAS...

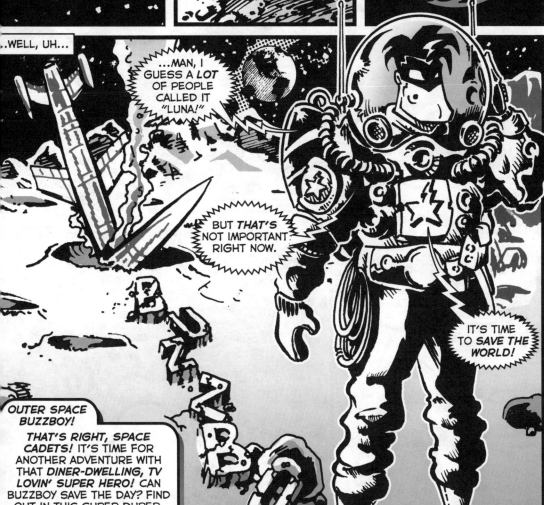

...WELL, UH...

...MAN, I GUESS *A LOT* OF PEOPLE CALLED IT *"LUNA!"*

BUT *THAT'S* NOT IMPORTANT RIGHT NOW.

IT'S TIME TO *SAVE THE WORLD!*

OUTER SPACE BUZZBOY!

THAT'S RIGHT, SPACE CADETS! IT'S TIME FOR ANOTHER ADVENTURE WITH THAT *DINER-DWELLING, TV LOVIN'* SUPER HERO! CAN BUZZBOY SAVE THE DAY? FIND OUT IN THIS SUPER DUPER SPACEY *SUSPENS*TORY!

STORY ★ ART
"JOLLY" JOHN GALLAGHER
ROBOY RED INKS BY "RIOTOUS" RICH FABER!

THIS STORY IS DEDICATED TO WILL EISNER & WALLY WOOD

page 01 OXYGEN E F

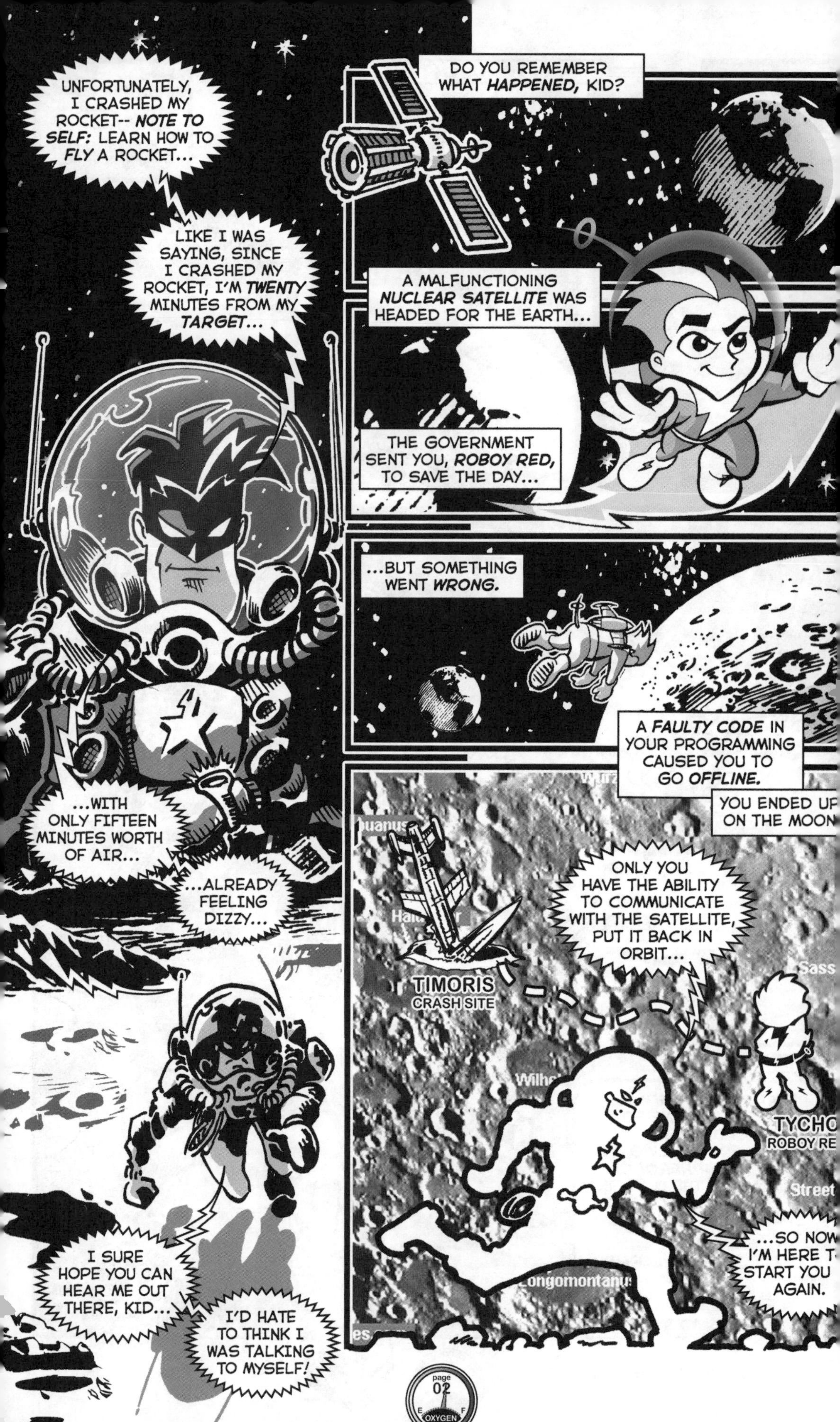
UNFORTUNATELY, I CRASHED MY ROCKET-- *NOTE TO SELF:* LEARN HOW TO *FLY* A ROCKET...
LIKE I WAS SAYING, SINCE I CRASHED MY ROCKET, I'M *TWENTY* MINUTES FROM MY *TARGET*...
...WITH ONLY FIFTEEN MINUTES WORTH OF AIR...
...ALREADY FEELING DIZZY...
I SURE HOPE YOU CAN HEAR ME OUT THERE, KID...
I'D HATE TO THINK I WAS TALKING TO MYSELF!
DO YOU REMEMBER WHAT *HAPPENED,* KID?
A MALFUNCTIONING *NUCLEAR SATELLITE* WAS HEADED FOR THE EARTH...
THE GOVERNMENT SENT YOU, *ROBOY RED,* TO SAVE THE DAY...
...BUT SOMETHING WENT *WRONG.*
A *FAULTY CODE* IN YOUR PROGRAMMING CAUSED YOU TO GO *OFFLINE.*
YOU ENDED UP ON THE MOON
TIMORIS
CRASH SITE
ONLY YOU HAVE THE ABILITY TO COMMUNICATE WITH THE SATELLITE, PUT IT BACK IN ORBIT...
TYCHO
ROBOY RE
...SO NOW I'M HERE T START YOU AGAIN.

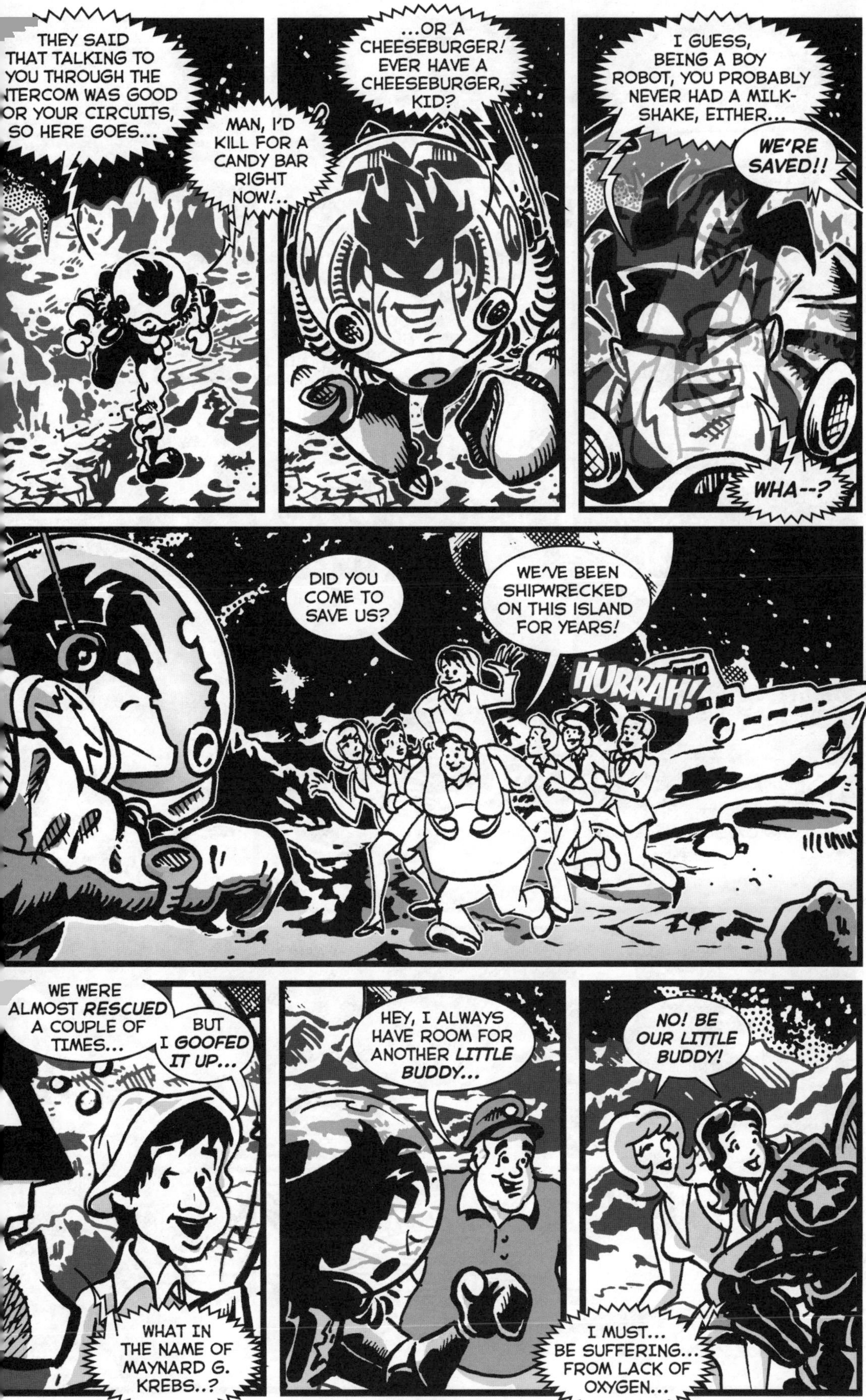
THEY SAID THAT TALKING TO YOU THROUGH THE INTERCOM WAS GOOD FOR YOUR CIRCUITS, SO HERE GOES...
MAN, I'D KILL FOR A CANDY BAR RIGHT NOW!..
...OR A CHEESEBURGER! EVER HAVE A CHEESEBURGER, KID?
I GUESS, BEING A BOY ROBOT, YOU PROBABLY NEVER HAD A MILK-SHAKE, EITHER...
WE'RE SAVED!!
WHA--?
DID YOU COME TO SAVE US?
WE'VE BEEN SHIPWRECKED ON THIS ISLAND FOR YEARS!
HURRAH!
WE WERE ALMOST RESCUED A COUPLE OF TIMES...
BUT I GOOFED IT UP...
WHAT IN THE NAME OF MAYNARD G. KREBS..?
HEY, I ALWAYS HAVE ROOM FOR ANOTHER LITTLE BUDDY...
NO! BE OUR LITTLE BUDDY!
I MUST... BE SUFFERING... FROM LACK OF OXYGEN...

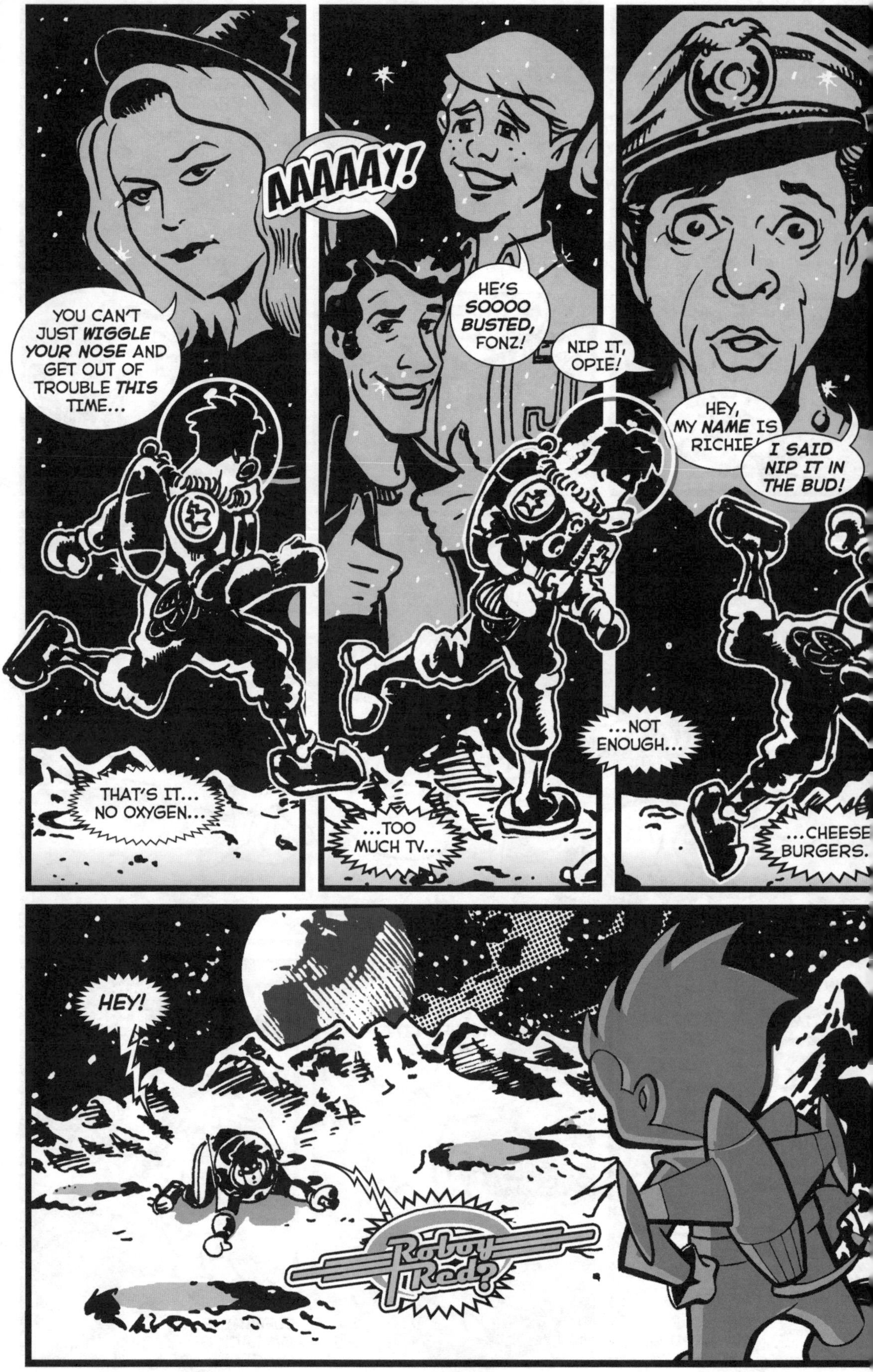
YOU CAN'T JUST WIGGLE YOUR NOSE AND GET OUT OF TROUBLE THIS TIME...
THAT'S IT... NO OXYGEN...
AAAAAY!
HE'S SOOOO BUSTED, FONZ!
NIP IT, OPIE!
...TOO MUCH TV...
...NOT ENOUGH...
HEY, MY NAME IS RICHIE!
I SAID NIP IT IN THE BUD!
...CHEESE BURGERS.
HEY!
Roboy Red?

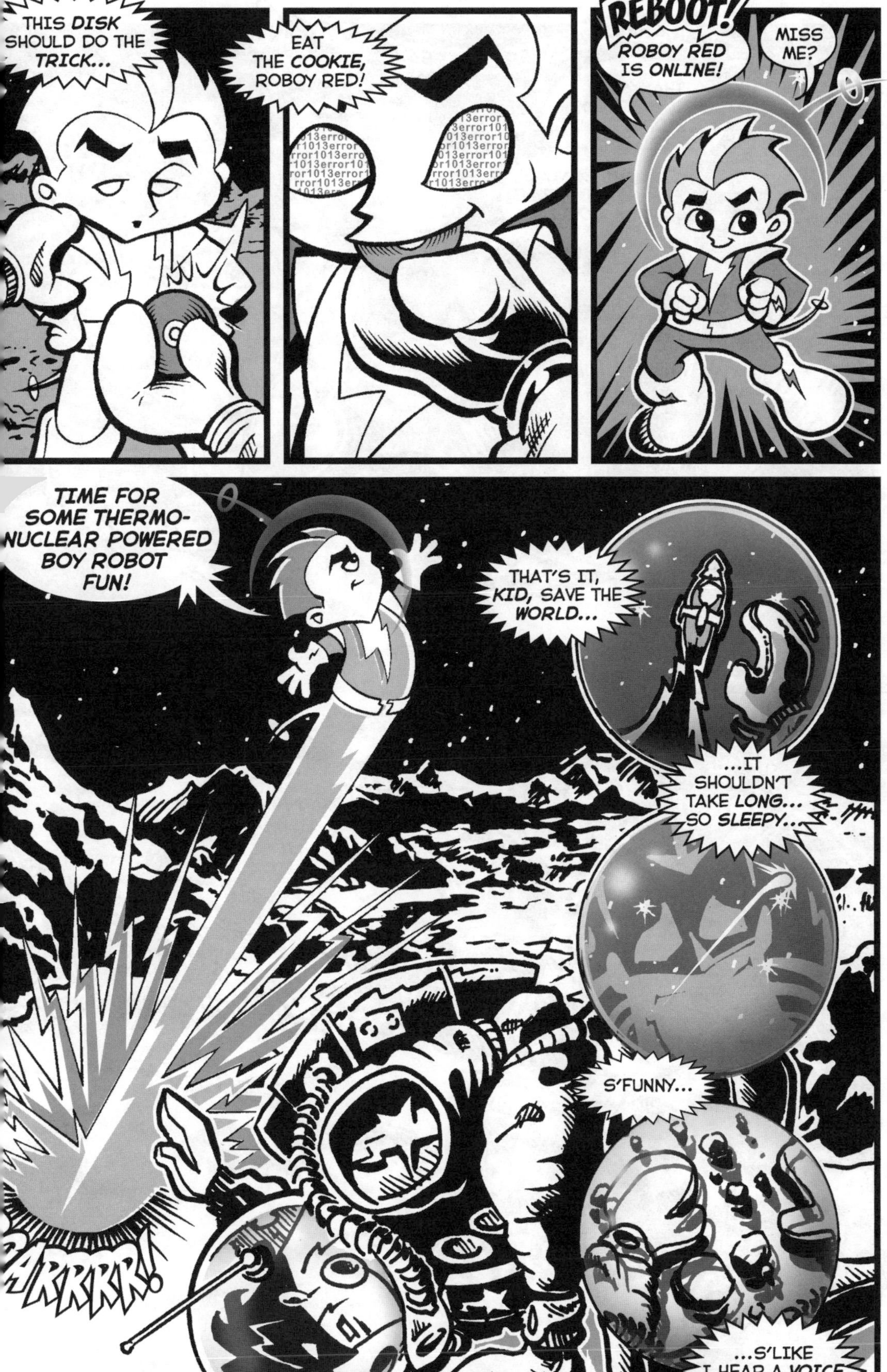
THIS DISK SHOULD DO THE TRICK...
EAT THE COOKIE, ROBOY RED!
REBOOT!
ROBOY RED IS ONLINE!
MISS ME?
TIME FOR SOME THERMO-NUCLEAR POWERED BOY ROBOT FUN!
THAT'S IT, KID, SAVE THE WORLD...
...IT SHOULDN'T TAKE LONG... SO SLEEPY...
ARRRR!
S'FUNNY...
...S'LIKE I HEAR A VOICE SINGING...

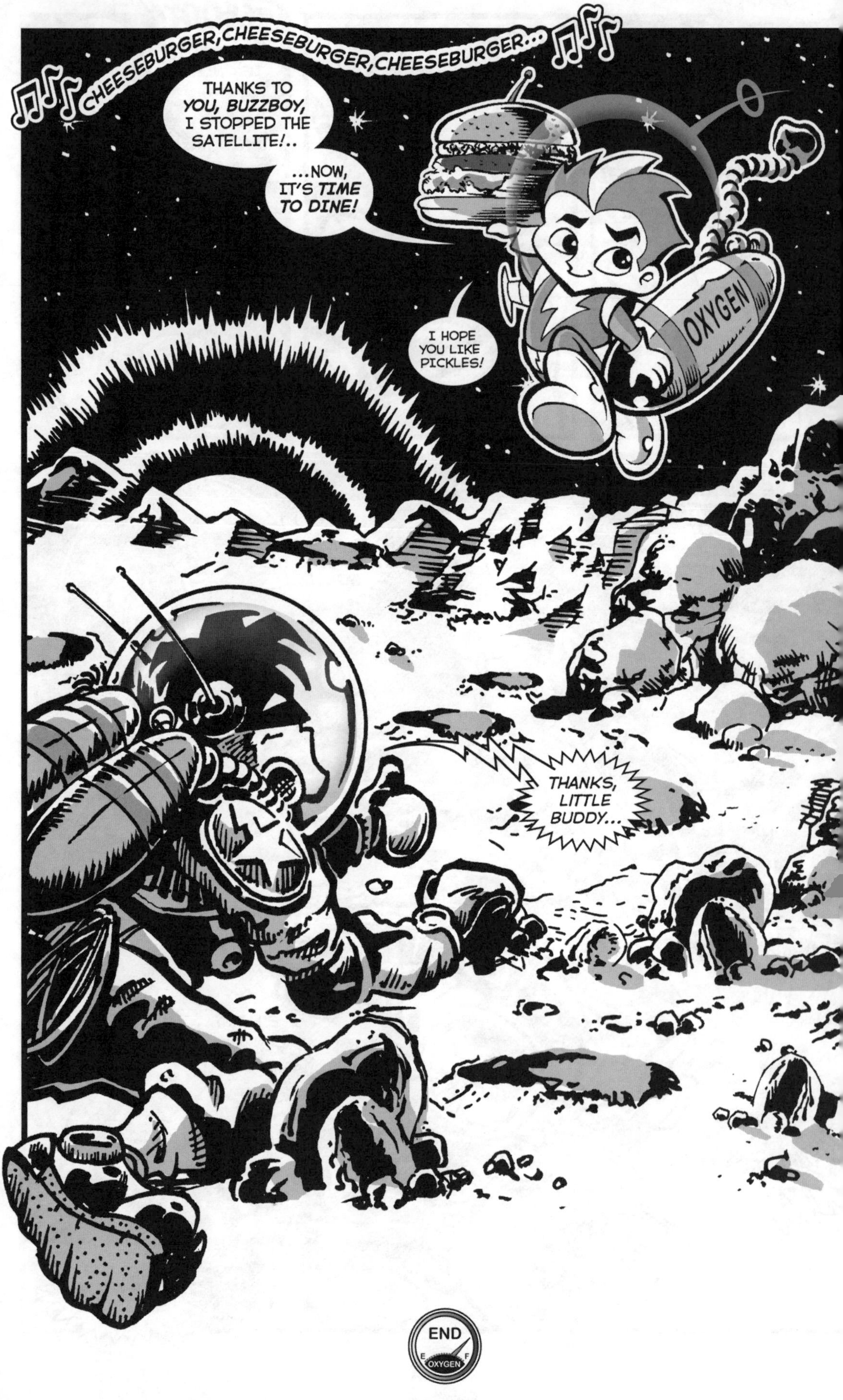
CHEESEBURGER, CHEESEBURGER, CHEESEBURGER...
THANKS TO *YOU, BUZZBOY,* I STOPPED THE SATELLITE!..
...NOW, IT'S *TIME TO DINE!*
I HOPE YOU LIKE PICKLES!
OXYGEN
THANKS, LITTLE BUDDY...
END
E F OXYGEN

Fourth Course

"This must be where pies
go when they die."
- Agent Dale Cooper
Twin Peaks

Side Dishes

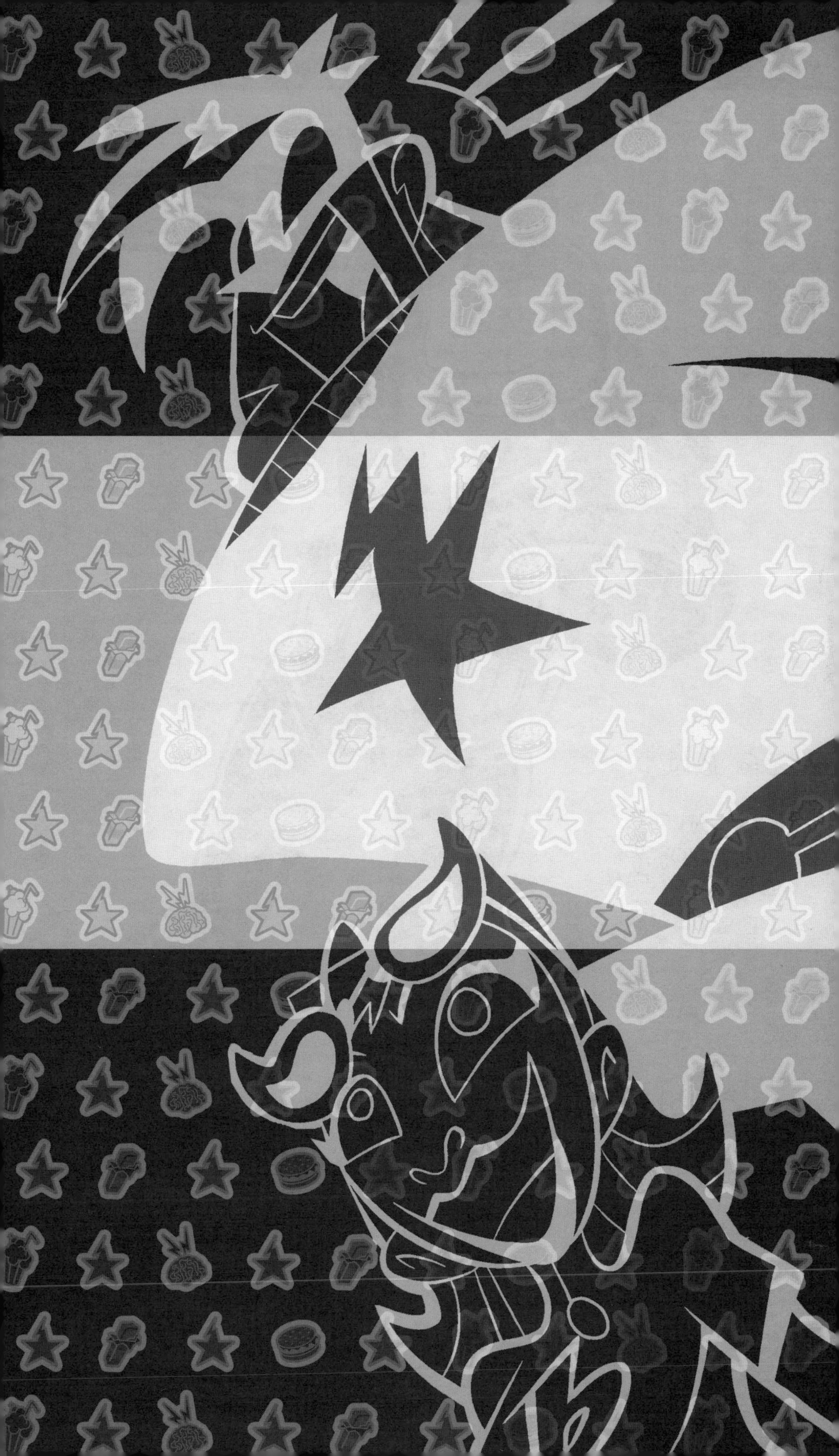

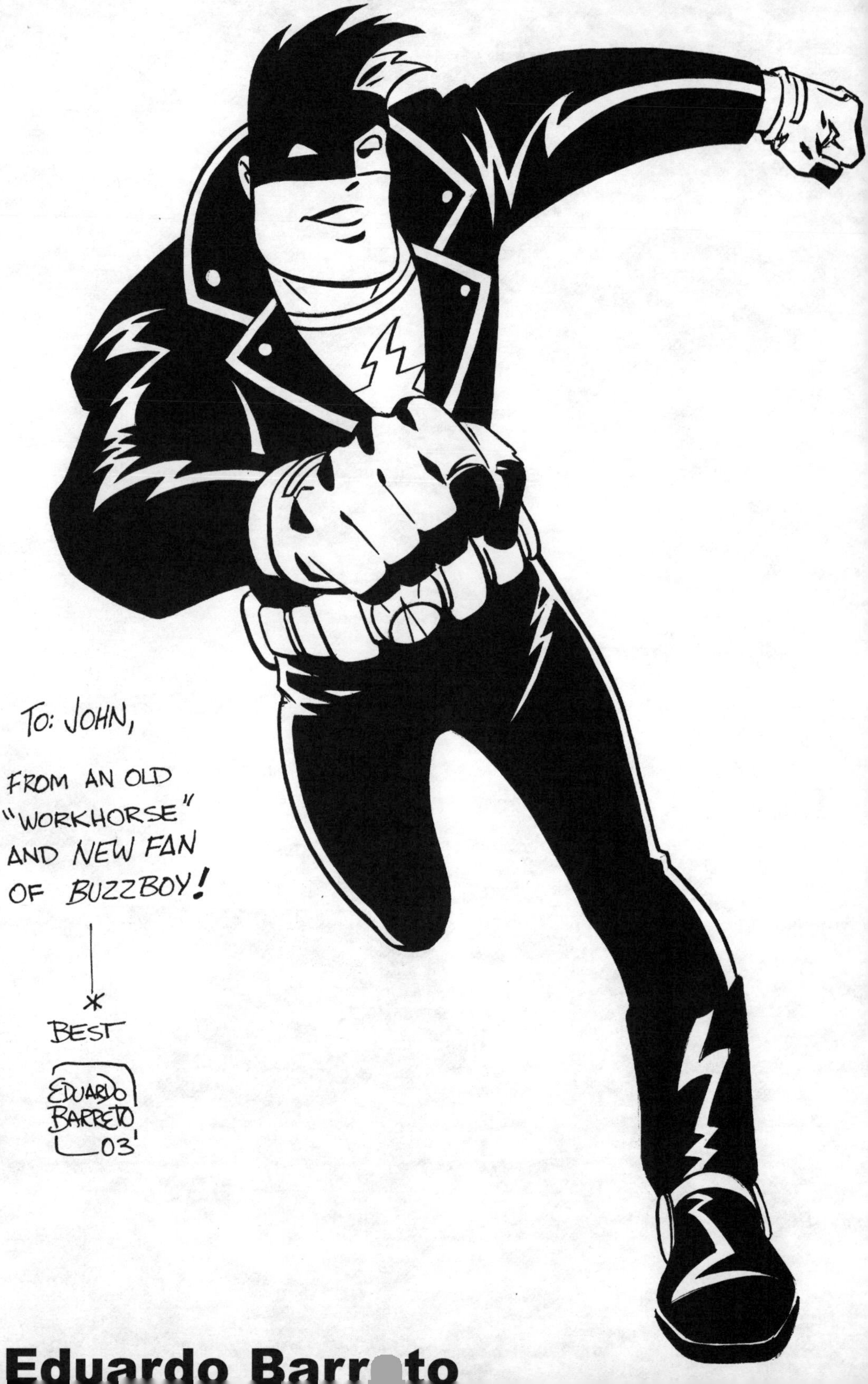
TO: JOHN,
FROM AN OLD "WORKHORSE" AND NEW FAN OF BUZZBOY!
* BEST
EDUARDO BARRETO 03'

Eduardo Barreto

Gene Ha

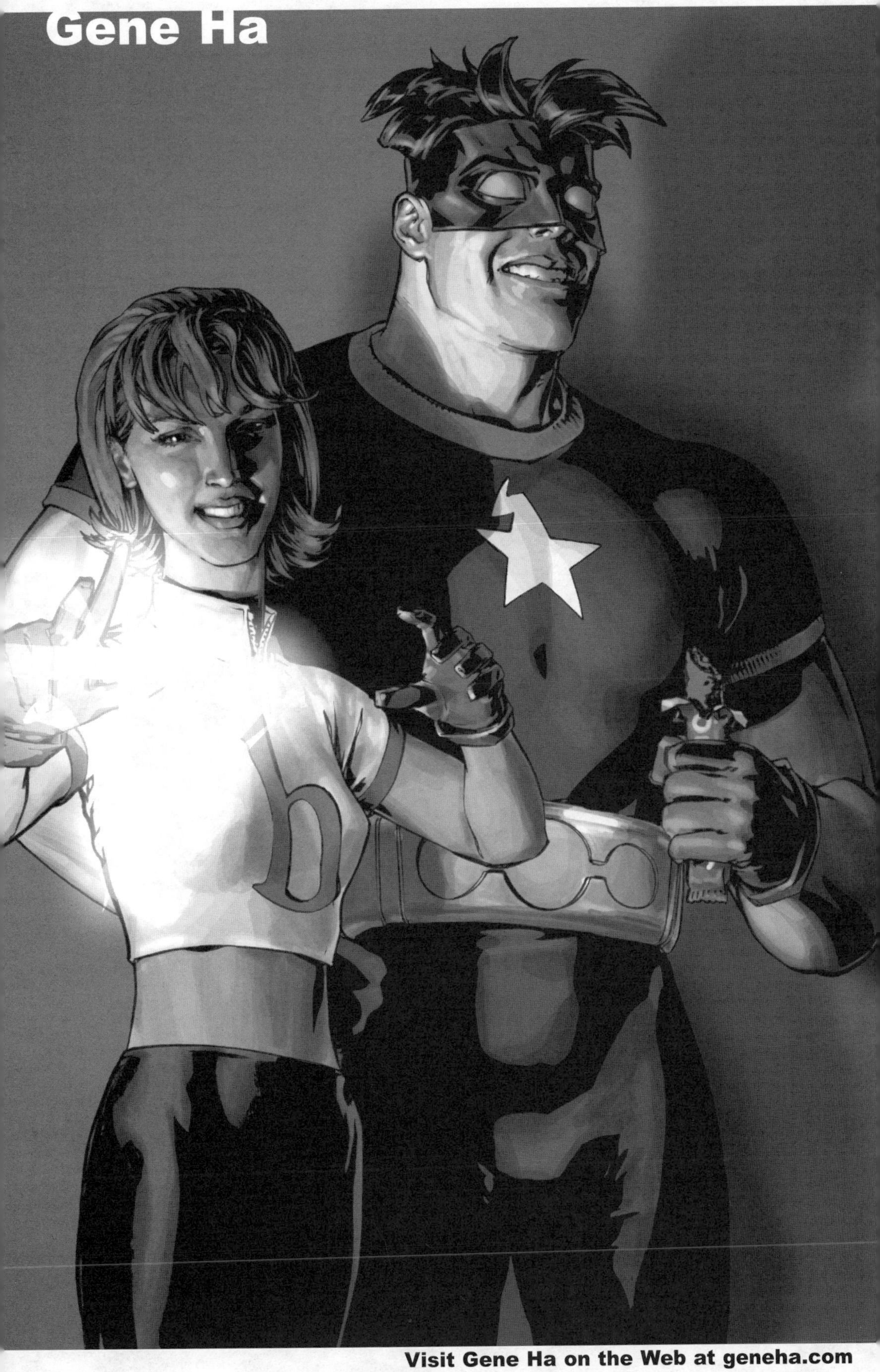

Visit Gene Ha on the Web at geneha.com

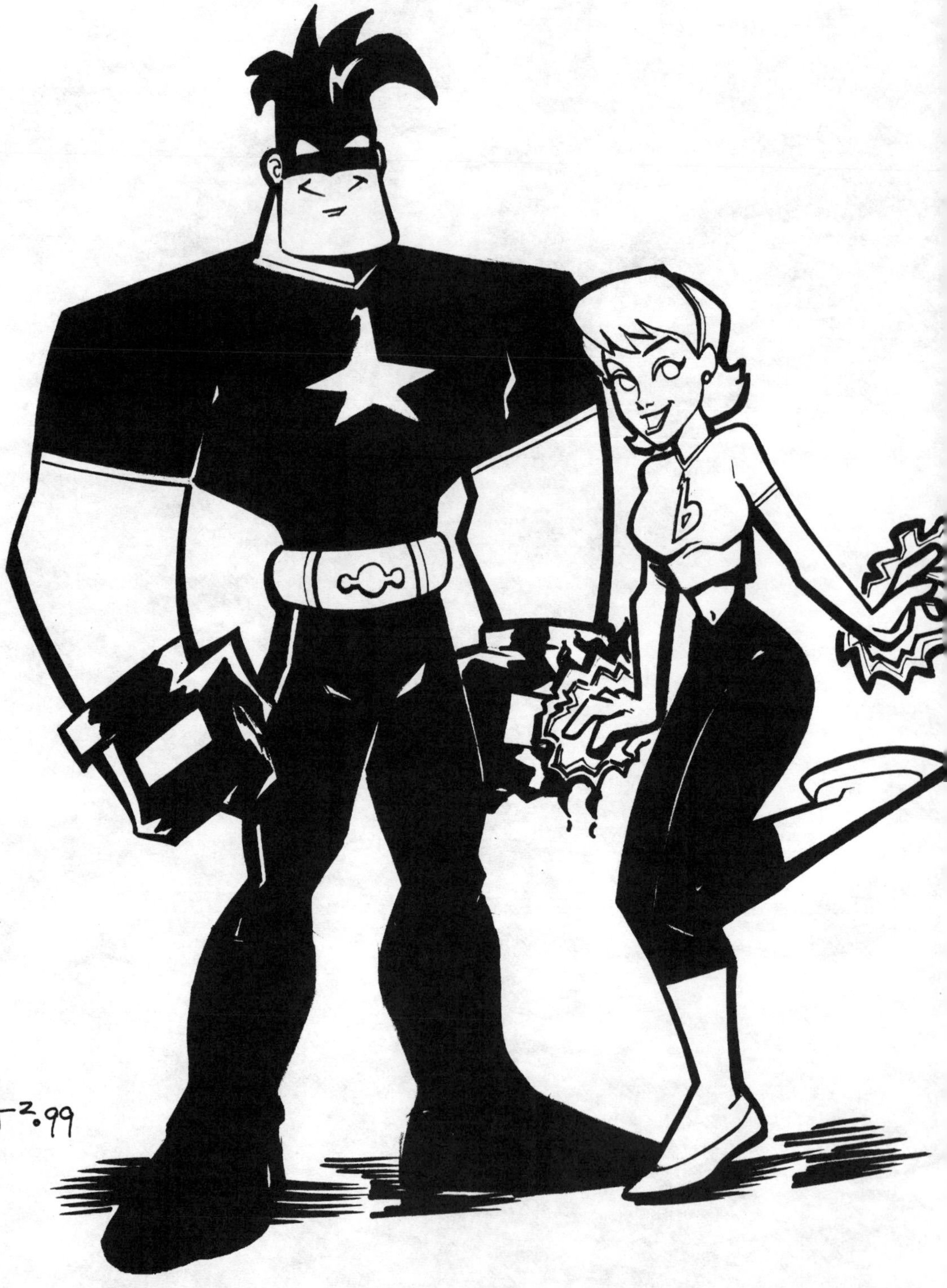

ed Tucker

Ronn Sutton w/ Rich Faber

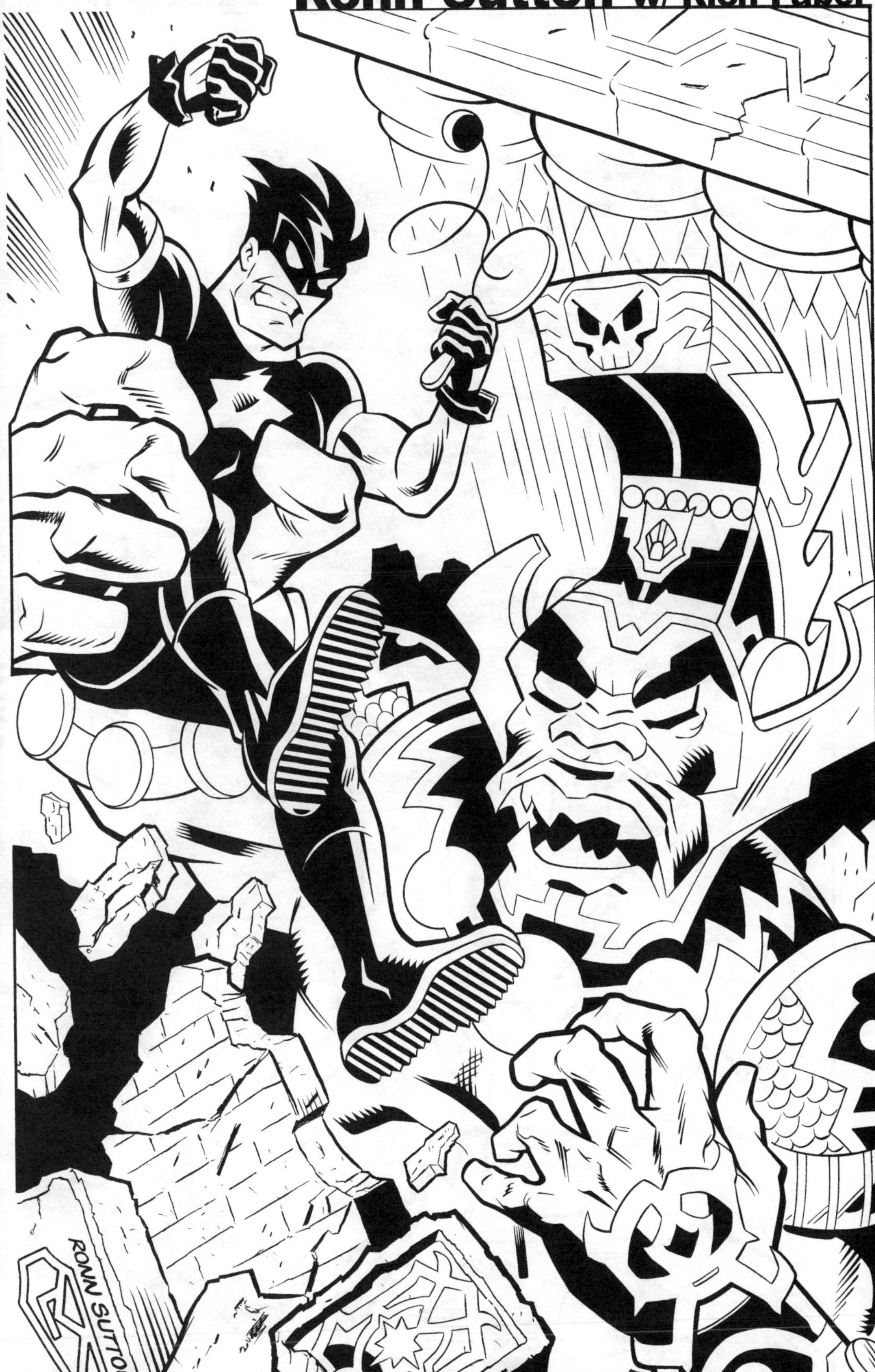
RONN SUTTON
RFABER

Visit Ronn Sutton on the Web at http://members.aol.com/eternalrom/
Visit Rich Faber's website at thinkinkstudios.com

Visit Joey Mason's website at steamrollerstudios.com
Visit Howard Shum on the Web at howardshum.com

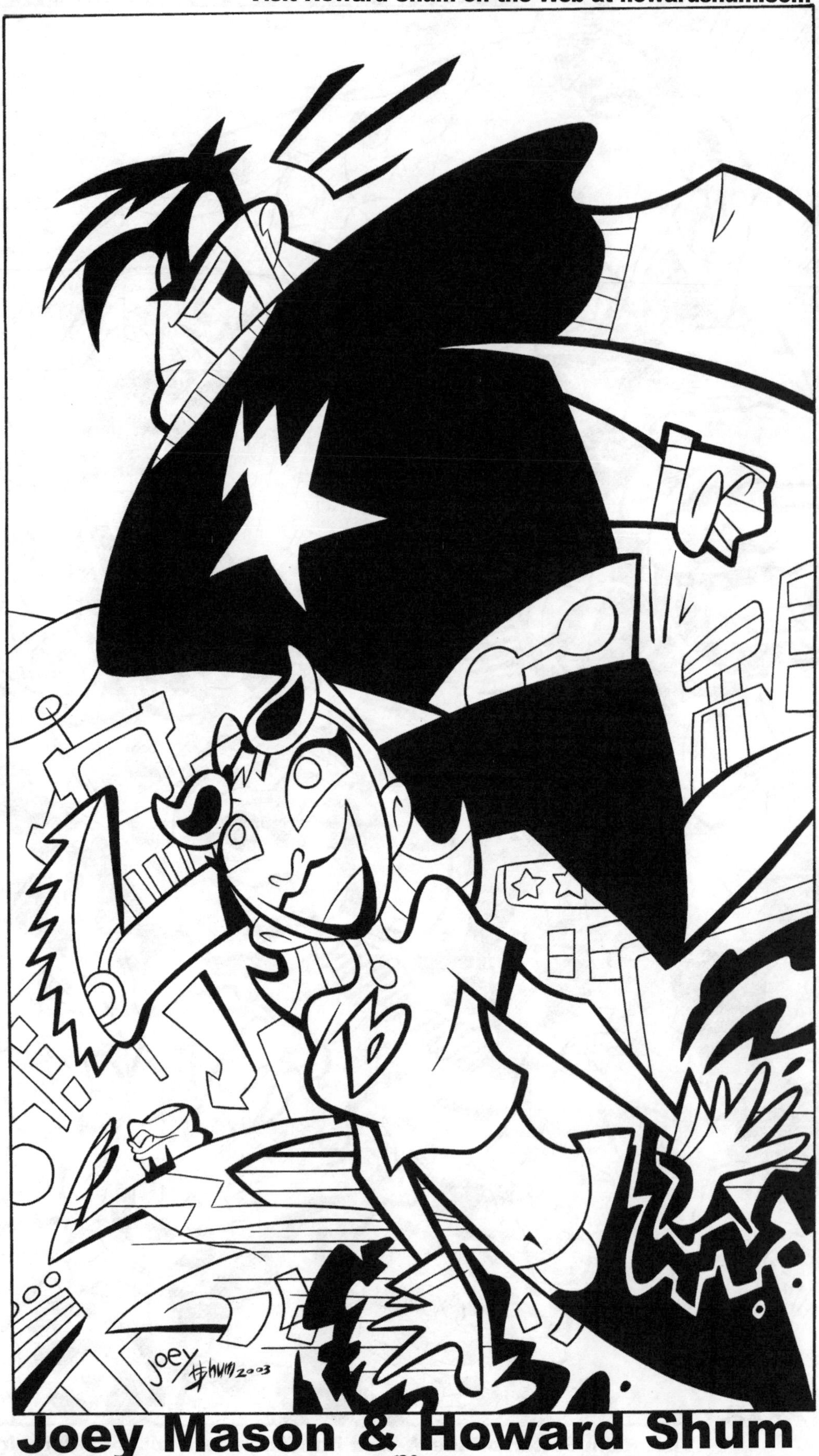
JOEY
SHUM 2003

Joey Mason & Howard Shum

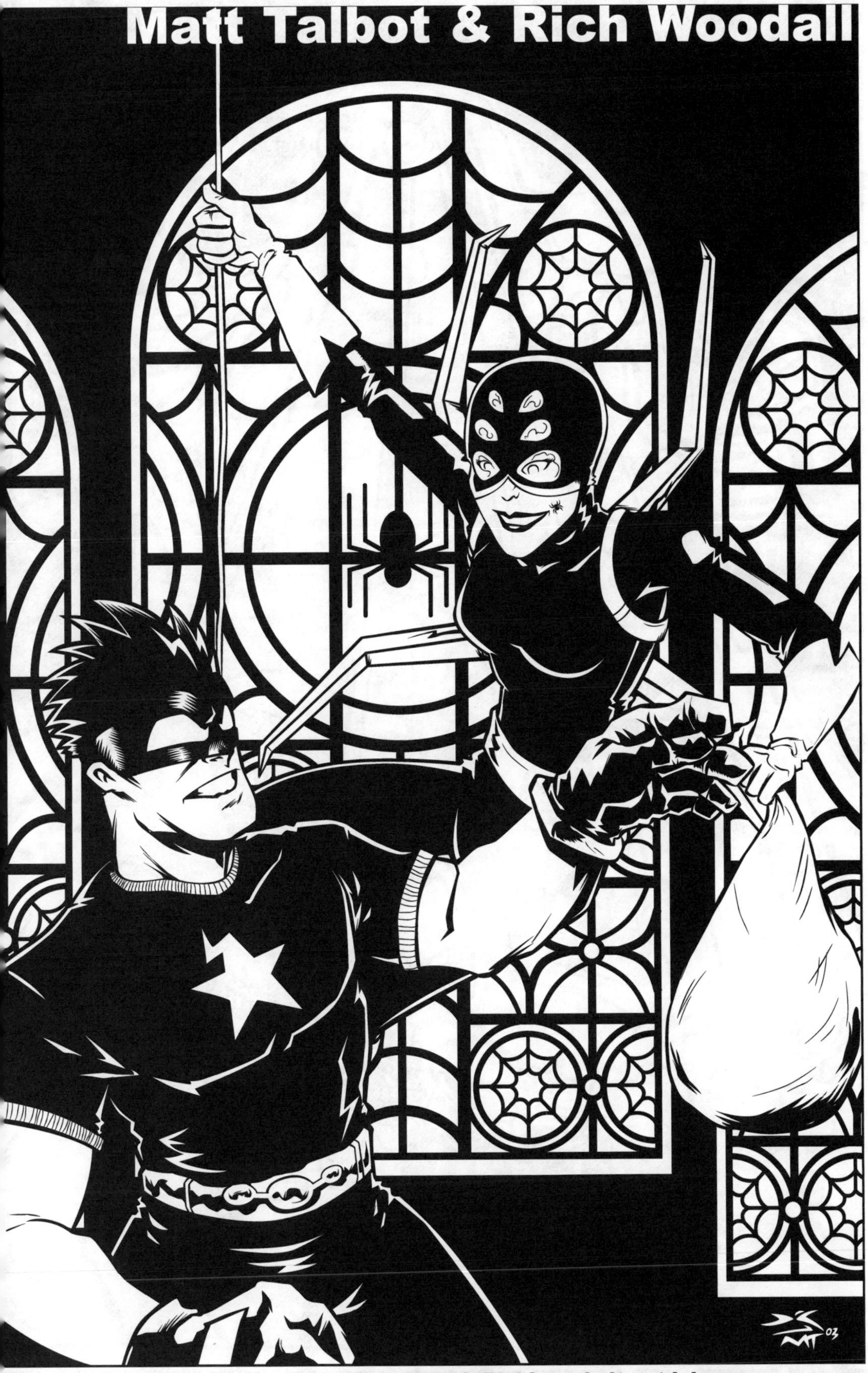
Matt Talbot & Rich Woodall

Visit Matt & Rich's website at johnnyraygun.com

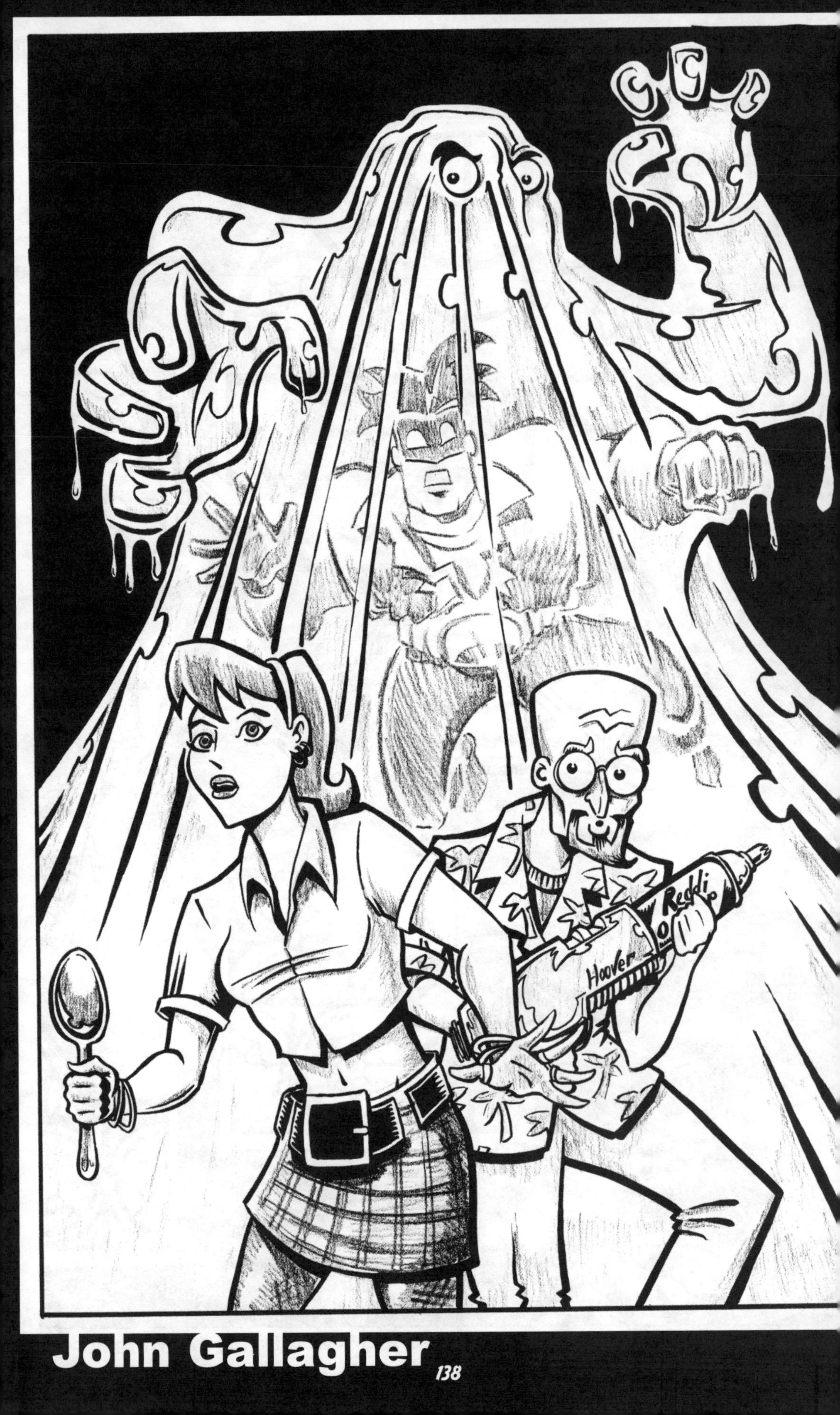
Hoover

John Gallagher

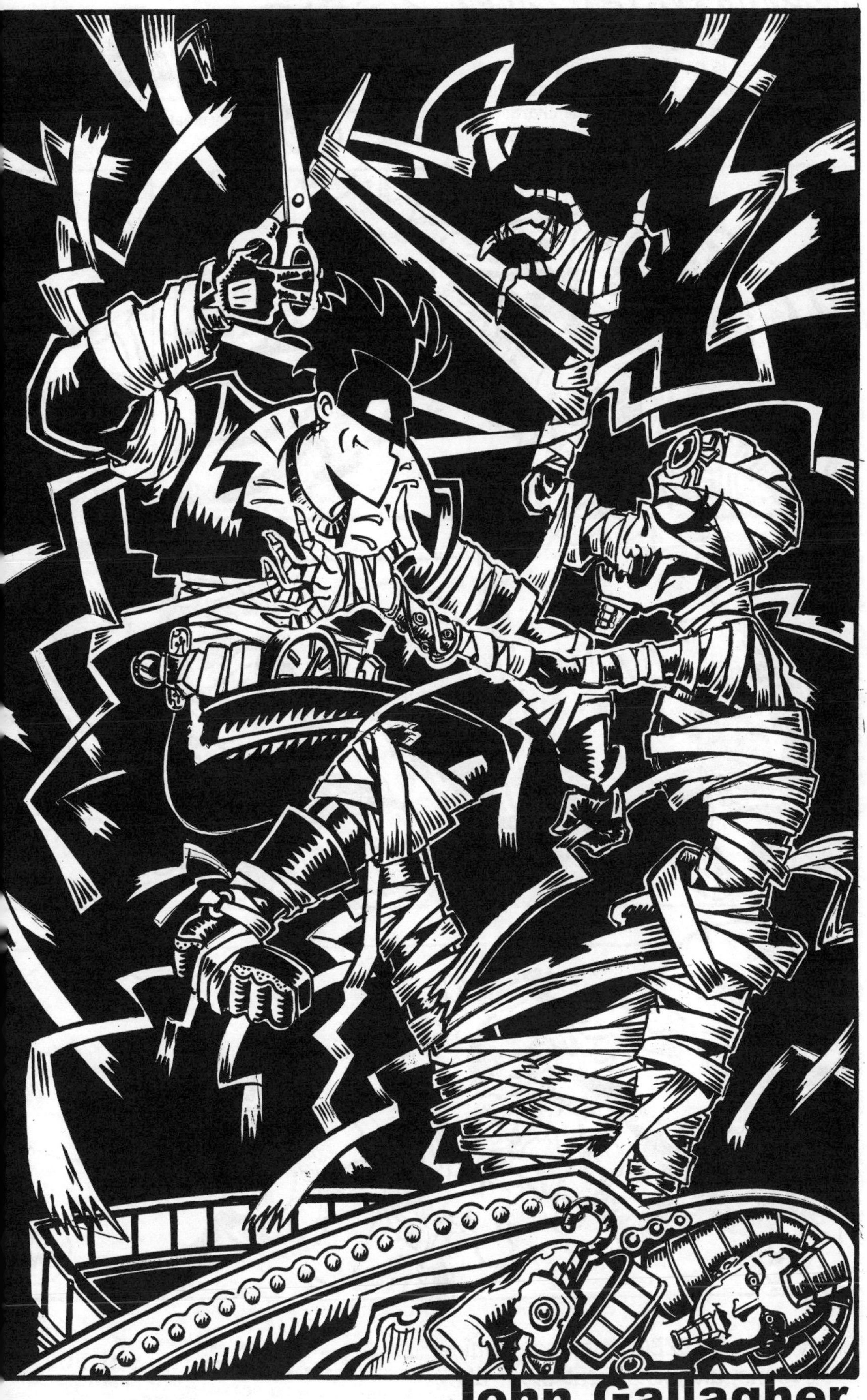

John Gallagher

WRITE-A-COMIC!

Yes! You, too, can write comics! Buzzboy is battling that fiery fiend, Sgt. Asbestos-- but what is he saying? Help out by putting words in the characters' mouths, then color in the pictures!

buzzboy

Buzzboy created by John Gallagher

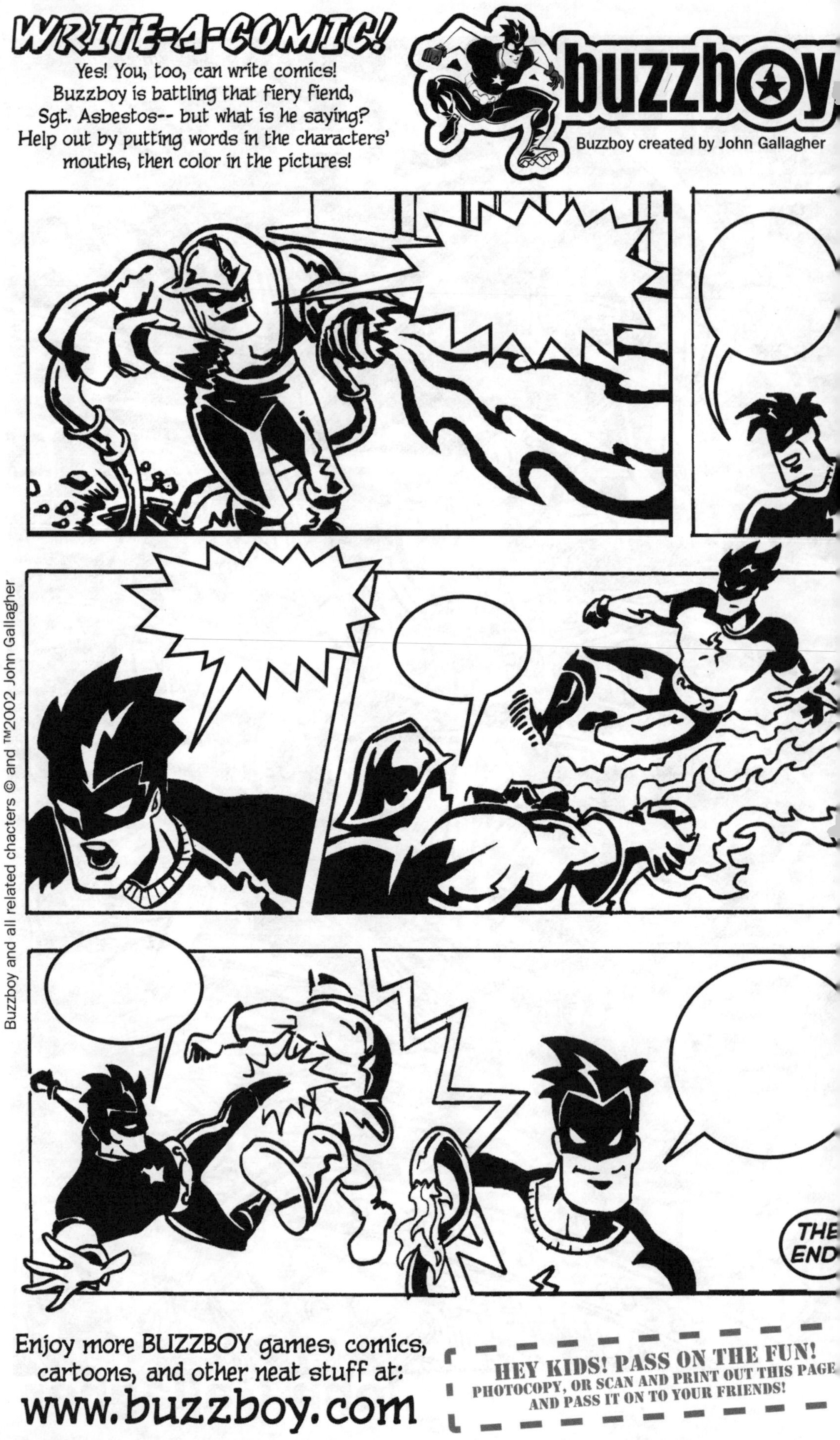
THE END

Enjoy more BUZZBOY games, comics, cartoons, and other neat stuff at:

www.buzzboy.com

HEY KIDS! PASS ON THE FUN!
PHOTOCOPY, OR SCAN AND PRINT OUT THIS PAGE AND PASS IT ON TO YOUR FRIENDS!

IOW TO DRAW buzzboy

ow these simple steps, and soon, you'll be drawing uzzboy, the "World's Most Upbeat Superhero!"

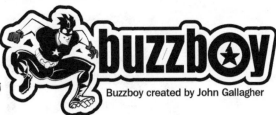

Buzzboy created by John Gallagher

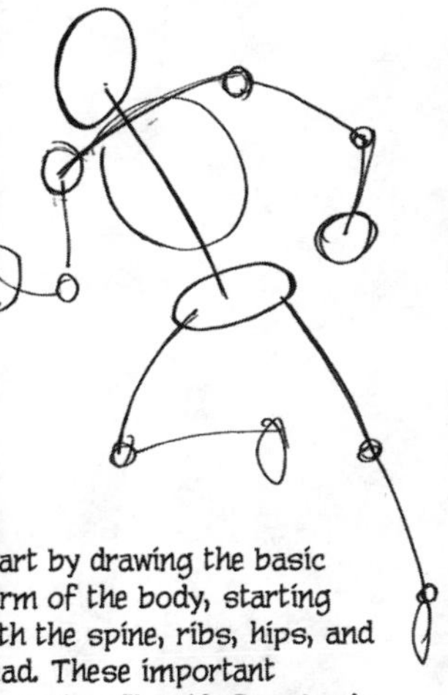

tart by drawing the basic orm of the body, starting ith the spine, ribs, hips, and ead. These important lements will guide Buzzboy's ose. Add the arms and the gs in stick figure form.

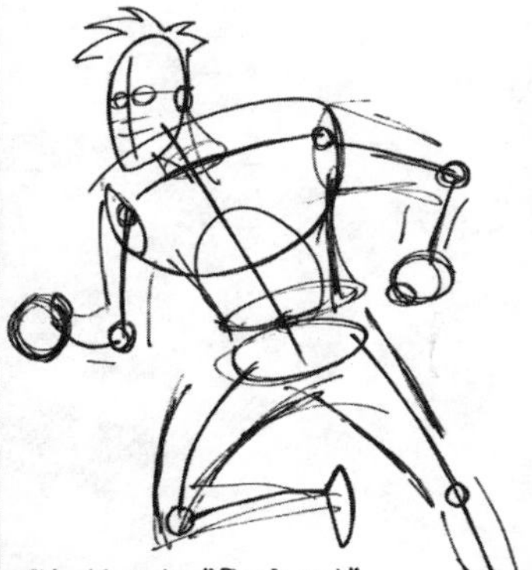

It's time to "flesh out" the drawing. Add the basic outline of Buzzboy's muscles. Remember to draw lightly with your pencil, so you can erase these lines later!

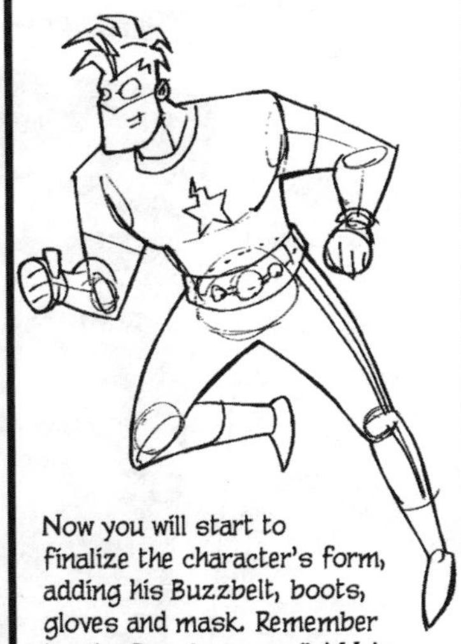

Now you will start to finalize the character's form, adding his Buzzbelt, boots, gloves and mask. Remember to give Buzzboy a smile! He's often drawn with just the suggestion of a smirk...

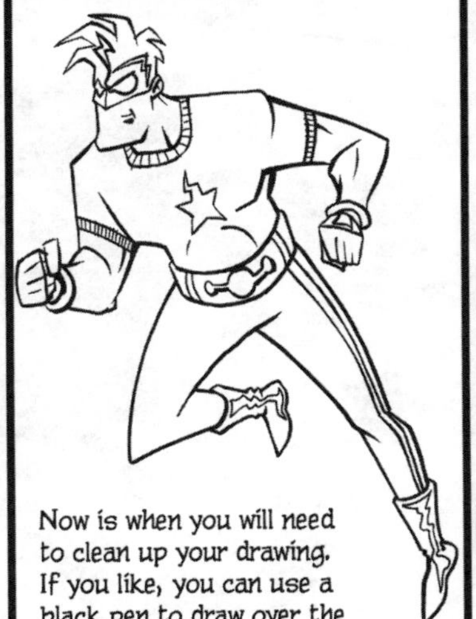

Now is when you will need to clean up your drawing. If you like, you can use a black pen to draw over the pencil drawing, then erase your pencil lines. This is called "inking."

Buzzboy is now ready to take on those pesky villains! Pull out some crayons, markers, or colored pencils, and help Buzzboy see the world in Technicolor!

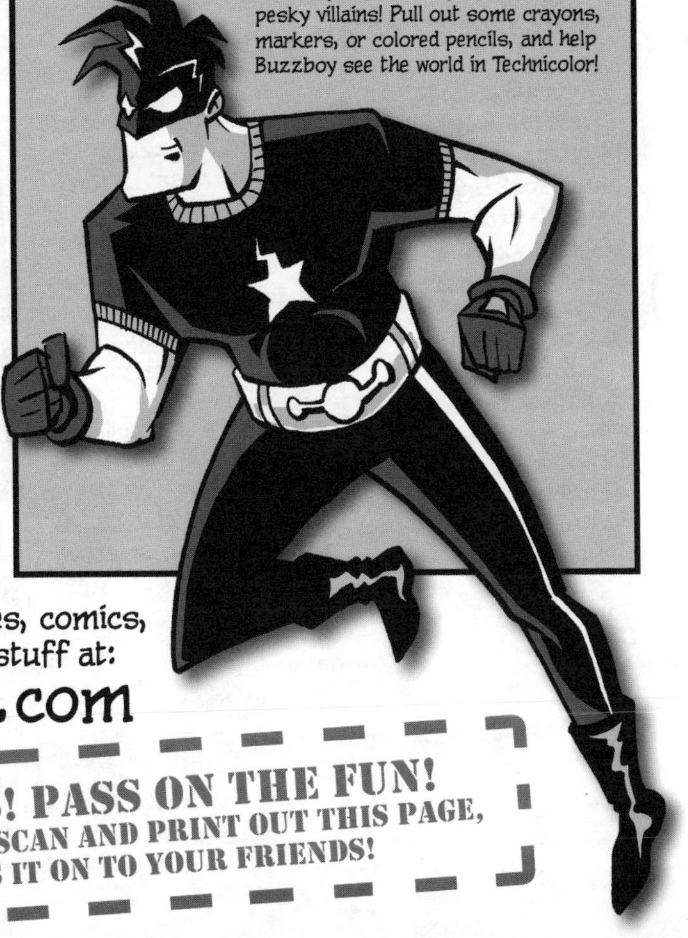

Enjoy more BUZZBOY games, comics, cartoons, and other neat stuff at:

www.buzzboy.com

HEY KIDS! PASS ON THE FUN!
PHOTOCOPY, OR SCAN AND PRINT OUT THIS PAGE, AND PASS IT ON TO YOUR FRIENDS!

Below: Gallagher and special consultant Katie mull over story ideas (and milkshakes) in the diner booth located in the Sky-Dog studio.

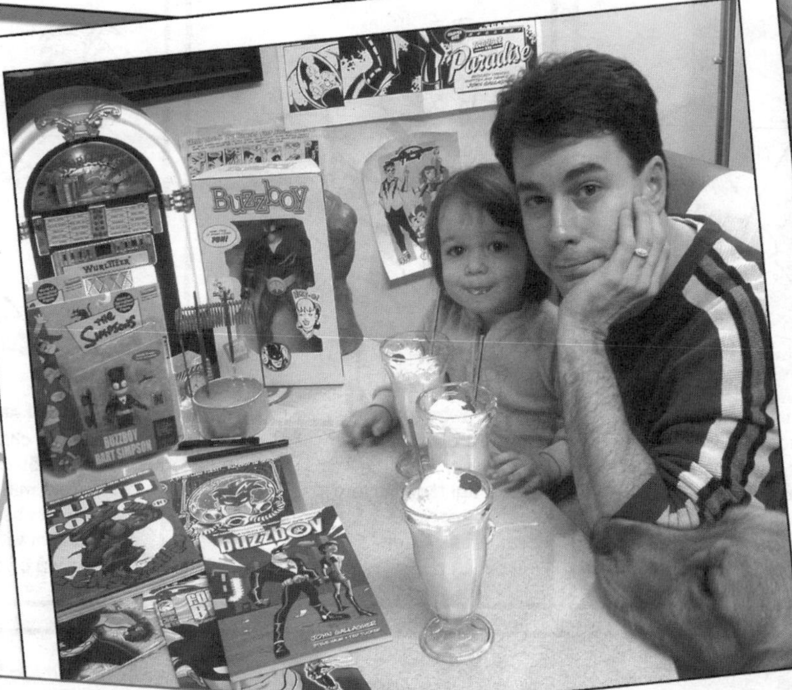
Paradise
BUZZBOY
WURLITZER
THE SIMPSONS
BUZZBOY BART SIMPSON
FUND COMICS
BUZZBOY
JOHN GALLAGHER

FROM THE FILES OF DOC CYBER...

John Gallagher entered the comics field in 1998, writing and drawing Buzzboy comics for his own Sky Dog Press. When not working on Buzzboy, John runs an award-winning design and custom comics company, most recently creating holiday giveaway comics comics for Westfield Shoppingtown malls, with a circulation of close to half a million copies.

Besides creating and packaging custom comics, John has worked on digital and print design for such clients as AOL/Time Warner, Ringling Bros. and Barnum & Baily Circus, Mobil Oil, Apple Computer, and UPS.

John lives in the Washington, DC area with his wife, Beth, daughter Katie, and his dog and cat, Sky and Meetu.

In 2001, tired of his incessant whining, Beth Gallagher bought her husband a diner booth, which resides in the Sky-Dog studio. Gallagher now uses it in place of a drawing table to write and pencil comics. Thanks, Hon!

THANKS

BETH & KATIE

MARC & BONNIE NATHAN

STEVE CONLEY

FRANK CHO

OFFICER MIKE WHITE

STEVE LEAF

MARK MCKENNA

AL NICKERSON

JOEL POLLACK

GREG BENNETT

ELIZABETH GORDON

TRACI FABER

MARK SULLIVAN

HAROLD BUCHHOLZ

CHRIS BAILEY

MIKE MANLEY

BRET BLEVINS

TIM BLEVINS

JM & RANDY LOFFICIER

JOE MURRAY

NEIL VOKES

MIKE OEMING

DAVID NAPOLIELLO

TIM OGLINE

JOHN SHINE

BILL BAKER

NATHAN MELBY

BRITT SCHRAMM

GARY ROSENTHAL

AND SPECIAL THANKS TO
RICH FABER, INKER OF THIS
VOLUME'S FIRST STORY.
PLEASE VISIT RICH'S SITE AT
THINKINKSTUDIOS.COM

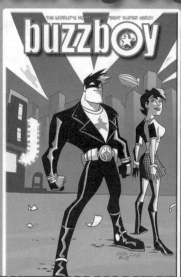

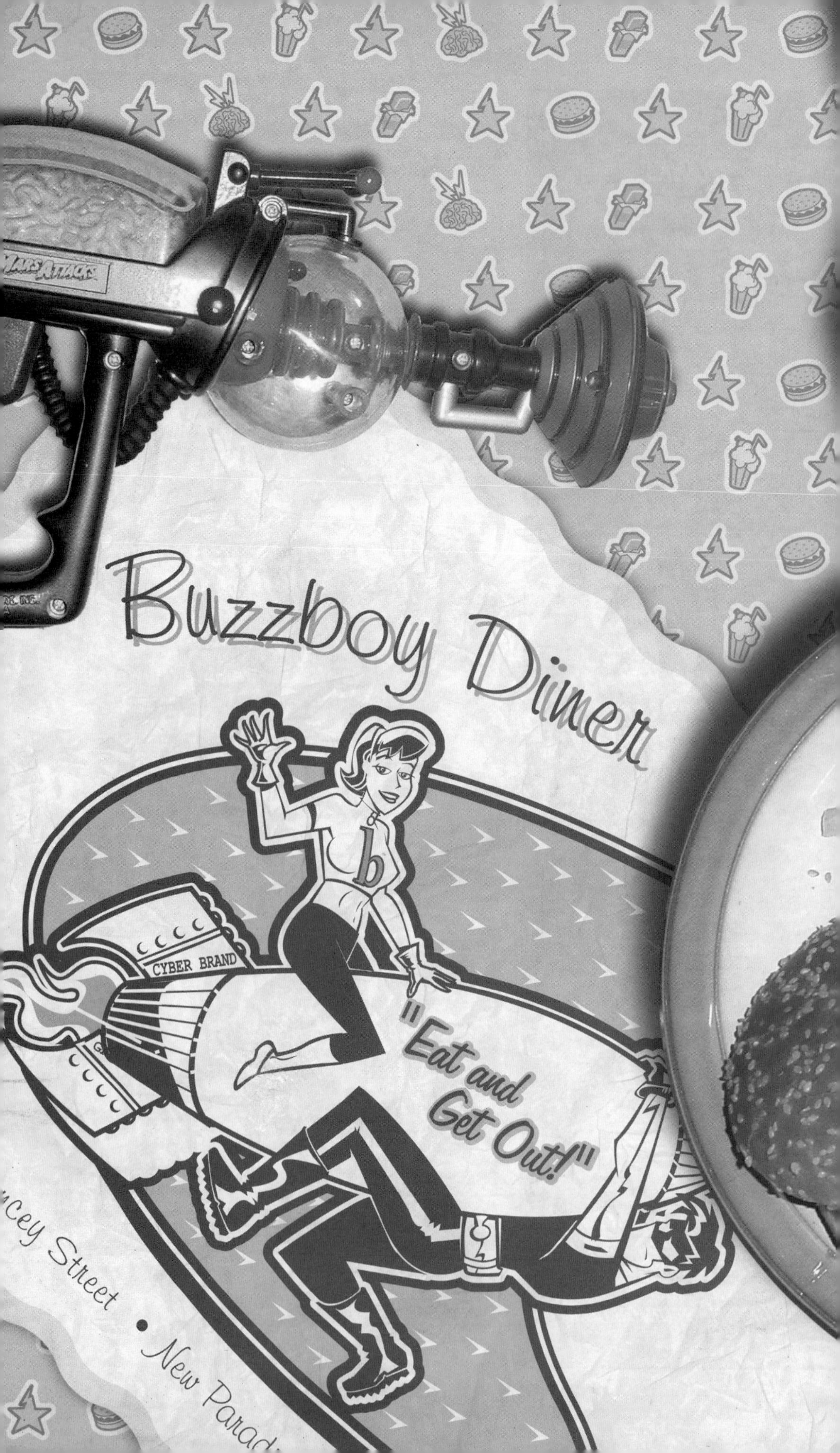
MARS ATTACKS
Buzzboy Diner
CYBER BRAND
b
"Eat and Get Out!"
ncey Street • New Parad